THE DISCOVERY
OF EGYPT

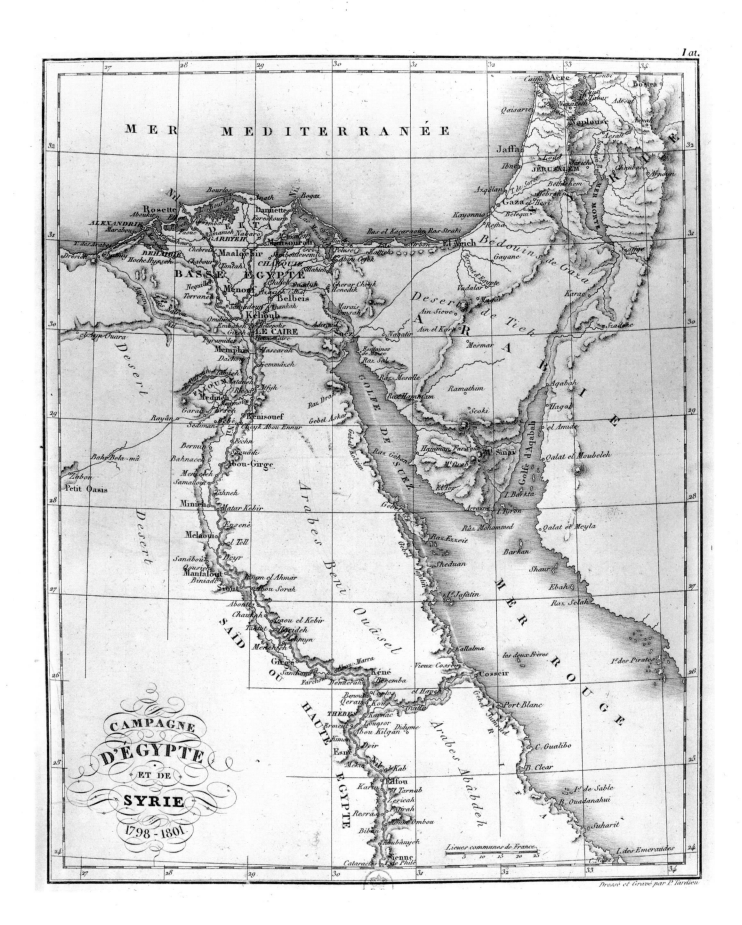

Map of the Egyptian and Syrian campaigns, 1798-1801.
Drawn and engraved by P. Tardieu. Paris, Bibliothèque Nationale.

THE DISCOVERY OF EGYPT

Fernand Beaucour
Yves Laissus
Chantal Orgogozo

Flammarion

Flammarion, 26 rue Racine, 75006 Paris

Translated from the French by Bambi Ballard

The translation of this volume was assisted by a grant
from the French Ministry of Culture and Communication.

ISBN 2-08-013506-6

I wish to extend special thanks to the staff of the Musée d'Aquitaine
and the Bibliothèque Municipale de Bordeaux
for their help during the preparation of this book.

Chantal Orgogozo

Design by Jehanne-Marie Husson
Picture research by Béatrice Petit
Composed by SCCM, Paris
Photoengraving by Bussière Arts Graphiques, Paris
Printed by the Imprimerie Jean Mussot, Paris
Bound by SIRC, Marigny-le-Chatel

CONTENTS

FOREWORD

If there is one single factor which can be said to have introduced ancient Egypt to Western civilization in modern times it must be the event to which the main part of the present work is devoted: the Egyptian Expedition, led by Napoleon Bonaparte.

On leaving France on 19 May 1798 Napoleon's brief was to obstruct the English in Egypt with a view to denying them access to India; to establish the French in the Mediterranean and the Red Sea; and to negotiate an agreement with the English which would, it was hoped, keep Europe at peace.

At that time Egypt was under Ottoman rule—in principle, at least. In fact the country was in the hands of local beys or princes. Although he planned to improve the conditions of the Egyptian population by introducing the benefits of Western civilization, Napoleon's primary objective was a military one. Hence it is the more surprising that it was decided to include a team of 'savants'—scholars, scientists, artists—in this potentially dangerous enterprise. But the work these men carried out, often in difficult circumstances and at the mercy of military requirements, was to have a far greater impact on posterity than the political schemes, which eventually failed. In backing up a military campaign with a study tour of new and unfamiliar ground, Napoleon took up an idea he had already tried out in Europe, bringing home to an increasingly curious public descriptions and drawings of people, places, plants and animals, not to mention objects of antiquity and works of art. In Egypt the ground was to prove richer than anyone could have imagined.

With the foundation of the Commission for Arts and Sciences of the Army of the Orient in March 1798 and the Egyptian Institute in Cairo in August the same year the foundations were laid for a new science: Egyptology. The fact that during the following years printing techniques were vastly improved to deal with the scholarly output of Napoleon's *savants* got the new subject off to a flying start, and the fruits of the many studies that followed became accessible to the public with unprecedented speed.

It is an interesting thought that, on setting out from France, these scholars had no precise idea of their destination. Most of them were scientists, whose knowledge would be applicable in a variety of geographical circumstances. Others were painters and draughtsmen who travelled with the army to provide a pictorial record of foreign parts and, hopefully, to celebrate the victories they achieved there. To bring along a whole printing press was a farsighted move. On looking through the early list of members, the only clue to the nature of the expedition is in the presence of a number of orientalists and interpreters, but again this gave no more away than the 'oriental' name of the army. A playwright was included, perhaps because he was an acquaintance of Napoleon, and he was joined by another writer and also by a professor of piano and a musicologist. Three days before the expedition was due to disembark the destination was officially announced: Alexandria.

Egypt must have been a cultural shock to them. They arrived in July, the hottest month of the year. The country was disorganized, and travelling without a military escort was unthinkable. The inhabitants were of a different creed and spoke a language that few in the expedition understood. To add to the anxiety, diseases were common, and soon the English were to present a serious threat along the coast. But the strangeness and the feeling of antiquity which permeates the country completely fascinated both scholars and soldiers. A travel library had been brought along, but the section on ancient Egypt would have been modest: a handful of classical writers and the works of a few early travellers to Egypt such as Claude Sicard, to whom we owe the identification of the city of Thebes in 1717, and Norden and Pococke, who left vivid descriptions of their ventures into Egypt in 1737. The Scottish traveller James Bruce, who visited Egypt in 1769, would also have been studied, as would the experiences of C. S. Sonnini, a French naturalist who came to Egypt in the 1770s. The efforts of the scholars were best spent in meticulous description and recording of what they saw, for when it came to interpretation they had little more than their intuition to rely on.

On studying the 900 or so plates of the *Description de l'Égypte* one marvels at the quality both of the work of the painters in the field and of the engravers at home. The work ran into several editions, and individual plates have been frequently reproduced in more recent times. The drawings and paintings on which it is based were all done *in situ,* and the artists were often obliged to leave them unfinished when the army demanded to move on. This makes the entire undertaking an astonishing achievement. So far, however, few students of the expedition have been able to bypass the copper plates of the engraver to study the original work of the artists themselves. The present book provides this opportunity. Here we can get to know the artists on their own individual merits. Some works appear as preliminary sketches which were then perfected by the engraver. Others are true works of art, which in publication kept their accuracy but lost their freshness. And in a number of drawings the original is more true to the ancient Egyptian motifs than the plates in the *Description.* Where monuments have now deteriorated, or have even completely vanished from the face of the earth, the records of Napoleon's draughtsmen are invaluable.

In the wake of the French expedition a number of individual travellers began to appear in Egypt. Many were heading for the Holy Land, others used the overland route to India, which entailed journeying upriver to Qena then branching off to Qusayr on the Red Sea coast. Few came as far south as Thebes, and although diaries were published few were of lasting scholarly significance.

First on the scene after the departure of the French in 1801 was the English diplomat W. R. Hamilton. He left one of the earliest descriptions of a Theban private tomb which has proved to be of real use to a modern scholar. When in 1816 Mohammed Ali became ruler of Egypt, travelling in the country was made easier. The consuls of England and France acquired key positions in matters concerned with antiquities. More or less trained artists continued to make drawings and paintings, but a significant breakthrough in epigraphical work did not occur until the early 1820s. Owing to the fact that the majority of the records of the time were either left unpublished or redrawn for publication, the quality of the original copies has often been underestimated. The team of draughtsmen brought together by Robert Hay of Linplum during his visits to Egypt between 1825 and 1833 made use not only of oiled tracing paper for facsimile copying but also of a drawing gadget called *camera lucida* which enabled the artist to project the outline of his motif on to his drawing pad. This was the foundation of modern epigraphy and of techniques which are still in use today. When the far better publicized expedition of Champollion and Rosellini arrived in 1828, scholarly work in Egypt was already in full swing.

The part played by Champollion in the decipherment of the hieroglyphs and the advance of the study of Egyptology can not be exaggerated. It is ironical that the object which symbolizes his achievements is now in the British Museum. The Rosetta stone, with its trilingual inscription, was discovered in the Egyptian delta by a French naval officer; then, when the fortunes of war changed, it was claimed by the English. But it will for ever be connected with the name of Champollion.

It would be fair to say that the French maintained a dominant role for many years afterwards in the organization of antiquities and in the establishment of learned institutions in Egypt. The English contribution excelled in individual, personal efforts. Outstanding among the early scholars was J. Gardner Wilkinson, an industrious, scholarly writer and draughtsman who lived in Egypt permanently from 1821 to 1833. Compared to works like the *Description,* his publications were small in size but great in their impact on the public. Giovanni Battista Belzoni, a resident in England, became famous for his discoveries and clearance of major tombs and temples between 1816 and 1823. He too was adept at publicizing his work through exhibitions and writing. It is less well known that he seems to have been the first writer whose travelogue was rewritten especially for young readers in 1821.

By 1850 the pioneering days of Egyptology were over. But the study of early records is as fascinating as the antiquities and hieroglyphs themselves. On reading the works of the members of Napoleon's expedition, we are reminded in a vivid and memorable way that these were the forerunners of generations of scholars who rediscovered for us one of the greatest civilizations of antiquity.

LISE MANNICHE

The painted monuments of Egypt. Coloured engraving after the painting by Charles Louis Panckoucke.
Frontispiece of the second edition of the *Description de l'Égypte*, 1821-6.

THE MILITARY
ENTERPRISE

In France, almost two hundred years after it took place, the Egyptian campaign remains one of the most popular events in the history of the Revolution. It is also the strangest and, paradoxically, the least well known of Napoleon's campaigns, and yet it immediately fires the imagination. It combines the allure of Egypt and the mysteries of antiquity with the dazzling aura surrounding the prowess and sufferings of the young Bonaparte and his 'Army of the Orient'—and, playing a major role in the expedition, an incongruous group of France's most eminent scientists and academics.

What were the motives, the execution and the fruits of an enterprise so rightly characterized by the French historian Jean Tulard as extravagant? For, although France was unable to maintain her military presence in Egypt, the campaign was to change the course of the development of that country and deeply influence the history of the East.

After the Treaty of Campo Formio of 17 October 1797, England became, in the eyes of France, the last remaining obstacle to peace in Europe. She had to be given a crippling blow to make her surrender: but where, and how? Her supreme naval strength excluded the possibility of a victory at sea, which left invasion as the only possible solution, especially since England's army was smaller and less experienced than the armies of the Republic, which had just proved their strength on the Rhine and in Italy—and there was also a reasonable chance of taking her by surprise.

England had been a thorn in the side of revolutionary France since as far back as 1793, when the Committee for Public Safety, led by Robespierre, had first examined the feasibility of an invasion. By 1797, after numerous plans had been studied, developed and then abandoned by both the Committee for Public Safety and, later, the Directoire, it was generally agreed that a decisive step had to be taken. As soon as it learned of the Treaty of Campo Formio the Directoire announced its plan to turn its forces against England, naming Bonaparte, the architect of the treaty, commander-in-chief in a decree dated 26 October 1797.

By the beginning of 1798 plans for the proposed offensive were well under way, and on 12 January the Directoire ordered the formation of the 'Army of England'. But on 23 February Bonaparte filed a report outlining the conditions under which the invasion could be successfully carried out, which led the Directoire to look for an alternative solution. It decided that an indirect attack, damaging England's commercial interests, would be the best way both to bring her to heel and to open up new opportunities for France.

During his victorious campaign in Italy in 1796-7 Bonaparte had proved himself a consummate politician. By taking the Ionian Islands he had given the Republic control of the Adriatic and, consequently, of Austria and Naples. This extension of French influence in the Mediterranean made Malta of great importance, for it would consolidate and strengthen France's hold on Corfu. On the other hand, were it to fall into hostile hands, it would give France's enemies a base in the Mediterranean from which, for instance, they could prevent the French Adriatic fleet from combining with its ships in the Mediterranean ports.

The Ionian Islands were also a key to the East, since they would allow France to support her oldest ally the Turkish Empire—or take her share of it for, noting the weakening of that state and foreseeing its partition, Bonaparte wrote to the Directoire on 16 August 1797:

> The day is not far off when we will realize that in order to destroy England we must seize Egypt. The rapid decline of the Ottoman Empire means that we must take the necessary measures quickly if we wish to preserve our commerce in the East.

The Directoire agreed, and on 23 September Foreign Minister Talleyrand wrote to Bonaparte: 'As for Egypt, your ideas on the subject are excellent'; he went on to say that he considered that such a measure would help put a stop to British and Russian intrigue over the Ottoman Empire, in recognition of which the Turks would be bound 'to give us the influence and commercial advantages we need in that country. Egypt, as a colony, would soon replace the products from our West Indies and, as a route, would bring us commerce with India for, as far as commerce is concerned, everything is a matter of time, and time here means five journeys as opposed to three by the ordinary route'—which was round the Cape.

On 14 February 1798, while Bonaparte was travelling along the coast between Boulogne and Holland, Talleyrand submitted a long report to the Directoire in which he advocated an expedition to Egypt. As far back as the reign of Louis XV, after the loss of France's colonies

André Dutertre,
Portrait of Bonaparte, 1798.
Graphite. Musée National
du Château de Versailles.

Pierre Paul Prud'hon, *Portrait of Talleyrand.*
Oil on canvas. Paris, de Castellane Collection.

in America and India, the great Foreign Minister the Duc de Choiseul had suggested that compensation could be found in Egypt, for were France to extend her commercial activities into the Mediterranean basin she could expect appreciable gains thanks to the position she already held there: the conquest of Corsica in 1768, for instance, had been a step in that direction. When Joseph II of Austria and Catherine of Russia seemed to be coming to an agreement on the partition of Turkey, it was suggested that Egypt could be given to France in order to maintain her preponderance in the East, which dated from the alliance between Francis I and Suleiman I in 1536. France's support for a weakened Ottoman Empire no longer had any advantage, and she was eager to take part in the share-out that was becoming inevitable. Furthermore, the influence of the Porte—the Turkish government—over Egypt was by now purely nominal, and the real masters of Egypt, the beys, were doing nothing to stop harassment of the French. Consul-General Magallon had already been forced to leave Cairo with the majority of the French colony there and take refuge in Alexandria, and since then had constantly reminded the Directoire of the need for a military intervention in the country, specifying the means by which it could be achieved. But an invasion of Egypt had to be put off to a later date, as were plans for the conquest of Rhodes and Cyprus, since at that time France was faced with more pressing dangers directly menacing her frontiers.

It was Bonaparte's report of 23 February 1798, dispelling hopes of an immediately successful military action in England, that led to the resurrection of the plan for an expedition to the East. Talleyrand formulated the means by which it could be put into action at once, while Bonaparte's knowledge of the earlier plans and the experience he had gained during the Italian campaign enabled him to assume responsibility overnight for an enterprise that would attack Britain's commercial interests, threaten her position in India, and eventually lead to peace negotiations whilst giving France colonial territories to replace the French West Indies and increasing her power in the Mediterranean.

It remained for Talleyrand to make the Porte accept a military intervention. He believed that he could do so through negotiation or, if that failed, by threatening to occupy Albania, Morea and Macedonia.

Speed and secrecy were of the essence. Bonaparte sent the Directoire a detailed breakdown of the measures to be taken, and on 5 March 1798 the decision was made. In the meantime Naval Minister Pléville le Pellay, at Brest, was instructed to continue overtly preparing for the invasion of England.

Charles Louis Balzac, *Toulon harbour,* 1797. Gouache. Paris, Musée de la Marine.

THE INVASION

Once Bonaparte was in charge, preparations for the expedition advanced rapidly: raising and fitting out war and transport ships, recruiting troops and organizing funds to equip the fleet became his main objectives. In order to disguise the real purpose of the expedition its directives went under the name of 'the Armament Committee of the Mediterranean Coast'. At the same time, for the benefit of British spies, the activities of the Army of England ostensibly continued, and on 31 March 1798 the Directoire issued a spurious order—deliberately leaked to the press—posting Bonaparte to Brest to take command of the invasion forces.

Meanwhile the government had set up other diversionary operations: General Augereau, in command of the 10th Division bivouacked at Perpignan, was ordered to prepare to march on Portugal, a British ally; preparations were also under way in Genoa for an army variously presumed to be destined for a march on Naples or an invasion of Algeria; and the Directoire spread yet another rumour, that the Toulon fleet was about to sail for Brest.

The Directoire had to move quickly if the secret preparations taking place in Civitavecchia, Genoa, Toulon, Marseilles and Ajaccio were to have a successful outcome. On 16 March they issued an order to set up two printing houses on the Venetian islands—one for Greek and the other for Arabic texts. Once again, this was aimed at confusing the issue. On the same day the Minister of the Interior was instructed to place engineers, artists and other personnel at Bonaparte's disposal, along with any equipment he might require for his expedition. Bonaparte was well aware that he would face many technical difficulties in Egypt and that scientists would be a valuable addition to the expedition. Since it was planned not only to invade but also to colonize Egypt, it would be essential to take with him men who were capable of organizing its administration. And as an enthusiastic member of the recently formed National Institute, he hoped to found a similar one in Egypt.

One of Bonaparte's first objectives was to extract the funds allocated to the project by the Directoire from the State Treasury. He was forced to put pressure on both the Directoire and the Treasury to get them to provide the money to cover the costs of the expedition, the soldiers' pay and two months' worth of supplies. Once this was done, the largest ships to be found in the ports of Civitavecchia and Genoa were chartered, and others destined for the transportation of troops and artillery were acquired in Leghorn, Nice, Antibes, Toulon, Marseilles, Bastia and Ajaccio. Chief Supplies Officer Sucy and Naval Supplies Officer Jean Jacques Sébastien le Roy busily gathered together all the requirements for the expedition, and troops mustered at the various embarkation points, though they still had no idea of their ultimate destination.

By the beginning of April preparations for the Genoa division were well under way; at Civitavecchia they were also in hand, although not quite so far advanced. General Brune, commander of the Army of Italy, which was providing much of the manpower, sent a request for reinforcements to the minister, asking in particular for superior officers to replace those seconded to the expedition, for Bonaparte had taken every single officer who had distinguished himself in the Italian campaign.

Within two weeks troop movements and maritime operations were so close to completion that final dispositions prior to departure could be made. On 12 April a series of secret orders was issued by the Directoire as to the organization, command and aims of the expeditionary army: 'An army will be formed which will be called the Army of the Orient,' we read in the first one; and 'Citizen Bonaparte, at present Supreme Commander of the Army of England, is named Commander-in-Chief of the Army of the Orient.' The title 'Commander-in-Chief, Army of England' nevertheless continued to appear in his correspondence. A special decree declared that, because the Turkish beys had taken over the government of Egypt, formed close alliances with the English and were perpetrating hostile and cruel acts against the French, it was the duty of the government of the Republic to pursue them wherever they were to be found. Equally, since England had taken possession of the Cape of Good Hope and 'rendered access to India via the usual route extremely difficult for the vessels of the Republic', it was now essential to open up another route for the Republican forces and to combat the allies of the British in order 'to stem the flow of her corrupting riches'—all of which made the intervention of France indispensable.

To this effect Bonaparte was ordered to proceed to Egypt with the land and sea forces under his command and to occupy the country. His mission was also to expel the British from any Eastern territories he might reach and, in particular, to destroy all their trading posts on the Red Sea so as to give France complete control of both the isthmus at Suez and the Red Sea. He was required to better the conditions of the Egyptians by all the means at his disposal and to maintain, as far as it was within his power, good relations with the sultan of Turkey,

Martinet, *Departure of the Army of the Orient for Egypt, 19 May 1798*. Pen, sepia and wash.
Providence, Rhode Island, Brown University Library.

Selim III, and his subjects. Another decree, also issued on 12 April, drawing attention to the hostility to France of the Order of Malta and the fact that the Grand Master, who had constantly supported the royal coalition, was placing Malta at the disposal of the enemies of the Republic, ordered Bonaparte to take the island. Still on the same day, Admiral Bruix replaced Pléville le Pellay as Naval Minister.

On 18 April Bonaparte issued instructions to all the staff officers and other personnel who had been stationed in Paris, along with the scientists and artists, to leave for Toulon. He followed on 9 May, and the convoy of troops from Marseilles joined him two days later. The entire fleet weighed anchor on 19 May. Bonaparte's chief-of-staff was Major-General Berthier. The other major-generals were Baraguey d'Hilliers, in command of the troops in the Genoese convoy; Desaix, in command of those in the Civitavecchian convoy; Reynier, in command of those in the Marseilles convoy; plus Bon, Dugua, Dumas, Dupuy, Kléber, Menou and Vaubois. The brigadiers were Andréossy, Belliard, Caffarelli, Chanez, Damas, Davout, Dommartin, Friant, Fugière, d'Hennezel, Lannes, Leclerc, Manscourt, Mireur, Murat, Rampon, Veaux, Verdier, Vial and Zayonchek. The total manpower from the various convoys, including the one from Corsica, was about 38,000 men.

The squadron, under the command of Admiral of the Fleet Brueys, was made up of 13

Andrea Appiani, *Major-General Desaix reading
an order of the day from Bonaparte to two Egyptians*, 1800. Oil on canvas.
Musée National du Château de Versailles.

André Dutertre, *Portrait of Major-General Reynier*.
Black chalk and stump on blue-tinted paper.
Musée National du Château de Versailles.

men-of-war, 6 frigates and 1 sloop; 2 men-of-war and 7 frigates were fitted out as storeships; the lightships included 8 advice ships, 4 bomb vessels, 6 tartans, 6 armed longboats and 2 armed feluccas. They shipped 13,000 sailors and gunners. There were about 300 convoy ships manned by 3,000 ordinary seamen. All in all, Bonaparte took a total of around 54,000 men to Egypt.

On 9 June the fleet arrived before Malta where it joined the Civitavecchian convoy, which had been there since the 6th and was growing anxious about the Toulon squadron. A single day's skirmishing followed by a day's negotiation sufficed to bring about the fall of the fortified town, and on 11 June Malta capitulated. News of this decisive action spread quickly through the Muslim states around the Mediterranean.

Meanwhile Nelson had crossed the Messina Straits and was sailing east. Bonaparte had hoped to have the advantage of a few days over him, but when he came in sight of Alexandria on 1 July he learned that Nelson had preceded him with fourteen men-of-war, declaring that he was looking for the French in order to attack them. The immediacy of the danger led Bonaparte to abandon his original plan to disembark at several points and was forced to order a hasty landing. By his mere presence Nelson had gained a major advantage. A landing at Damietta and Rosetta would have provided the French troops with the immediate protection of the terrain against an attack by the cavalry of the mamelukes—the warrior-princes of

Egypt—and the two branches of the Nile would have provided an easy route to Cairo. The route from Alexandria to the Nile, on the other hand, entailed leading tired and hungry men across the desert under constant threat from the Arabs and mameluke cavalry charges.

Despite the darkness of the night and a violent sea swept by strong winds, the troops landed at Marabut, near Alexandria. Much of the scientific equipment had to be abandoned when the *Patriote* ran aground. At dawn Bonaparte proceeded to the town with his army on foot, for it had not been possible to land the horses.

In Alexandria it was generally assumed that the French naval expedition was hostile, and when Bonaparte attempted to parley he was ignored. Storming the gateway to Rosetta, Menou on the left, Kléber in the centre and Bon on the right took the walls of the town and by nightfall the forts had fallen. Kléber was seriously wounded in the head during the scaling of the walls.

Desaix's and Reynier's divisions landed that same morning, 2 July, and marched on Alexandria. The horses were made to swim to land, their bridles held by the men in the boats. Now that Alexandria was taken, Bonaparte entrusted Desaix with the formation of the advance guard for his march on Cairo.

Before landing Bonaparte had written to the pasha of Egypt assuring him of France's friendly intentions towards the Porte, and that very evening he published a proclamation in Alexandria inviting the inhabitants to receive the French as friends, though with a warning that anyone who took up arms on behalf of the mamelukes would be punished. All the subject

Nicolas Jacques Conté, *View of the fort at Alexandria*, 1798-1801. Watercolour. Private collection.

François Henri Mulard, *General Bonaparte gives a sword to the military head of Alexandria, July 1798*, 1808 Salon. Oil on canvas.
Musée National du Château de Versailles.

villages were ordered to fly the French and Ottoman flags. The inhabitants, who were quite used to being ruled by conquerors, were largely reassured by this proclamation, and the influence of the religious leaders, whose privileges Bonaparte respected, helped maintain the peace. On 4 July the leading sheiks in Alexandria signed a solemn declaration in which, taking note of Bonaparte's promises, they agreed to exert their authority on behalf of the French army.

André Dutertre, *Alexandria seen from the esplanade, or great square, of the new port and the Arab quarter.*
Engraving from the *Description de l'Égypte*, 1809-26.

Local resources were required to keep the army properly supplied and Bonaparte issued fair and precise rules to replace the arbitrary practices of the mamelukes. This was to be his invariable principle in all his administrative measures.

Alexandria became the central depot of the army. Bonaparte immediately set about organizing the defences and the administration and intelligence services of the town. Kléber, whose wound disabled him from the command of his division, was made military governor.

Now that the army was on dry land the fleet had accomplished its principal duty, but it was decided to keep it in the vicinity until a decisive victory had crowned military operations. Its presence would also facilitate the arrival of a second expedition which Bonaparte had ordered to be readied to bring reinforcements to Egypt. Furthermore, it appears that Bonaparte intended to return to France as soon as Egypt was conquered, leaving the occupation and colonization of the country in the hands of one of his generals, for he anticipated a revival of the plan to invade England. Wanting therefore to protect the fleet, he suggested that it should anchor in the old port, but soundings indicated that the channels were impracticable so it was decided to anchor it instead at Aboukir.

Before leaving Alexandria, Bonaparte wished to reaffirm his policy of conciliation and consideration towards the local population. To this end he maintained the status of the sherif, Koraim, who had been in command of Alexandria before the landing, by appointing him civil governor of the town, under Kléber's authority.

There were two possible routes from Alexandria to Cairo. The shortest followed the Alexandrian canal across a practically deserted region, past Damanhur to join the Nile at al Rahmaniya, whence it followed the left bank of the river. The other led to Rosetta, near the west side of the mouth of the Nile. Bonaparte decided to send a division to Rosetta, commanded by Dugua in place of Kléber, to occupy the town and then join the troops at al Rahmaniya. Dugua was to take the fort at Aboukir on his way, and was under instructions, once in Rosetta, to facilitate the entry of Admiral Perrée's reserve flotilla into the Nile to control the river traffic.

OVERLEAF:
Charles Louis Balzac, *Rosetta, view of the boghaz or mouth of the Nile,* 1798-1801. Watercolour. Paris, Bibliothèque Nationale.

The occupation of Rosetta would give the army control of one of the mouths of the Nile, opening up a navigable route for the march on Cairo. Menou was put in command of the town.

Desaix, who was engaged in forming the advance guard, was ordered to march the next morning, 3 July, and follow the Alexandrian canal. He was followed by Reynier's division on the night of the 4th. It had now become possible to assemble two cavalry corps, so Brigadier Leclerc was put in command of them and sent forward to place himself under Desaix's orders.

Vial replaced Menou, wounded in Alexandria, at the head of his division and was sent, in the company of Bon's division, along the route that the advance guard had taken. Bonaparte left Alexandria for Damanhur at 5 a.m. on 7 July, passing Bon and Vial on the way. The army then regrouped at Damanhur.

Although the soldiers were delighted to be on dry land after their uncomfortable passage, they now had to face the desert with its dried-up cisterns and silted wells from which little water could be drawn. The canal too was dry, and there were many hardships involved in the transportation of equipment. There was also the constant threat of attack by bedouin.

There were endless false alarms, and the troops soon became demoralized. It is difficult to give an idea of the army's discontent and despair during those first few days in Egypt. Bonaparte's influence and inspiration alone kept them in order. Damanhur provided enough relief to enable them to forget the days of discomfort and privation, but one of the soldiers was murdered there, and on 9 July Brigadier Mireur, walking alone, was also murdered.

Reynier's, Vial's and Desaix's divisions left Damanhur for al Rahmaniya on the night of the 9th and at dawn on the 10th; Bon's division was kept at Damanhur with the dismounted

Dominique Vivant Denon, *View of Rosetta*, 1798-9. Pen and wash. London, British Museum.

Dominique Vivant Denon, *Vignette: French soldiers under a palm tree*, 1798-9.
Pen and wash. London, British Museum.

cavalry which Zayonchek was reorganizing. The march towards the Nile saw some action: the nimble mamelukes and bedouin around Damanhur were joined by mamelukes sent from Cairo by the Turkish commander Murad Bey. The French were attacked in the flanks and rear.

The sight of the fertile banks of the Nile gave rise to celebrations: the army would now be free of the main discomforts of the journey, and the flotilla, which had been on a parallel course upriver, would lighten their loads. On 10 July, at al Rahmaniya, Bonaparte took command of Desaix's, Reynier's and Vial's divisions, to which he added Bon's and Dugua's the following morning. He learned that Murad Bey, supported by an armed flotilla, had advanced as far as

François André Vincent, *The Battle of the Pyramids*. Pen and wash heightened with white on bistre paper.
Paris, Musée des Arts Africains et Océaniens.

<small>OPPOSITE:</small> Louis François Lejeune, *The Battle of the Pyramids, 21 July 1798* (detail), 1806.
Oil on canvas. Musée National du Château de Versailles.

Shubra Khayt to bar the way to Cairo. He decided to move the army forward at nightfall on the 12th in order to be in a position to attack the enemy the next morning. Faced with the mameluke cavalry, Bonaparte immediately decided on a battle formation in squares, with each division flanking its neighbour. The mamelukes suffered heavy losses at each charge of these formations and left the battlefield in disarray.

The next day the army was back on the march. The advance guard was formed by Desaix's and Reynier's divisions, while Bon's and Vial's, with whom Bonaparte marched, formed the battle corps and Dugua's the reserve. The troops complained continually at the arduousness of the march. The sky was burning hot, the land even hotter, the nights damp. They camped late and set off again before dawn. Cairo was now very close and the local inhabitants showed themselves to be friendly: sometimes, as they neared a village, the men would bring them water to drink and bread and watermelons to eat.

After their defeat at Shubra Khayt the mamelukes concentrated their forces around Cairo ready for a decisive battle. The inhabitants of the town were in total confusion. Bonaparte resolved to open the attack on the 21st, once the majority of his troops had assembled. The mamelukes had dug entrenchments covered by artillery at Imbabah on the left bank of the Nile. Murad Bey was positioned there, with his co-commander Ibrahim Bey on the right bank. A section of Murad's cavalry charged Reynier's and Desaix's divisions and was repulsed. Bon's

André Dutertre, *Cairo, view of the square known as al Rumeyleh and the citadel*, 1798-1801.
Pencil and watercolour. Paris, Bibliothèque Nationale.

and Vial's divisions attacked the entrenchments and took them: the mameluke camp, forty cannon and 400 laden camels passed into the hands of the French. The enemy burned a number of their warships. Murad Bey disappeared and Ibrahim Bey fled east with his mamelukes and the pasha of Cairo that night. Murad's house in Giza became the general headquarters: the town had surrendered. It was the Victory of the Pyramids.

Bonaparte entered Cairo on 24 July and moved into the home of Mohammed Bey al Elfi, the palace of Azbakiyyah. From there he sent the Directoire his report on the victorious march of his army.

The defeat of the mamelukes had caused the collapse of the entire governmental structure of Egypt. Now that victory was assured, it was essential to set up new town and provincial authorities. At first there were fears that the Egyptians would assume the French had come, as in the days of St Louis, to impose religious domination, but Bonaparte, who was sensitive enough to respect the religion and the customs of the country and to involve its ulema, the custodians of Mohammedan law, soon put these fears to rest. Following the principles he had established in Alexandria, Bonaparte chose agents who were prepared to work with the French administration from amongst the various ethnic groups. On 25 July he entrusted the government of Cairo to a Divan, or ruling council, of nine members, and created a Turkish regiment to police the town, placing it under the orders of Major-General Dupuy, military governor of Cairo. On the 27th he established similar provisional administrations throughout Lower Egypt. Exploitation of public revenue and the confiscated possessions of the mamelukes provided the army with its necessary supplies; to which was added a heavy tax imposed on the merchant classes. On the military front, the first orders concerned the planning and administration of all the various services, which were to be centralized in Cairo.

With the mamelukes gone, the major towns of Lower Egypt could now be brought under

26

French control. Bonaparte quickly reestablished his communication lines with the coast which, broken during his advance, had left him out of touch with Alexandria and Rosetta. He immediately replaced Vial with Lannes as commander of Menou's division, ordering him to occupy Damietta so as to deprive the mamelukes of their last Mediterranean port. Zayonchek was sent to Minuf to subdue the southern half of the delta, and Admiral Perrée was put in command of navigation on the Nile, with offices at Bulaq, in order to establish communications between Cairo and the various provinces.

As he multiplied the points occupied by the French troops, Bonaparte ensured that they were able to keep each other regularly informed of any eventuality by creating a postal service using both branches of the Nile, under the supervision of Sucy. He then set about the practical requirements of the troops and scholars. Supplies, fresh mounts, the setting up of a printing press, chemical and physics laboratories, an observatory, as well as hospitals and other essential

André Dutertre, *The citadel at Cairo, view from inside the gate known as Bab al Gabal*, 1798-1801. Pen and wash. Paris, Bibliothèque Nationale.

services, gave rise to a great number of ordinances. On 28 July he formed a group to study the question of proper clothing, for the troops' ordinary uniforms were hardly suitable for the torrid Egyptian climate.

After the Battle of the Pyramids, Ibrahim Bey and Murad Bey had fled in opposite directions. The majority of the mamelukes had fled with Murad, and, although they had become disorganized due to their great losses, Murad began to rebuild his army in Upper and Middle Egypt. Lacking both in cavalry and transportation, Bonaparte had no hopes of following him, which gave Murad Bey time to reorganize his force. Desaix was posted south of Giza in a defensive position even though it was known that Murad had retreated a great distance away and posed no immediate threat. The respite enabled Bonaparte to mobilize sufficient troops against Ibrahim Bey, who had halted at Bilbays, a mere 40 km north-east of Cairo. Meanwhile the imminent arrival in Cairo of the hadj, the great caravan returning from Mecca full of pilgrims from Morocco, Algeria, Tunisia, Tripoli and Egypt, was of considerable political and economic importance. It was essential that the pilgrims should view the French conquest without fear and make it known in their respective countries.

Bonaparte sent Carlo Rosetti, a frequent visitor to Egypt, to open up negotiations with Murad Bey, with whom Rosetti was on friendly terms, while sending a forward guard to Bilbays to prepare for the army's next march. He sent Major Junot to reconnoitre the routes to the Suez isthmus on 4 August. Sending Reynier's, Lannes's and Dugua's divisions on ahead, Bonaparte set off in turn for Bilbays on the 7th, leaving Desaix's and Bon's divisions behind to cover Cairo. The three divisions met the pilgrims' caravan at Bilbays on the 9th, and on the 11th, after a forced march, the army came into contact with some of Ibrahim Bey's troops at Salihiyya. Because the French were exhausted by the march, the combat that followed was not decisive and Ibrahim was able to flee to the outskirts of Gaza in Syria. Again, Bonaparte decided it would be useless to follow him. But one major result had been achieved: Ibrahim was out of Egypt. It would merely be necessary to block his return by a powerful occupation of the country. Wishing to open up negotiations with him, Bonaparte proposed the pasha of Egypt, who had followed him, as mediator.

Bonaparte left for Cairo on 13 August, leaving a single division—Reynier's—plus Leclerc's cavalry unit at Salihiyya with orders to build fortifications and gather the necessary provisions for an expedition to Syria and Suez. He reached Bilbays late that night, where he found an aide of Kléber's waiting to inform him of the naval disaster at Aboukir.

The previous May, Nelson and his squadron had been detached from the Cadiz blockade and sent to patrol the Gulf of Lions to keep an eye on the movements of the Toulon fleet. On the night of 20 May, as the French fleet sailed for Genoa, Nelson's squadron was caught in a storm and it was not until after he had repaired the damage to his ships that he learned, on the 31st, of the departure of the French fleet for an unknown destination. He followed the Italian coast as far as Naples, which he reached on 17 June, only to learn that the French were at Malta. He immediately set off in pursuit, reaching Messina on the 20th in time to hear of the fall of Malta and to learn of the departure of the fleet for the East. He hastened to Egypt, arriving at Alexandria on the 28th, two days ahead of the French. Not surprisingly, he was unable to obtain any information as to their whereabouts. It did not cross his mind that the French might arrive after him, so he headed for Syracuse to replenish his supplies and anchored there on

20 July. The Neapolitan crown promptly provided the necessary fresh supplies, enabling him to leave Syracuse a few days later. He set sail for Morea, where he learned that the French fleet had been sighted sailing south-east from Crete. He immediately turned back in the direction of Egypt which he reached, under a crowded sail, on 1 August. Sighting the French fleet still at anchor off Aboukir, he immediately prepared to attack.

Suspicious-looking sails had been sighted by the French as far back as 20 July, but Admiral Brueys had seen no need to improve his position. The squadron was strung out along a single line 2 km from the coast at a depth of seven fathoms: had they been closer to land there would still have been enough depth for manœuvre and the land batteries could have afforded some protection, but at 1 km—the distance of the flagship from the island of Aboukir—the effectiveness of the two mortars installed there was illusory. And yet the French fleet had been in daily expectation of the arrival of the enemy.

As they had feared, twelve enemy sail were indeed sighted at two in the afternoon of 1 August, heading at full speed in their direction. At three o'clock Brueys cleared the decks for

Nicolas Jacques Conté, *The citadel at Cairo, Joseph's Well,* 1798-1801. Watercolour. Private collection.

action. At four, two more ships joined the English squadron. Brueys, seeing them sailing towards him under a fair wind, realized that they would attack that very evening and gave the order to engage combat while at anchor, having decided that the insufficient number of his crews made it impossible to sail and fight at the same time; Admiral Blanquet du Chayla alone was to put up a vigorous fight under sail.

Nelson decided to concentrate his offensive on the head and centre of the French line. The distance at which Brueys had anchored from the coast permitted the enemy to round the head of the French ships and catch them between two salvoes, which they did at six o'clock. The mortars on Aboukir opened fire but had no effect at all. Then the ships against which the offensive had been particularly directed were boarded, and hand-to-hand fighting spread like wildfire, becoming general in the space of half an hour. The English manœuvres consisted in several ships attacking one of the immobilized French men-of-war and overwhelming it while the rearguard stood helplessly by. Brueys was wounded at seven o'clock. At seven-thirty his left thigh was blown off. He died on the bridge. At half past nine his flagship *Orient* caught fire and had to be abandoned. It exploded an hour later. By this time the English had put more than half the French fleet out of action.

By the end of the day the French squadron was almost totally destroyed and the loss of life was considerable: 1700 men killed or drowned, 1500 wounded and over 3000 taken prisoner, with Brueys's death in action leaving the fleet without a commander. The English fleet had not come out of it unscathed: nine men-of-war had been dismasted, and two of these were very seriously damaged.

It is not surprising that Brueys should have been taken so totally unawares by Nelson. He made no use of the defensive possibilities of the island of Aboukir and his awkward positioning of the squadron compromised its safety. He was incapable of enforcing discipline on board and never personally inspected his ships. He was also short of men. Nevertheless, there were many acts of heroism and the English fleet was badly battered. By regrouping the rearguard with the ships that had not seen action that day, a good admiral might have been able to turn the next day into a victory; instead, the rearguard, led by Captain Decrès and Vice-Admiral Villeneuve, abandoned the field. (Curiously, we shall find those two together again in 1805, Decrès as Naval Minister investing Villeneuve with the command of the English invasion fleet!)

In the aftermath of the battle—the Battle of the Nile—there were fears that the English would round off their victory with an attack on Rosetta and Alexandria, but they had paid dearly for their victory and were in no position to attack the French defences. The destruction of the French fleet and the departure of its rearguard gave Nelson the necessary time to set about repairing his ships before going back to sea. He temporarily occupied the island of Aboukir, and later blockaded the Egyptian ports, but his real victory was in gaining supremacy over the Mediterranean.

Kléber, in Alexandria, had immediately taken the necessary measures to oppose the English, and informed Bonaparte in a letter dated 10 August that 'the English are sure to come and shell our ports, [and will not] hesitate to sail up the channels that our seamen find so dangerous and impracticable'. Menou was in Rosetta with a handful of men in the midst of a superficially docile population which English intrigue could turn against him at any moment. He had already been forced to make an example of one village, where some Frenchmen had been killed, by burning it to the ground.

The English maintained an active surveillance of the coast and intercepted all sea communications between Alexandria and Rosetta. The Battle of the Nile put an end to any French thoughts of draughting further troops to Egypt and particularly to the proposed

André Dutertre, *Portrait of Murad Bey.*
Engraving from the *Description de l'Égypte,* 1809-26.

expedition to India, as Nelson hastened to announce to the governor of Bombay, thereby saving him the expense of preparing for its defence. The news of the victory also spread rapidly to Constantinople and throughout the East, where it was to have important repercussions.

The conquest of Egypt, which Bonaparte had so successfully carried out, was now affected by a very different set of circumstances. The remains of the navy had to be reorganized, the coastline had to be protected against the English, preparations for a possible offensive by returning mamelukes had to be got under way, and hostile acts by the population had to be prevented or suppressed. On 10 August the garrison at al Mansurah was massacred: the delta had yet to be conquered. It was also important not to allow the army to become discouraged in the face of this disaster, and to ensure that the new colony became self-sufficient now that free passage between France and Egypt was no longer possible. Bonaparte had become the prisoner of his own conquest.

While still occupied with the subjugation of the delta, Bonaparte had to turn his attention to Upper Egypt. Negotiations with Murad Bey had broken down after the bey, hearing of the defeat of the French at Aboukir, rejected proposals he was about to accept and set about preparing for battle. Luckily the defeat of Ibrahim Bey had released enough troops for action in Middle and Upper Egypt. Bonaparte put Desaix at their head and, taking advantage of the flooding of the Nile for the transport of men and equipment, Desaix sailed upriver from Cairo towards Bani Suwayf on 25 August.

Bonaparte tried without success to establish peaceful relations with the pasha of Acre, Ahmed Djezzar, who exerted fierce control over Syria, and sought contact with the sherif of Mecca whose religious influence over Egypt he hoped to enlist. He also attempted to establish direct contact with the Porte by writing to the Grand Vizier, Yussuf Pasha, and he wrote similar letters to the pashas of Damascus and Egypt: all remained unanswered.

In Constantinople the defeat at Aboukir had turned the scales in favour of England and Russia and encouraged Selim III to go to war against France. Ruffin, the French chargé

Michel Rigo, *Abd Allah Cherkaoui, president of the Cairo Divan and sheik of the al Azhar mosque*, 1798-1800.
Oil on canvas. Musée National du Château de Versailles.

32

d'affaires in Constantinople, was imprisoned in the Castle of the Seven Towers, and repressive measures were taken against the French throughout the East. The disaster at Aboukir had put an end to any hopes that a peace could be founded on Turkey's hesitation over joining forces with her ancient enemies. The new state of affairs profoundly altered the conditions of the struggle and caused a resurgence of Muslim fanaticism. Also, Turkey would soon have the support of the Russian fleet, which was on its way to the Mediterranean from Sebastopol. The eastern islands were to be the first objective of a combined Russian-Turkish offensive, and the pasha of Rhodes was ordered to join the English squadron before Alexandria in a show of solidarity between Turkey and England which would weaken the effect of French assurances of their friendly intentions towards the Porte. Meanwhile the Directoire was not able to send enough men and arms for the defence of the eastern islands, though Corfu managed to hold out until March 1799.

Troops were being slowly assembled in Syria. English and Portuguese squadrons were laying siege to Malta, where a revolt broke out supported by Naples. The Directoire had not yet abandoned hope of avoiding a break with the Porte and believed that the situation would drag on unchanged until Descorches, the new ambassador in place of Dubayet, who had died in 1797, could reach Constantinople. Talleyrand had briefed Descorches to represent France's grievances to the Porte, suggesting two plans which could result in a treaty of alliance and offering France's services as mediator with Passwan Oglou, at that time leading a rebellion in Bulgaria. But the arrest of Ruffin and the declared hostility of the Porte presented the Directoire with a *fait accompli*, and Descorches's departure was put off; from now on the Army of the Orient would have to manage on its own in Egypt.

It was therefore becoming more and more essential that Bonaparte should win over the

Dominique Vivant Denon, *The military divan*, 1798-9. Pen and wash. London, British Museum.

local population and conciliate the Arabs in order to form a coalition. The best advice the Directoire could offer was sent to Bonaparte in a letter of 4 November: 'You have three possibilities: to stay in Egypt and establish a colony that can be protected from the Turks; to go inland to India; or to march on Constantinople: the choice is yours.' This letter, of which several copies were sent by different means, only reached Bonaparte on 25 March 1799, some five months later.

EGYPT UNDER BONAPARTE

For a time Egypt became relatively peaceful: the Porte was not yet able to mount an offensive against the French; Ibrahim Bey, exiled in Syria, was occupied with the reorganization of his troops; and in Upper Egypt Murad Bey had only a small force which Desaix easily contained. Bonaparte therefore had his hands free to establish the government and administration of the country.

Mediators had to be selected to act as liaison officers between the authorities and the local population, and on 2 September 1798, Bonaparte promoted the conductor of the Mecca caravan and one-time lieutenant of the pasha of Cairo, Mustapha Bey, to the position of Emir al Hadj. The sheiks and ulemas of Cairo conveyed their approval of this choice, which they considered

Edme François Jomard, *View of the Qasr Qarun temple situated at the western edge of the lake known as Birkat al Qarun*, 1798-1801. Watercolour. Paris, Bibliothèque Nationale.

to be favourable to Muslim interests, to the sherif of Mecca. On the 4th Bonaparte gave instructions for a general assembly of the Egyptian chiefs to be held in Cairo. On the 5th he condemned sherif Koraim to death for intriguing with the enemy, and had him executed the next day in the square of the citadel; his head was paraded round the streets of Cairo with a placard threatening all traitors and perjurers with the same fate. Bonaparte set up tribunals to settle commercial disputes in all the squares of Cairo, Alexandria, Rosetta and Damietta. On the 16th, in order to regulate land ownership and to prevent disputes over property, he established land offices where all owners had to register their properties and any subsequent transactions. On the same day he obliged everyone engaged in trade to take out a licence.

Bonaparte already felt sure enough of his position to add a Turkish foot company, under the command of Janissary Omar, to the Guide Corps. Other local companies were formed, and all the young mamelukes were drafted into the army. Ten companies of National Guards were formed in Cairo.

Bonaparte, based in Cairo with Lannes's and Bon's divisions, devoted himself to overseeing military arrangements, gaining the cooperation of the local dignitaries, encouraging the development of industry and reorganizing municipal services. The sheer number of details he attended to personally is astounding: hospitals, clothing, supplies, transport—all came under his scrutiny. Finance was one area in which everything had to be turned to account. Mounts for the army caused endless miscalculations due to the lack of horses and the ill will of the inhabitants, so Bonaparte turned to camels as a means of transport. Artillery, arms for the infantry and

Noël Dejuine, *The Battle of Sediman*. Watercolour. Paris, Bibliothèque de l'Institut.

cavalry, the discipline and duties of the troops and the organization of the defences of Cairo all received Bonaparte's personal attention.

By 8 September he was able to write to inform the Directoire:

I am in daily expectation of news from Constantinople. I shall not be able to return to Paris in October as I had promised, but I should not be delayed more than a few months. Everything is going perfectly well here. The inhabitants have been subdued and are beginning to get accustomed to our presence.... No other colony has had so much to offer, and I am convinced that, thanks to Egypt, you are in a position to make peace with England on your own terms. Once she controls Egypt, France will end up master of India. The Cabinet in London is perfectly aware of the fact. I therefore have no doubt that this is the guarantee of a general peace.

After the failure of his earlier attempts to communicate with the Turkish Porte, Bonaparte sought to open up relations by other means. Bearing a letter for Constantinople, his emissary Mailly de Châteaurenard set off for Latakia in Syria with orders to spread the information along the way that the French expedition was over, that were it not for the British attack on their fleet the army would already have left, that commerce could now be safety resumed, and so on. As soon as he reached Latakia, however, Châteaurenard was thrown into prison. He was later executed by Djezzar during the course of the Syrian campaign.

On 19 September Bonaparte visited the pyramids in the company of his officers and scholars. After having celebrated the feasts of the Nile and the Prophets in Cairo, he organized the feast of 1 Vendémiaire as a means of forming a bond between the Egyptian and French peoples.

The pacification and administration of Lower Egypt continued. In Alexandria the building of defences, protection for the canal and refitting of the surviving ships were progressing.

Bonaparte on the tallest pyramid in Egypt. Engraving. Artist unknown. Paris, Bibliothèque Nationale.

though the British blockade had put a stop to all commercial activity. To punish the villagers of Birkat Gitas, who had been springing leaks in the canal to prevent the waters of the Nile from reaching Alexandria, Kléber sent a detachment of troops to burn the village and parade the heads of the rebels on pikes. He followed this act of repression with a proclamation threatening any village that caused the slightest damage to the canal with the same fate.

In Rosetta, Menou had his hands full protecting the mouth of the Nile against the English, keeping the lines of communication with Alexandria open and administering the province. In the provinces of Mansurah and Damietta a complicated system of canals and approaches to Lake Manzalah had to be reconnoitred to facilitate communications and intercept Ibrahim Bey's emissaries. There were frequent attacks, underlining the general unrest. Andréossy, charged with scouting the lake area, found it necessary first to destroy the power base of Hasan Tubar, an ally of Ibrahim Bey and only apparently friendly to the French. Hasan Tubar eventually gave up the struggle and departed for Gaza.

In the province of Charkia, Reynier watched over the mameluke refugees in Syria and prepared the defences of the province, while Bonaparte gathered provisions for him in Salihiyya.

When the negotiations with Murad Bey broke down, Bonaparte decided to mount an attack against him and the mamelukes who had taken refuge in Upper Egypt. Desaix's division, which had left Cairo on 25 August via the Nile, reached Bani Suwayf on the 31st and set off in search of him. Murad Bey had retreated to the interior, to the east near Abu Girg, between the mountain and Joseph's Canal, where he had gathered his djerms and his provisions. Desaix followed the Nile as far as Abu Girg where a thorough but fruitless reconnaissance was carried out amidst great difficulties, finally forcing him to continue up the Nile to Joseph's Canal. Desaix's push into Upper Egypt gave rise to disturbing rumours: it was said that Murad Bey had intercepted the French and was now preparing a return offensive against Cairo, but this was without foundation. Despite the difficulty of navigation and the constant threat of Arab

Anne Louis Girodet-Trioson, *A wounded Turk*, study for
The Cairo Revolt.
Coloured chalk and pastel. Paris, Musée du Louvre.

OPPOSITE: Anne Louis Girodet-Trioson, *The Cairo Revolt,
21 October 1798* (detail), 1810.
Oil on canvas. Musée National du Château de Versailles.

39

and mameluke attacks, the division pursued Murad Bey and defeated him, after a bloody battle, on 7 October at Sediman, where he was entrenched. The mamelukes charged several times with great speed and ferocity, but always in vain; Murad Bey had to withdraw his cannon from the field and he himself ended up in flight. This important victory temporarily put Murad Bey out of action and Desaix was able to take control of the province of Fayyum.

At the beginning of October deputations of chiefs, sent from the various provinces at Bonaparte's request, arrived in Cairo to form a government; Abd Allah Cherkaoui was elected president. But news was beginning to filter into Egypt that, contrary to the claims of the French, the Porte, far from acquiescing to the occupation of the country, was preparing for war. Emissaries from Syria and other Ottoman provinces were sent to stir up religious fanaticism and distribute incitements to insurrection to be read out in the mosques. The leaders of the rebellion seized the proceeds of a house tax that had just been ordered. On 21 October the revolt spread through the whole town, and the insurgents established their headquarters in the Great Mosque of al Azhar. Major-General Dupuy, Cairo's military governor, was among the first casualties of the day. The next day the Arabs surrounded the town and the cavalry was sent to keep them in check. Bonaparte's aide-de-camp, Sulkowski, was hacked to pieces during the engagement. Bonaparte retaliated by shelling the town, which persuaded the insurgents to parley; the barricades were opened and the troops penetrated as far as the Great Mosque. Both sides had suffered greatly during those two days. Bonaparte accepted the surrender of the insurgents and did his utmost to reestablish peace, wishing above all to limit the repercussions of the revolt. Insurgents caught carrying arms were summarily executed. Several leaders of the movement, who had been in contact with the mamelukes and the emissaries of the Porte, were captured. The sheiks thus compromised were condemned to death. After putting down the insurrection, Bonaparte reactivated the work of ensuring communications throughout Cairo and the protection of military establishments. On 21 December he reconvened the Cairo Divan which had been suspended during the uprising.

The unrest that led to these tragic events was not confined to this one town: agitation and occasional acts of hostility had been noted in several places, but the failure of the Cairo uprising was to intimidate those who harboured similar plans.

The intentions of the Porte were still unclear in October, although Bonaparte had used every means in his power to discover what the joint military activities of the Turks and the English might be. On the 19th two Turkish frigates appeared before Alexandria. On the 24th they were reinforced by a further sixteen men-of-war, two of which flew Russian colours. The defences had to be hastily completed. The enemy made an unsuccessful attack on the Aboukir fort. In the hope of throwing some light on the contradictory information he had been receiving about Ottoman policies, Bonaparte sent two mediators on board the combined squadron. He also tried to enter into relations with Derna and Tripoli in order to obtain news from Europe. And in December, in a further effort to make direct contact with the Turks, he sent the astronomer Pierre Joseph de Beauchamp as consul to Constantinople.

Meanwhile he carried on with the organization of Egypt which had been interrupted by the Cairo uprising. Once again, no detail was too insignificant for his attention: a hospital for the Cairo poor, the establishment of concerts and shows and the building of a Tivoli—a vast pavilion for meetings and amusement.

In November the French naval forces in Egypt were reorganized into three divisions, of which Captain Ganteaume was appointed commander. In December the plague made its

Antoine Jean Gros, *Bonaparte pardoning the Cairo insurgents.*
Pen and pencil. Private collection.

appearance in Alexandria, which would further hinder the already difficult relations between this town and the rest of Egypt.

In the Fayyum, Desaix, hampered by the activities of the mamelukes, was nevertheless succeeding in organizing the province and even managing to find horses there. He then returned to Cairo to expedite reinforcements for his division. On 2 December Bonaparte reviewed the entire cavalry on the plain of al Qobbet. He established that they were ready to fight the mamelukes and, on the 6th, a column of cavalry was put at Desaix's disposal which he led back up the Nile, reaching Bani Suwayf on the 9th.

Suez had not yet been occupied by the French. As this port was doubly important, for commercial relations with Arabia and in view of combining operations with mainland France, a column from Bon's division occupied it on 7 December. On the 11th Bonaparte dispatched a convoy to transport the supplies and arms that Bon required. Before setting off himself he took measures for the protection of Cairo and the defence of the coast, ordering the construction in particular of a fort at Lesbeh, at the mouth of the Nile near Damietta, and another at Qatia, towards Syria.

He left Cairo on 24 December leaving Kléber in command of the town during his absence. He reached Suez on the evening of the 26th. Through his occupation of Suez, Bonaparte intended to organize a naval force in the Red Sea capable of overseeing commerce and preventing assistance from Arabia reaching the mamelukes. During his stay he prescribed the necessary measures. We know that he also searched for the remains of the ancient Suez Canal. He returned to Cairo on the evening of 6 January 1799; he had just taken the decision to launch an offensive against Syria.

The campaign which was to lead Desaix's division as far as the cataracts opened on 16 December. He intended to travel up the Nile as fast as possible in order to overtake Murad Bey and force him to join battle, but his men and artillery were subjected to delays which enabled the mamelukes to slip away. There were some rough days' marches for the troops, who were frequently deprived of the support of the flotilla. On the 29th they reached Girga, which the mamelukes had hastily abandoned the night before leaving their boats, magazines and flocks behind them. In order to survive, the mamelukes seized provisions, beef and camels from the villages they passed through; whenever the villagers refused to cooperate fierce fighting broke out as the mamelukes plundered the village.

At Girga, Desaix waited patiently for the flotilla and prepared a new series of operations against Murad Bey. His immobilization, lasting three weeks, allowed the mamelukes time to reorganize their men, receive reinforcements and foment uprisings that threatened to cut the communications lines to Cairo. Davout's cavalry was ordered to disperse any such hostile gatherings.

On 20 January the division left Girga. Murad Bey had been able to add Hasan Bey's mamelukes to his own, as well as Arabian horsemen and bands of Arabs from Mecca, amounting to a total of 14,000 men, whom he intended to lead against the French. Not wishing to be forestalled, Desaix marched on Samhud, south of Girga, on the 22nd, where, at the end of the battle, he dispersed the mamelukes but was unable to recapture those who escaped. The mameluke cavalry had been incapable of breaching the French infantry and Murad Bey had desired nothing better than to escape, once again, from his conquerors. Desaix continued his march and reached Esna, with his cavalry vigorously pursuing the mamelukes up ahead. He left Friant's brigade at Esna and continued the pursuit, followed at half a day's march by Belliard.

On 2 February Desaix reached Syene (Aswan). Murad Bey's retreat beyond the cataracts proved that he was again temporarily out of action, but it was necessary to be prepared for a return offensive. Desaix entrusted Belliard with the occupation and fortification of Syene, followed on the 20th by the occupation of the island of Philae.

Meanwhile, bands of Meccans had assembled near Qena, on the Nile, at the end of the Qusayr route. Davout managed to catch up with Osman Bey on 11 February near Radisah where he joined him in bloody combat, chasing him into the desert towards Qusayr. On the

OPPOSITE: Jean Charles Tardieu, *The French army halts at Syene, Upper Egypt, on 2 February 1799* (detail), 1812 Salon. Oil on canvas. Musée National du Château de Versailles.

André Dutertre, *Portrait of General Desaix*. Black chalk heightened with watercolour and gouache. Musée National du Château de Versailles.

night of the 12th a Meccan offensive against Qena was repulsed after a lively engagement. This showed the need to occupy Qusayr, which Desaix was thinking of taking. Bonaparte himself had considered ensuring the occupation of the town by means of a small flotilla departing from Suez, but not until after the Syrian campaign since he would need to concentrate all his available resources there.

A fresh gathering of Meccans attacked the flotilla that had fallen behind on the Nile, depriving the division of almost all its reserve munitions and compromising the communication lines with the troops stationed in the upper valley of the river. Although Belliard routed the Meccans and Hasan Bey's mamelukes in a violent combat at Benut on 8 and 9 March, the division was placed in a very difficult position by the loss of the flotilla and the constantly renewed attacks from the mamelukes, the Meccans and the local inhabitants.

Desaix therefore directed his military operations in a new way in an attempt to destroy his enemies. He deployed his troops in successive columns aimed at forcing the enemy either to stay in the desert or face a long march before reaching cultivated lands. He directed his first action against Hasan Bey and the Meccans, who had taken refuge in Laqeita on the way to Qusayr, then he occupied both the outlets leading to the Nile, leaving a single long and painful means of retreat. The engagement took place at Bir al Bar on 2 April, and Desaix narrowly missed being taken prisoner when he pushed too far into the desert. Nevertheless, this battle stopped the advance of the mamelukes, who retreated towards the upper part of the Nile.

The capture of Qusayr was the best way, in Desaix's opinion, of ensuring French supremacy in Upper Egypt, for there was a danger that the English on their way back from India, who

Dominique Vivant Denon, *Combat and death of Brigadier Duplessis*, 1799. Pen and wash. London, British Museum.

Letterhead of the Dromedary Regiment. Paris, Bibliothèque Nationale.

were constantly appearing in the Red Sea, might otherwise capture this port. Desaix urged Belliard to put together the means to occupy Qusayr, one of which was to be the use of dromedaries to transport the expedition.

Establishing a base at Asyut, Desaix busied himself with the organization of Upper Egypt and the pacification of the country through just and firm means, but he was constantly obliged to make enormous efforts to overcome the lack of men and ammunition. Peace was maintained only by force, by taking hostages from the villages and by continual exhausting marches. Desaix organized a rapid and safe communication system throughout Upper Egypt, carried out by men on horseback.

Two military operations remained to be executed in order to protect the conquered provinces against attack: the occupation of Qusayr and an expedition against Murad Bey in his refuge in the Great Oasis. Belliard took Qusayr on 29 April with 350 infantry and artillerymen. He at once wrote to the sherif of Mecca assuring him that the French favoured relations and commerce between Mecca and Egypt, that they considered themselves the friends

Dominique Vivant Denon, *The French arrive at Qusayr*, 1799. Pen and wash. London, British Museum.

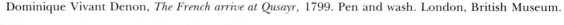

Jean Duplessi-Bertaux, *The Army of Egypt*. Pen and wash. Paris, Musée des Arts Africains et Océaniens.

of the Ottoman Empire and the Muslims, and that their only enemies were the English. Major-General Donzelot was left at Qusayr, the occupation of which completed the conquest of Upper Egypt and crowned the efforts of Desaix and his soldiers. They had overcome every enemy they had faced from the Fayyum to the cataracts.

On his return to Cairo from Suez, Bonaparte had decided upon an offensive against the forces mustering on the Syrian border. By driving out Ibrahim Bey and preventing enemy armies from threatening him from that quarter by a joint action with the European forces on the Egyptian coast, he would secure the conquest of the country. His plan had added advantages:

the English ships would be prevented from revictualling in Syria, and the Ottoman Empire would be forced into negotiation.

At almost the same moment that Bonaparte decided to make war on Syria, the Porte signed two treaties for a defensive alliance, one with Russia, on 23 December 1798, the other with England, on 5 January 1799, stipulating their formal protection of all the territories of the Sublime Porte.

Bonaparte had already given instructions for the occupation of Qatia and the building of a fort there. Recognizing their extreme mobility, he created a dromedary regiment. By various means he was able to procure enough horses to mount the cavalry and supply the needs of the artillery. By the end of January 1799 part of the artillery material had been sent to Salihiyya and Qatia. Bonaparte had the necessary troops for the infantry, but transporting a full siege depot across the desert behind the army not only required a great number of horses but risked presenting insurmountable difficulties because of its sheer weight. He decided therefore to organize a small flotilla which could carry the siege artillery he needed for Syria by sea.

Bonaparte left Cairo on 10 February. Al Arish, Gaza and Jaffa fell one after the other. In Jaffa the plague appeared; Bonaparte fearlessly went among plague victims offering what help he could. On 14 March he left Jaffa and marched on Acre, after first taking Haifa. On 28 March he thought that the moment had come for action and ordered the assault on Acre, but it was not practicable and the assault failed.

The pasha of Acre, Djezzar, raised an army of all Muslims able to bear arms, from Damascus, Nablus and Aleppo. Kléber reached Nazareth on 8 April. On the 11th he attacked the enemy gathered at Canaan and flung it back towards the Jordan. On the 16th the Battle of Mount Tabor took place, during which Bonaparte, in a rapid intervention in support of Kléber, carried a victory in which the mameluke camp was captured and the pasha's armies put to flight. This battle led the Druzes and the Maronites to declare themselves more openly on the side of the French. The English commodore Sidney Smith, who had come from Constantinople with his fleet, did everything in his power to support besieged Acre. During the night of 16 April Perrée's division brought the eagerly awaited siege material from Alexandria to Jaffa. Bonaparte expected to become the master of Acre on the 24th or 25th, and announced his imminent return. On the 24th a mine was laid to bring down the Great Tower, but although it destroyed a large section of the tower the upper floor was only slightly damaged and the enemy was able to blast anyone that went into the attack. It was another setback.

A fleet of thirty Turkish men-of-war arrived, bringing considerable reinforcements to the pasha. On 8 May a fresh assault penetrated the fortified town, but the entrenchments that a French émigré, Colonel Phélipeaux, had advised the pasha to prepare became an obstacle which separated the French troops inside the town. The support of the English, the barricades in the streets, the burning houses—including Djezzar's palace—made it impossible to hold the town.

On the 10th, Kléber's division returned to renew the assault, but the French troops came up against new entrenchments. They had to retire under fire from the palace and the houses across from the breach and from the batteries in front of the mosque and the lighthouse. This setback showed the growing inequality between the means at the disposal of the French army and those of the besieged, to which the support of the English men-of-war had by then been added. To prolong the campaign was to risk the very survival of the army. Bonaparte did not hesitate to take the decision that circumstances imposed upon him: he raised the siege on the night of the 20th.

The condition of some of the plague victims at Jaffa did not permit their evacuation.

Armand Caraffe, *The Battle of Nazareth, 8 April 1799*, 1801.
Line and wash. Paris, Bibliothèque Nationale.

Anticipating their massacre by the Turks, Bonaparte ordered them to be given an overdose of laudanum, but after protestations from Chief Medical Officier Desgenettes he merely had them heavily sedated.

The joy of the troops at being back in Egypt was as great as if they had returned to their mother country. Bonaparte prepared them for a triumphant entry into Cairo, and on 14 June they were fêted like a victorious army as they entered the town. Bonaparte tried in vain to present the raising of the siege of Acre in a favourable light. The army had lost some of its best men; the losses in campaign and siege artillery were very great; and the navy, already weak, found itself reduced even further.

Prisoners of their conquest, the French troops could only look forward to hollow victories and to becoming the certain prey of an enemy who, master of the sea, merely had to bide her time—unless France could find a means to come to the aid of her soldiers in Egypt.

For three weeks at the beginning of 1799 the English fleet had intermittently shelled Alexandria; then Bonaparte's advance into Syria had led them to anchor at Acre to support the besieged Djezzar. On 3 March Rear Admiral Troubridge had been replaced by Sidney Smith as commander of the English squadron. Bonaparte had taken the emir al hadj, Mustapha Bey, and the sheiks with him on his way to Syria, but they went no further than Salihiyya. This was significant. An insurrection had been brewing in Lower Egypt, but energetic measures had been taken and peace appeared to have been assured. The emir's intentions became more and more hostile and bands of Arabs attacked the French convoys with his support, but he was vigorously pursued and overcome before his revolt could spread.

No sooner was Charkia delivered from the emir's clutches than a new danger arose in the Bahayra area. A fanatical chief from Derna, Ahmed al Madhi, proclaimed himself an envoy from the Prophet sent to help the true believers triumph over the infidels. He claimed to be invulnerable and his inflamed preaching drew hordes of Arabs to his side. On the night of 24

OPPOSITE: Louis François Lejeune, *The Battle of Mount Tabor, 16 April 1799* (detail), 1801 Salon. Oil on canvas. Musée National du Château de Versailles.

Louis François Lejeune, *The Battle of Aboukir, 25 July 1799,* 1804 Salon. Oil on canvas. Musée National du Château de Versailles.

April, al Madhi took the small garrison of 1500 men at Damanhur by surprise and butchered them all. Emboldened by his success, he made for the Nile and fomented an uprising in the delta just as mamelukes and Meccans from Upper Egypt reached the outskirts of Cairo. On 5 May Dugua, who had succeeded Dupuy as military governor of Cairo, wrote to inform Bonaparte that fanaticism and treachery were leading the entire population of Egypt to revolt. Military quarters were under attack and communication lines were in danger of being cut. In short, it was necessary for the Syrian army to return.

At Dugua's behest, Davout left Bani Suwayf for Cairo on the 3rd. It was difficult to gather sufficient forces to fight al Madhi, for Alexandria was in constant expectation of an English offensive from the sea and its garrison was being sorely tried by the plague. However, al Madhi's troops were dispersed at Damanhur on 9 May and the town was looted, burned and sacked.

On 11 July the enemy fleet appeared before Alexandria; the English strength was supplemented by the Turkish fleet and a corps of 20,000 men under Mustapha Pasha. They disembarked at Aboukir on the 14th. Bonaparte received the news on the 15th in his camp at the pyramids; he immediately decided to march on the threatened area and concentrate sufficient forces at al Rahmaniya.

The Turks attacked the redoubt a kilometre from the fort that cut Aboukir island more or less in two, and the few French who survived were beheaded before the pasha. The fort capitulated on the 17th. The capture of Aboukir cut all communications between Alexandria and Rosetta.

Bonaparte reached al Rahmaniya on the 19th and set off for Alexandria on the 23rd to determine the strategic position of the town and the advantages it might afford before deciding

Antoine Jean Gros, *Murat at the Battle of Aboukir* (detail), *c* 1805.
Oil on canvas. Detroit, Institute of Arts.

The Fall of Aboukir. Pen and wash. Artist unknown. Paris, Bibliothèque Nationale.

on his offensive against the Turks. The troops gathered about 7 km outside Aboukir during the evening of the 24th. On the 25th the French army was on the march before daylight; Murat and Destaing led the advance guard with Lannes on the right flank and Lanusse on the left, while Kléber headed the reserve. The redoubt was taken and Mustapha Pasha was captured. Kléber, who was unable to join Bonaparte until the evening, could not resist kissing Bonaparte and exclaiming: 'General, you are as great as the world itself.' The Turks fled towards the sea. The fort still had to be taken; it was immediately surrounded. Bonaparte left for Alexandria on the 27th and on the 29th he announced the Victory of Aboukir to the Directoire even though it was not until 2 August that, overwhelmed by the shelling and exhausted by privation and above all by thirst, the defenders of the fort finally surrendered.

The speed at which Aboukir had been recaptured warded off the principal danger—an explosion of Muslim fanaticism and a reawakening of hostility which only savage repression could contain. Bonaparte's victory happened too quickly for the enemies of France to be able to react.

Meanwhile, Murad Bey had been fleeing up the Nile valley pursued by the French columns. He was surprised not far from Samhud during the night of 11 August by Morand, who captured his camp; despite being wounded, Murad managed to escape under cover of darkness and remained elusive. The English attacked Qusayr on the 14th, 15th and 16th, but were repulsed by Donzelot.

For the next few months peace descended on Egypt and it would be long time before the Turks were able to renew their offensive. However, Mustapha Pasha, now a prisoner, informed Bonaparte that the French armies had been defeated everywhere in the renewed European war, and this was confirmed by newspapers sent by Sidney Smith. It was clear that no help would be forthcoming from France for the Army of the Orient.

The idea of returning to France had long been on Bonaparte's mind. The French army was trapped in Egypt and no longer had anything to gain from the East, and he knew that the Directoire needed him to head the armies of the Republic. The victory at Aboukir provided a respite during which he could return to France.

He left Alexandria for Cairo on 5 August. He intended to spend no more than a few days there, during which time Ganteaume was to complete the fitting out of the men-of-war he would require and keep a watch on the movements of enemy squadrons in order to choose a propitious moment for his departure from Egypt. When he arrived in Cairo on the 11th, the entire population gathered at Azbakiyyah where they were able to see Mustapha Pasha and many other Turkish officers whom Bonaparte had brought with him as trophies of his victory. The town remained calm despite a number of incitements to hostility. On the 15th Bonaparte wrote to Desaix telling him to resume the occupation of Upper Egypt and the pursuit of Murad Bey in order to defeat and force him to negotiate.

Bonaparte wished to ensure the best possible defences for Egypt but he also still hoped to renew negotiations with the Turkish Empire. He knew that his army was being reduced in number and that it could not withstand another combined operation. He chose one of the prisoners taken at Aboukir, Mehemet Effendi, as a mediator and made him the bearer of a letter to the Grand Vizier on 17 August:

> The Sublime Porte declared war on the French Republic without awaiting the arrival of Ambassador Descorches. Your enemies are not in Egypt but on the Bosphorus. We could settle everything in two hours of conversation.

But England, by virtue of her treaty with the Porte, would not permit these negotiations, from which she would have been excluded.

Despite the care with which Bonaparte disguised his planned departure, rumours of it began to spread. On 14 August Ganteaume apprised him of the departure of the enemy ships from Alexandria; Bonaparte received his letter on the 17th and decided to leave that same night. He went to the general headquarters at Bulaq at midnight and, embarking at 3 a.m., he followed the Rosetta waterway to Minuf, where Lanusse was in command. He stayed there for twenty-four hours, denying the rumours of his departure and inviting Kléber to confer with him on 'some vitally important issues' at Rosetta on the 24th: he was about to hand over the supreme command of the army.

Bonaparte then descended the Nile as far as al Rahmaniya where it appears he arrived on the evening of the 20th. Menou was ordered to join him by the fountain near the general headquarters of the battle at Aboukir. Awaiting Bonaparte and his escort were horses to take them to the coast. He reached Birkat Gitas on the evening of the 21st. Only Berthier and Bourrienne were in on the secret. The next day they made a halt at the Beydah well, 12 km from Alexandria, whence they reached the coast.

While Bonaparte was travelling from Cairo to the coast, Ganteaume and Marmont had continued their watch for movements of the enemy vessels, which were no longer patrolling Alexandria: because of this Bonaparte decided to embark on the 22nd without entering the town. He had arranged to meet Menou and Ganteaume between Alexandria and Aboukir, 4 km from its fort. During the meeting he gave Menou a number of letters and documents concerning his departure, the transfer of the supreme command to Kléber, and a short proclamation to the army. His instructions were amplified in a long report on the defence and political administration of Egypt.

On the 22nd the frigates *Muiron* and *Carrère* appeared offshore and that night Bonaparte and his escort embarked. The frigates got under way at eight the following morning. Bonaparte was aboard the *Muiron* with Berthier and Andréossy; Lannes, Murat and Marmont were aboard the *Carrère*.

On 30 September they entered the roads of Ajaccio, reaching St-Raphael Bay in France at 10 a.m. on 9 October, where they were greeted enthusiastically. Bonaparte left for Paris the same day, arriving there on the 16th.

The success of Bonaparte's passage had depended on its secrecy. He had even asked Menou to wait forty-eight hours before publishing the news and Dugua was still writing to Bonaparte after he had gone. Kléber had received no counter-orders about his meeting with Bonaparte on the 24th and was furious when he learned of his departure at Rosetta. He opened the letters Bonaparte had sent with Menou then, after conferring with him, left for Cairo on the 27th.

His arrival dissipated anxiety there and he was received with pomp. Saluted by the guns of all the forts, he established himself in Bonaparte's quarters. His nomination was unanimously acclaimed and he even succeeded in earning the trust of the Divan and the chiefs of Cairo. The town was peaceful and, once people got used to the idea, Bonaparte's departure led to hopes of relief within a few months and even to an amicable evacuation. Desaix was to write:

Louis Meyer, *General Bonaparte's arrival in France on his return from the Egyptian campaign on 9 October 1799*, 1843. Oil on canvas. Paris, Hôtel de Lassay.

If the commander-in-chief reaches France, knowing his talent as we do, we can expect an improvement in our situation.

The Directoire meanwhile was seeking a basis for negotiation with the Porte using Spain as the intermediary. Reinhart, the new Minister for Foreign Affairs, was commissioned to inform Bonaparte of this. It appeared that the Turks were ready, after the victories of the French, to conclude a separate peace on the single condition of the evacuation of Egypt. Back in France Bonaparte was soon to seize power. He also intended to rescue the army he had left behind, though circumstances would prevent him from sending immediate relief.

THE END OF THE ADVENTURE

Kléber had never seen eye-to-eye with Bonaparte on the occupation of Egypt, and had taken the ascendancy of a man so much younger than himself very badly. He regretted having followed him and had resigned himself to the idea that this expedition had been Bonaparte's alone. Much loved by his men, he had constantly fuelled their longing to return to France. Now that Bonaparte was gone, leaving him in charge of Egypt, he decided it was time to evacuate a country that had become a trap.

Bonaparte had not ignored the possibility of the army being forced to leave Egypt when he had made his final overtures of peace to the Porte, but he had calculated on producing enough of a conflict of interest between Turkey and England to gain time in which to consolidate the occupation of the country.

The Turkish offensive reopened on 1 November 1799, when a force disembarked at Damietta. Brigadier Verdier, the military governor there, repulsed them with his meagre troops, despite English artillery fire, in a brilliant feat of arms.

Meanwhile, malicious gossip about Bonaparte—that irresponsible young man on the subject of whom Kléber sent the Directoire a report written by the administrator Poussielgue—had sufficed to justify Kléber's fatal decision to prepare for immediate evacuation. Neither Kléber nor Poussielgue had the slightest inkling that the report and Kléber's letters would be given to Bonaparte in person—now First Consul of France following the *coup d'état* of 18 Brumaire (9 November)—whom they half expected to have been captured at sea by the English.

On his own initiative Kléber had sent one of his officers to make fresh overtures for peace to Yussuf Pasha, the Grand Vizier, by then back in Syria, and Sidney Smith, thinking to take advantage of this moment of weakness of the French to wrest the conquest of Egypt from their grasp before their government had a chance to react, advised the Grand Vizier to listen to Kléber's request. At the same time, in the hope of ensuring a safe passage to France for the army, Kléber sent Desaix and Poussielgue on an embassy to Sidney Smith himself, though without previously examining Smith's powers of negotiation. At this precise moment Bonaparte was seizing power in France.

Kléber had made it a condition of the negotiations that the Grand Vizier's army should halt its advance through Syria at the frontier with Egypt, but Yussuf, as soon as he came into the presence of the French army at al Arish, summoned the garrison to surrender. Its commandant, Cazals, rejected the summons, but dissension amongst the men, exacerbated by the evacuation having been announced as decisive, resulted in disagreements amongst the troops defending the fort. It fell on 30 December, opening the gates of Egypt to the Turks.

André Dutertre, *Portrait of General Kléber.*
Black chalk heightened with wash, watercolour and gouache.
Musée National du Château de Versailles.

On learning what had happened, Kléber demanded a fresh suspension of hostilities and, leaving Cairo, travelled to Salihiyya. Desaix and Poussielgue reached the Turkish camp at al Arish on 13 January 1800, where they found Sidney Smith and agreed a convention stipulating the departure of the French army, which was to pull back to Alexandria, Rosetta and Aboukir to embark for France. Davout opposed the agreement altogether, but Kléber ratified it on the 28th. The convention also stated that England would provide the necessary safe conducts for the passage of the army, but Sidney Smith, with whom Bonaparte had never dealt directly and whose intervention Kléber had solicited on his own initiative, would not commit his government by signing it. Kléber's great mistake was to sign a document that went beyond the powers invested in him. The British Cabinet had meanwhile discovered the contents of Poussielgue's report and was in possession of letters from the men expressing their longing to leave Egypt. It was now perfectly placed to crush an army which it believed to be at its last gasp, and ordered that no capitulation was to be signed that did not include the French army being taken prisoner. But by then Kléber had given all the positions on the right bank of the Nile back to the Turks

Anne Louis Girodet-Trioson, *Turk wearing a turban*.
Charcoal, chalk and sanguine on grey paper. Paris, Musée du Louvre.

and the division in Upper Egypt had done the same with its positions on the upper Nile: Kléber
had been outmanœuvred.

Desaix was recalled to France, and, just as he was boarding ship with Davout, who no
longer felt able to support Kléber after the treaty of al Arish, dispatches arrived from France
informing the Army of the Orient that a consular government was to be established in Egypt.
This was a further blow for Kléber, who had just learned of the failure of the convention by
which he had hoped to withdraw the army from Egypt. He now had not only to defend himself
under circumstances that were infinitely worse than those he had already considered unbearable
but to achieve what he had thought impossible a few days earlier. He was condemned to stay
on in Egypt.

Kléber reacted to the situation by immediately countermanding all his orders to the army and ordering back to Cairo a part of the troops which had already descended the Nile. He summoned the Grand Vizier to halt his march on Cairo under pain of an immediate resumption of hostilities. The Grand Vizier reminded him of the al Arish convention and demanded that it be fully complied with, and continued his march on Cairo. At the same moment Kléber received a letter from Lord Keith telling him that the British government would not accept a French capitulation unless they laid down their arms and surrendered as prisoners of war. So much for the convention he had signed entrusting Sidney Smith with the safety of the army;

Jean Julien Deltil, *The Battle of Heliopolis* (detail). Wallpaper. Paris, Musée des Arts Décoratifs.

now he had no choice but to turn and face the Grand Vizier's army and a population on the brink of an uprising.

On 20 March the French army sortied from Cairo towards the ruins of ancient Heliopolis and took up a formation of squares. Kléber harangued the troops and ordered a charge against an enemy detachment which was manœuvring on the French left in an attempt to enter Cairo, and put it to flight. He then ordered Reynier to attack the entrenched village of al Matariyyah, while he and Friant took up a position between there and Heliopolis to prevent the bulk of the Turkish army from intervening. Al Matariyyah was taken and the Turks fled in disarray in the direction of Cairo, led by Nassif Pasha, the Grand Vizier's lieutenant. The greater part of the Grand Vizier's army still had to be faced and was preparing for a general offensive. The French formations remained calm, firing continuously and accurately; the Turks fell under the volleys and finally retreated towards al Khankah. The French gave chase; seeing them closing in, the enemy fled, abandoning its baggage and supplies. Meanwhile Nassif Pasha and Ibrahim Bey had entered Cairo, where Kléber had left only a garrison in the citadel and the forts. He sent Lagrange to their rescue that very evening.

During the battle Murad Bey had remained out of the action on the fringes of the Turkish army and then had plunged into the desert and disappeared. Realizing that the Turks wanted to recover Egypt for themselves and would not be giving it back to the mamelukes, he had thought to get close enough to the French to be able to become their ally if they were victorious.

Claude Louis Desrais, *The death of General Kléber, murdered in Cairo on 25 Prairial Year VIII* (14 June 1800). Engraving. Paris, Bibliothèque Nationale.

André Dutertre, *Portrait of General Menou.* Black and white chalk on blue-grey paper. Musée National du Château de Versailles.

Kléber, not wishing to give the Grand Vizier a respite, rested for only a few hours and then marched on Bilbays, which he reached the next day. Yussuf Pasha had already escaped, but the Turkish corps that was still there was captured. The next day Kléber continued the pursuit towards Salihiyya and, while still on his way there, received a message from the Grand Vizier asking to negotiate. He refused and, at Koraim, the Turkish cavalry's lightning charges put him in great danger from which he was rescued just in time by Belliard. The French troops reached Salihiyya at the end of the day expecting to see action against the Grand Vizier the following morning. But he had fled into the desert and Arab looters were seen escaping from his camps as the French army arrived. At the sight of the rich booty the penniless troops no longer felt themselves to be condemned to perish in Egypt.

Kléber immediately set about retaking the positions at Damietta, Fort Lesbeh and in the delta lost through the al Arish agreement. Leaving Reynier at Salihiyya, he returned to Cairo, arriving there on 27 March to discover that there had been serious troubles during his absence. The people of Cairo, seeing Nassif Pasha and Ibrahim Bey and assuming them to be the victors of the battle, had attacked the French garrisons. Duranteau and the general headquarters staff in the palace of Azbakiyya managed to hold out until Lagrange came to relieve them, and Cairo was reconquered by the 25th after a bloody battle. The inhabitants feared that Kléber would punish them harshly; instead he pardoned them and merely levied a tax on the town, as he did on all those who had revolted.

At the end of March the English landed troops and, on 19 April, Kléber sent a detachment to retake the port, routing the English. The alliance with Murad Bey was at last beginning to take form; Kléber granted him the province of Upper Egypt, with the title Prince of Said, under the sovereignty of the French, as Bonaparte had planned. Murad undertook to cease fighting the French and drove Dervish Pasha's occupation corps out of Upper Egypt. In Syria, meanwhile, the defeated Grand Vizier was searching for a fanatic to send to Cairo to assassinate his conqueror. He found him in Suleiman al Halebi, a young Muslim aged twenty-four from Aleppo, who had spent three years in Cairo. He reached Cairo from Gaza on 14 May and spent the next month studying Kléber's habits. The general headquarters had been damaged during the fighting and Kléber was having it repaired by the architect Protain. In the meantime he was staying in Murad Bey's palace at Giza. On 14 June he went to Cairo to lunch with his chief-of-staff, Auguste Damas (brother of the brigadier). First he visited general headquarters in the company of Protain, then they lunched with Damas. Rising from the table at about two o'clock, he asked Protain to go back with him to take another look at the work in progress. Suleiman had followed from Giza and was now waiting on the terrace leading from Damas's home to general headquarters. Kléber and Protain were deep in discussion together, and frequently stopped during their walk. It was during one of these halts that Suleiman stabbed Kléber; Protain was also stabbed several times. Kléber died almost at once. Suleiman was condemned to death and impaled on the 17th, but the Grand Vizier had his revenge: Kléber was dead.

Menou, as the senior major-general, was automatically Kléber's successor. It is conceivable that Desaix would have been as good as or better than Kléber at governing Egypt, for we have seen how well he had handled both military and civil events in Upper Egypt. But he had left the country three months earlier and had fallen at Marengo on the very day of Kléber's assassination. Menou, however, although he had the required administrative ability, had none of the qualities of a Kléber or a Desaix on the military front.

Kléber's loss saddened the Arabs, who had come to respect him, and there were no disturbances following his death. It was a blow too for the army, and whilst awaiting France's decision on a new commander there were more and more disturbances among the men, for they wanted Reynier to take command. The First Consul's confirmation of Menou's position finally reached Cairo on 6 November. Menou's title was now assured, but this did not give him the authority or the military ability required of the successor of leaders such as Bonaparte and Kléber. Menou was only interested in the pleasures of government and, seduced by the magic of the East, he tranquilly settled down to enjoy it, keeping well away from anyone who warned

Cécile, *Thebes, Karnak, view of the ruins of the hypostyle hall and granite apartments of the palace,* 1798-1801. Watercolour. Paris, Musée du Louvre.

him of the dangers of an attack. The army continued to be torn between him and Reynier, but, secure in the presence of the army in Cairo, Menou refused to listen to anything that might stir him out of his complacency. As it happens, Menou would have governed Egypt well in times of peace; unfortunately the country was at war.

On 3 February 1801, two frigates sent by the French government carrying artillery and munitions reached Egypt. They also brought news that the enemy were preparing further offensives and that the government would be sending more substantial assistance. In fact, early in 1800, Napoleon had tried to bring about a naval armistice with England in order to save

Egypt, using the negotiations that were under way with Austria as an argument, but England had consistently refused. Then on 5 September England took Malta and immediately prepared to invade Egypt. Napoleon had already been sending as much assistance as he could spare; now an expedition, said to be for Santo Domingo but actually for Egypt, was preparing at Brest. Under the command of Ganteaume, the squadron sailed from Brest on 23 January 1801 but, after reaching Gibraltar, it took refuge in Toulon. Nevertheless, a number of frigates reached Alexandria on 1 March: there was yet hope.

Despite their alliance, Menou was incapable of making use of Murad Bey as a source of information, nor did he reopen the negotiations with the Grand Vizier which might have created the necessary dissension between England and the Porte. Instead, the English offered to join the Ottoman Empire in a coastal invasion during which the Grand Vizier would march his army on Egypt from Gaza while another English corps, from India, would enter Egypt from the Red Sea.

By assembling the bulk of his troops in Cairo, Menou had left insufficient men on the coast to defend Alexandria, Aboukir and Rosetta; even so, he should have been able to deploy his troops at the first sign of danger. But he was basking in a sense of total security when the messenger sent by Friant, the military governor of Alexandria, reached him on 4 March and announced that the English fleet had appeared along the coast. The force landed near Aboukir on the 8th. Under such circumstances Bonaparte or Kléber would have rushed to the endangered area. Menou stayed put and was content to send Lanusse towards Aboukir. The army's amazement at this troubled him not at all, and it was not until 11 March, on learning that Friant had been defeated and had fallen back on Alexandria, that Menou made a move. On the 12th he left Belliard in Cairo and ordered the troops there to leave for al Rahmaniya. Meanwhile the English had extended their positions and tried to take Alexandria by surprise, but Lanusse, who had reached al Rahmaniya on the 8th, had managed to stop them. Menou reached al Rahmaniya in the evening of the 15th, spent the 16th resting, slept at Damanhur on the 17th, spent the day of the 18th there and finally reached Lanusse's camp in the evening the 19th. Aboukir had capitulated the night before.

Caricatures of the time show Menou riding on a tortoise, and his slowness gave the English time to increase their forces and strengthen their positions. Even worse, once he found himself face-to-face with the enemy, Menou had no idea of what to order his army to do. On the 21st they marched to combat but Menou followed up the movements badly and the battle of Canopus was lost, forcing them to fall back on Alexandria. Menou's inertia aroused consternation in the army. His lack of action as he waited for assistance from France had opened up Egypt to the enemy.

The English at once blockaded Alexandria and proceeded to take Rosetta. Menou, mournfully awaiting Ganteaume's squadron, did not make a move. The English then brought a large flotilla into the Nile alongside their troops, and on 10 May al Rahmaniya was taken. Lagrange, whom Menou had stationed there, was able to retreat to Cairo where he joined Belliard on the 13th.

When the troops from Upper Egypt returned to Cairo, Belliard invited Murad Bey to join them. Murad Bey had every intention of doing so but was struck down by the plague on 22 April. Belliard then thought of mounting an attack, with Lagrange's help, on the Grand Vizier's troops advancing towards Cairo, in the hope of a decisive battle which would then enable him to fall on the English corps as it travelled up the Nile. But the English had instructed the Grand

Théodore Géricault, *Incident during the Egyptian campaign*. Black chalk, Indian ink and gouache on bistre paper. Paris, Musée du Louvre.

Vizier to avoid combat with the French and to fall back to the delta should they appear. When he came before Belliard, Yussuf Pasha dispersed his corps, leading Belliard to pull back to Cairo for fear that the town might be taken and occupied by the English and the Turks.

Damietta was taken by a Turkish corps and Lesbeh fell shortly afterwards. General Hutchinson, who had replaced General Abercromby, killed at Canopus on 21 March, had been very circumspect in his movements. On 15 June the English force from India had anchored before Qusayr where it had learned of the victory at Canopus. It landed on the 16th under the command of General Baird and marched on Qena on the 18th.

Now back in Cairo, Belliard had received no further instructions from his commander. He took the initiative of conferring with the enemy and, on 27 June, he signed an agreement whereby he was to evacuate Cairo and all other areas occupied by the French and lead his troops to Rosetta. Once there they were to embark and be transported with their arms and baggage as far as the French ports in the Mediterranean. Belliard ratified the agreement on 28 June after the English and the Turks had signed it, and it was carried out without obstacle. General Kléber's body was exhumed to the sound of English and Turkish artillery salutes from the forts.

On 9 June the corvette *Héliopolis* from Ganteaume's squadron arrived from Toulon, but Ganteaume did not attempt to approach Alexandria. Sailing to Benghazi, he headed back to Toulon while Menou continued to live in vain hope of relief. On 5 July Menou learned of the agreement signed by Belliard and refused to ratify it. The English took the Marabut fort on the night of 21 August and gained control of the channels in the old port. The situation had become impossible, forcing Menou to call a council of war which met in Friant's house on the 28th, during which he laid the blame on the Cairo convention—in other words, on Belliard.

On 2 September Menou capitulated: the French army was to be evacuated to France. The town was handed over to the English and the French troops prepared to leave. Embarkation was carried out in stages and by the end of September there were hardly any French left in Alexandria. Menou himself embarked on 18 October.

Preliminary peace agreements with England were signed in London on 1 October, followed by a peace treaty signed on 25 March 1802 in Amiens. The English insisted upon the ending of the Egyptian expedition as a major condition. They also wanted to hold on to Malta in order to control the route to the East.

Hutchinson was of the opinion that Menou had been incapable of defending Egypt and

André Dutertre, *View of Birkat al Hagg*, 1798-1801. Pen and wash. Paris, Bibliothèque Nationale.

that Kléber's death had delivered the country to the English. Bonaparte was fully aware of Menou's incompetence but bore him no animosity for that: recognizing his administrative ability, he appointed Menou general administrator of Piedmont as early as 1802, and later made him a count, appointing him to the governor-generalship of Tuscany, followed by that of Venice, where he was to die in 1810. Kléber, on the other hand, had never been a courtier, and when his body was sent back to France by Belliard it was placed in the Château d'If—in which Alexandre Dumas was to imprison his Count of Monte Cristo—and remained there throughout Napoleon's reign. Nevertheless, during his exile on St Helena, Napoleon was to fully concur with Hutchinson's appreciation by saying that it was Kléber's death alone which led to the loss of Egypt.

The Egyptian expedition was to be truly valuable on a very different plane from the military one. Pierre Montet, the French Egyptologist to whom we owe the discovery of the intact tombs of the pharaoh Psusennes and others at Tanis, wrote in *Isis ou À la recherche de l'Égypte ensevelie* (1956):

> When Bonaparte undertook his great expedition his priorities were political, but his claim to glory is not the military victories over the mamelukes that were so quickly effaced by the disaster at Aboukir, the murder of Kléber and the capitulation of Menou, but the fact that he took with him to Egypt the most distinguished names in the sciences and the arts available in France at that time.

André Dutertre, *The Alexandrian sailor*, 1798-1801. Watercolour heightened with pastel. Paris, Bibliothèque Nationale.

THE SCHOLARS IN EGYPT

An account that describes only the military events of the Egyptian expedition does not tell the full story of this extraordinary episode in the history of revolutionary France. The sciences were strongly represented, and the members of the Commission for Arts and Sciences who travelled with the Army of the Orient—indiscriminately referred to as 'the scholars' by the men—played an essential role alongside the soldiers and sailors.

THE CREATION OF THE COMMISSION FOR ARTS AND SCIENCES

The birth of the Commission for Arts and Sciences of the Army of the Orient can be precisely dated to 16 March 1798, for it was on that day that the Directoire issued the following instruction to the Minister of the Interior:

> The Executive Directoire, Citizen Minister, instructs you to put the engineers, draughtsmen and other personnel under the authority of your ministry at the disposal of General Bonaparte, as well as any articles he might require to serve the expedition with which he has been entrusted.

Bonaparte had in fact been strongly attracted to the sciences for a long time, and ever since he had been made a member of the First Class of the National Institute on his return from Italy in December 1797 he had dreamed of forming a Commission and giving it a prominent role in his conquest of Egypt. The idea was not entirely new: in 1794-5 a small group of painters and botanists had been sent to the Rhineland and the Low Countries to collect paintings and sculptures for French museums and to study the local flora and fauna, and during the Italian campaign of 1796-7 a Commission for Arts and Sciences had been formed to requisition works of art for the Republic. Two members of that Commission, the mathematician Gaspard Monge and the chemist Claude Louis Berthollet, were to play a major role in Egypt at the head of the artists and scientists who set off with the invasion forces.

Gaspard Monge (1746-1818), a Burgundian from Beaune, had greeted the Revolution with enthusiasm. After the events of 10 August 1792 he became Naval Minister for a few months, and during that time had interviewed a young artillery captain called Bonaparte who was thinking of moving to naval artillery. Monge, like Berthollet, was among the academics mobilized for the defence of the nation by the Committee for Public Safety. Put in charge of casting cannons, he oversaw six foundries scattered around the edges of Paris, and in 1794 published his thesis *L'Art de fabriquer les canons*. Two years later he published *Leçons de géométrie descriptive,* a series of lectures he had delivered at the École Polytechnique, of which he was a founding member. In 1796, on an artistic mission across the Alps for the Directoire, he was received graciously by Bonaparte.

Claude Louis Berthollet (1748-1822), born in Talloires, by the Lac d'Annecy in Savoie, made his mark early in his career as a talented chemist. The revolutionary period brought him in contact with Monge, his colleague at the National Institute. At that time he was making valuable discoveries about powder and explosives and held the chair of chemistry at the École Normale.

The two friends became close companions of the young commander-in-chief. He confided in them his dreams of the Orient, and when the Egyptian expedition was decided, he let them in on the secret. It was doubtless following their advice that he persuaded the government to create a commission of scholars, technicians and artists of all sorts to assist him in the enterprise.

Monge and Berthollet became the pillars of the Commission for Arts and Sciences. Their friendship grew so close, and their names were so frequently linked, that more than one soldier on the expedition would take 'Mongéberthollet' to be a single person.

Little by little the Commission was formed round the two friends. Although it was under Bonaparte's authority it was mostly recruited by its two founding members who, being well known themselves, had many useful connections. Brigadier Caffarelli du Falga of the Engineers, chosen to command the Commission, prepared an initial list of names and submitted it to Bonaparte. Towards the end of March 1798 a recruitment circular was prepared by the Ministry of the Interior which guaranteed that the selected scholars' posts would be kept open for them until their return and that their salaries would be paid to their families, whilst they themselves

André Dutertre, engraved portraits: Brigadier Caffarelli, Jean Joseph Fourier, Dominique Vivant Denon, Pierre Simon Girard, Edme François Jomard and Prosper Jollois.

would be remunerated in accordance with the nature of their new services. Meanwhile the purpose of the expedition remained a secret.

All the major scientific institutions of the capital—the École Polytechnique, the École Normale, the École des Mines, the Ponts et Chaussées, the Conservatoire des Arts et Métiers, the Muséum d'Histoire Naturelle and the Observatoire—were asked to propose their candidates. Some candidates declined, others accepted with enthusiasm. One professor at the École Polytechnique, Jean Joseph Fourier, was so keen that he managed to enrol five of his colleagues and about forty students or ex-students, among them Édouard de Villiers du Terrage, a civil engineer who was to become one of the best chroniclers of the Commission, and his colleague and intimate friend Aimé Dubois-Aymé. At the Natural History Museum Georges Cuvier politely refused but Berthollet easily persuaded Étienne Geoffroy Saint-Hilaire, a professor of zoology aged twenty-six. He in turn convinced Henri Joseph Redouté, younger brother of the painter of roses and an excellent draughtsman in his own right, as well as the zoologist Marie Jules César Savigny and the botanist Hippolyte Nectoux, who had just returned from Santo Domingo but did not hesitate to set off again for an unknown destination. As for the geologist Déodat Dolomieu, he promised to go along as soon as Berthollet assured him that 'there are mountains and stones to be found where we are going'. From the Observatory came the astronomer François Marie Quesnot and the student Jérôme Méchain (son of Pierre Méchain, the renowned inventor of the meridian circle), who would team up with a third astronomer, Nicolas Auguste Nouet. The surveyors and civil engineers attached to the Army of Italy were ordered to Genoa to embark, and several interpreters and orientalists were recruited from the École des Langues Orientales, among them Jean-Michel de Venture de Paradis.

A number of writers and artists were added to these scholars and technicians, the most prominent of whom was Antoine Vincent Arnault, author of a successful tragedy, *Marius à Minturne*, who had become friendly with Bonaparte when he crossed into Italy in 1797. Bonaparte asked him to see if he could enlist the poet Jean François Ducis, the composer Étienne Nicolas Méhul and the singer François Lays, but all three declined. They were replaced

Nicolas Jacques Conté, *Masons' tools,* 1798-1801.
Watercolour and wash. Private collection.

by the author François Auguste Parseval-Grandmaison, the pianist Henri Jean Rigel and the singer and musicologist Guillaume André Villoteau. Gabriel Legouvé, the poet, could not be persuaded, but Baron Dominique Vivant Denon did everything in his power to be accepted, and finally succeeded through the intercession of Arnault and Joséphine Bonaparte, of whom he was a friend. An excellent draughtsman and a witty companion who knew 'every court anecdote from the reign of Louis XI to that of Barras inclusively', this fifty-year-old combined a vast knowledge of the arts with the curiosity of a seasoned European traveller. Other recruits were the draughtsman Jean Gabriel Caquet and his colleague André Dutertre, who was also an accurate and realistic portrait painter, plus the painters Joly and Michel Rigo and the sculptor Jean Jacques Castex. Bonaparte even considered adding a troupe of actors and dancers to his suite, but the idea turned out to be impracticable at that stage.

While this multifarious body of experts was being recruited, the equipment required for the Commission's activities was being gathered from wherever it could be found. Caffarelli collected scientific instruments and a wide range of other tools for the use of the astronomers, surveyors, civil engineers, doctors, surgeons, pharmacists, naturalists, aeronauts, carpenters and mechanics. Nothing was forgotten, not even a four-pedalled Érard piano which he politely requested the naval supplies officer at Toulon, Najac, to purchase and stow on board as soon as possible.

Caffarelli, Arnault, Bonaparte's secretary Bourrienne, the economist Jean Baptiste Say (who was not part of the expedition) and his brother Horace, a captain in the Engineers (who was), gathered together a large campaign library composed of works of all kinds: history, geography, literature, pure and applied mathematics, physics, chemistry, medicine, surgery, natural history and architecture. They chose the smallest editions they could find and built cases lined with thick flannel, which could later be converted into shelves, to transport them. Maps were of course indispensable, and they discovered that the Anville atlas luckily contained the best ones available—as far as Egypt was concerned, at least.

Constructing a printing press met with some difficulty: the director of the Presses of the Republic, Dubois-Laverne, obstinately clung to the precious Arabic and Greek fonts that

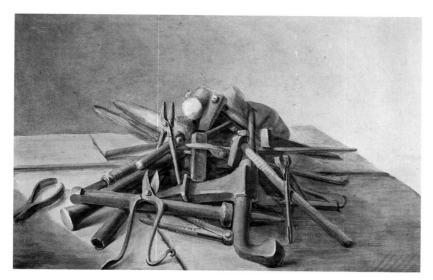

Nicolas Jacques Conté, *Ironmongers' and tinsmiths' tools,* 1798-1801.
Watercolour and wash. Private collection.

Bonaparte was claiming, and the orientalist Louis Mathieu Langlès, whom the general insisted upon taking with him, was equally insistent about not going. The intervention of the Minister of the Interior finally made Dubois-Laverne give in, but nothing could make Langlès change his mind, so he was replaced by another orientalist, Jean Jacques Marcel, as head of the press.

The press now had all the necessary typefaces except for an Oriental font. Bonaparte therefore asked Monge, who had left for Italy to prepare the foundation of the short-lived Roman Republic, to requisition the typographical riches of the Propaganda Office at the Vatican—and, while he was about it, to recruit some interpreters to add to Marcel's staff. As Monge himself was still hesitant about embarking on the voyage, Bonaparte wrote to him on April 1798: 'I am counting on the printing press of the Propaganda and on yourself, even if it entails sailing the squadron up the Tiber to fetch you.' How could anyone resist such a blandishment?

By now the recruitment of the Commission for Arts and Sciences was complete. According to the list prepared by Estève, the paymaster of the army, 167 members had been gathered together. On 2 April they received orders from the Minister of the Interior to be ready to leave for Toulon; then, on 18 April, under instructions from Bonaparte, Caffarelli requested each member to be in Lyons inside five days, where they would be given further orders.

The scholars set off as soon as they had collected their passports from the École Polytechnique. The choice of route was left to each individual, so groups of old or new friends formed for the four days it took to travel by coach to Lyons, where they boarded packet boats and sailed down the Rhône to the Mediterranean coast. Most of them reached Toulon on 30 April. The town was full to overflowing and bustling with all manner of preparations for the voyage. The scholars managed to house themselves somehow, in lodgings that were mostly far from comfortable, and occupied themselves with last-minute arrangements before embarking.

The town was rife with conjecture since, for obvious military and diplomatic reasons, the destination of the expedition was still a secret. A number of the scholars—Dolomieu for one—guessed or suspected it, and there were the inevitable rumours in which the word 'Egypt' constantly recurred. When Parseval-Grandmaison was asking to accompany Arnault he cried: 'You are going to Egypt, the whole world knows that!' England, however, was to remain in doubt up to the last minute. The same probably goes for many of the scholars who, although they had no idea where it would take them, had enlisted in the adventure with all the enthusiasm of youth. Monge and Berthollet at fifty-two and fifty respectively, Nouet nearing his sixties and Venture de Paradis at over sixty must have seemed like patriarchs amongst such people as the engineer Alexandre Saint-Genis, twenty-six, and his colleague, mining engineer Hippolyte Victor Descotils, twenty-five, Étienne Louis Malus, an Engineers officer, and Louis Madelène Ripault, a student antiquarian, both twenty-three, Jean Baptiste Prosper Jollois and Michel Ange Lancret, both civil engineers of twenty-two, Edme François Jomard, a surveyor, twenty-one, Aimé Dubois-Aymé, nineteen, Édouard de Villiers du Terrage, seventeen, and Joseph Viard, a student at the École Polytechnique, a mere fifteen. Bonaparte, their commander-in-chief, was not yet thirty.

Towards the middle of May the scholars embarked and faced the first, somewhat rough experience of their new life. Unfavourable winds held up the fleet in Toulon harbour for about eight days, during which the many inconveniences of shipboard life made themselves felt. Worst of all, it became clear that the army regarded the members of the Commission for Arts and Sciences with open contempt.

Soldiers of all ranks watched jealously as Bonaparte placed his title as member of the National Institute before that of Commander-in-Chief, never missing an opportunity to show his respect for the sciences and their representatives. There were, of course, exceptions: some of the men were flattered to be in the company of such illustrious scholars as Berthollet or Dolomieu, and General Reynier struck up a warm friendship with Geoffroy Saint-Hilaire; but Brigadier Lannes would have loved to see the scholars thrown overboard by his grenadiers, and Caffarelli himself, despite being head of the Commission, openly displayed his preference for military engineers over civil ones.

Bonaparte had foreseen this kind of dissension, and to prevent quarrels over precedence he had divided the Commission into five groups with different pay—6000 francs for the first, 5000 for the second etc.— in accordance with army grades. The members of the first class, equivalent to the rank of superior officer, were allocated comfortable cabins; the rest had to content themselves with hammocks and suffer all the discomforts of the ratings.

On 19 May the wind finally turned and the Toulon squadron weighed anchor in brilliant sunshine. On a signal from the flagship *Orient*, almost 300 ships unfurled their sails and the huge fleet set off to the sound of the crowds cheering on the shore, the artillery in the forts answering the ships' guns, and the bands playing the music of the regiments on board. The adventure had begun; but with ships onto which three times as many troops had been crammed as were needed for their defence, and with bridges, bulwarks and rigging encumbered with land artillery, the expedition was at the mercy of an attack by Nelson.

The fleet took twenty-two days to reach Malta. Arguments frequently broke out between civilians and servicemen, even on board the *Orient,* in which Bonaparte was sailing. Then boredom struck. Occasionally the military bands gave a concert of the airs written by Méhul for the expedition, and the scholars seized every opportunity for distraction: reaching Corsica, Arnault accompanied Berthier, Bonaparte's chief-of-staff, on a short mission to Bastia. Later, when they were again on the open sea, they took advantage of calm weather to exchange visits from ship to ship. Geoffroy Saint-Hilaire turned the catching of a shark to good account by carrying out experiments on it before the admiring passengers and crew of the *Alceste*. Jollois, the architect Jean Constantin Protain and several colleagues on board the *Guerrier* busied

Cécile, *View of Alexandria's Great Bazaar.*
Engraving from the *Description de l'Égypte,* 1809-26.

themselves learning physics and Italian. The chief surgeon, Dominique Jean Larrey, who guessed they were heading for Egypt, questioned Venture de Paradis and Charles Magallon, both of whom had been there before (the latter as consul-general), about all the details of interest to his department.

Nor was Bonaparte himself idle for a moment. When weather permitted he was to be found on the stern of the *Orient* conversing with Admiral Brueys, Berthollet and Caffarelli. Arnault would read to him, then they would discuss literature together. Every evening Bonaparte convened what he called 'his Institute', gathering together the generals and the most eminent members of the Commission, namely Berthollet, Arnault, Regnault de Saint-Jean-d'Angély, Chief Medical Officer Desgenettes and Venture de Paradis. A subject was then proposed, and the discussion began. Bonaparte listened, only intervening when the debate flagged or degenerated into dispute. Sometimes there were farcical incidents, such as when Major Junot inquired why Brigadier Lannes was not present at the assembly when his name alone should have ensured his inclusion,* or when Junot—again—snored loudly and, on being woken up, declared to Bonaparte that 'his rotten damned Institute would send anyone to sleep'. At last

*TRANSLATOR'S NOTE: the pronunciation of 'Lannes' is identical to '*l'âne*', an ass.

André Dutertre, *Abyssinian priest*, 1798-1801. Watercolour heightened with pastel.
Paris, Bibliothèque Nationale.

OPPOSITE: André Dutertre, *An Egyptian*, 1798-1801. Watercolour
heightened with pastel. Paris, Bibliothèque Nationale.

Bonaparte would decide that the discussion had gone on long enough, and everyone would retire to their cabins, while the immense fleet slipped quietly through the night.

On 9 June, before Malta, the bulk of the fleet joined up with the convoy from Civitavecchia under Major-General Desaix; Monge, who was with him, left the frigate *Courageuse* for the *Orient* where Bonaparte greeted him warmly. On 10 June the French troops landed on the island; on the 12th the capitulation of Malta, negotiated on the French side by two members of the Commission, Poussielgue, the financial administrator, and the geologist Dolomieu, was signed at midnight on board the *Orient*. Malta had become French territory.

76

The scholars, delighted to be on dry land, disembarked on 13 June and explored the artistic riches of the island and its capital. 'This town,' wrote Nicolas Jacques Conté in a letter to his wife, 'is large and very beautiful... full of very ancient buildings.' The musicologist Villoteau ransacked the bookshops for antiphonals and other musical works. Denon, who already knew the country, revisited the frescos in the cathedral of St John and sketched various *objets d'art* preserved in the library. Night overtook Villiers du Terrage, Ripault and several others, and after requesting the hospitality of a local inhabitant they slept on the floor of 'a hall fifty feet long, hung with the portraits and arms of the Knights of Malta'.

Within a mere six days Bonaparte totally remodelled the political, social and religious structures of the island, while Monge and Berthollet were given the task of making an inventory of the treasures confiscated on behalf of the Republic, those of the cathedral of St John in particular. Knights under sixty were forbidden to remain on Malta, so many of them joined the expedition. One of them was André Louis Saint-Simon, brother of the renowned socialist. Regnault de Saint-Jean-d'Angély, on the other hands, abandoned the expedition in order to become government commissioner in Malta: the general opinion of his colleagues was that he was to be envied. Dubois-Aymé and the naturalist Ernest Coquebert de Montbret seriously considered staying behind too, but in the end they followed their comrades. As for Arnault, he so longed for his lost freedom that, when his brother-in-law fell ill, he abandoned the adventure to be at his side, and sailed for France a few days later.

On 19 June the Commission reembarked and sailed away from Malta. On its way the fleet was passed one foggy night by Nelson's squadron, which failed to see it from a distance of a mere six leagues. On 28 June Marcel printed a proclamation on board the *Orient* officially confirming their destination to be Egypt, and Bonaparte announced proudly that 'The first town we shall reach was founded by Alexander.' Three days later, at dawn, Alexandria was in sight; on the same day the first tricolour floated over Africa.

Alexandria was in a state of utter confusion and, when the troops left for Rosetta and al Rahmaniya, the scholars were totally forgotten amidst the general disorder. They complained

Henri Joseph Redouté, *Outskirts of Rosetta*, 1798-1801. Pen and wash. Paris, Bibliothèque Nationale.

to Berthier, who referred them to Kléber, military governor of Alexandria. Dolomieu became their spokesman. For their part the engineers paid a visit to Caffarelli, who amiably promised them that the situation would improve in Cairo. It was not until five days later that they at last managed to get common soldiers' rations from on board the ships, though these turned out to be barely edible. The heat, the mosquitoes and every imaginable difficulty conspired to make these first few days intolerable for the Commission. For one of them, the Egyptian adventure was already at an end: the orientalist Panhusen, Kléber's secretary and interpreter, disappeared, perhaps murdered; in any event he was never heard of again.

Otherwise, there was plenty to keep the scholars occupied. The chief surgeon, doctors and pharmacists were busy creating a permanent lazar house with their military colleagues. Marcel and his team installed their press in the Venetian consul's house and immediately began printing 4000 copies in Arabic of Bonaparte's proclamation to the Egyptians of 2 July; this proclamation, 'printed in the French camp in Alexandria', was the first text ever to be printed on Egyptian soil. Brigader Conté and his men were salvaging the ballooning equipment and scientific instruments that went down with the *Patriote* when it ran aground in the port.

Monge and Berthollet were among the first to leave Alexandria. Joining Bonaparte on the terrible desert crossing under a beating sun, they reached the Nile four days later, on 10 July, at al Rahmaniya. They then embarked on the xebec *Cerf* with Bourrienne and Chief Supplies Officer Sucy to travel upriver and, after a skirmish when their flotilla was attacked, they at last reached Giza where they rejoined Bonaparte, fresh from his victory at the pyramids. On the 24th Bonaparte made his entry into Cairo.

The other scholars formed into two groups. On 8 July about twenty of them, under the command of General Menou, sailed to the town of Rosetta at the western end of the Nile delta. Fourier, Parseval-Grandmaison, Denon, Geoffroy Saint-Hilaire, Jollois, Villiers du Terrage, Villoteau and Joly were among this group. They relished in the shade of the palms and sycamore trees which border the Nile and took full advantage of the abundant fruit and game to be found in the area, though they suffered from the heat and the mosquitoes. Very few of them were bored, however: Fourier, Parseval-Grandmaison and the former Knight of St John le Groing, formed a 'Commission of three' responsible for the purchase of foodstuffs for the

Nicolas Jacques Conté, *Cairo, view of Sultan Hasan's mosque*, 1798-1801. Watercolour. Paris, Bibliothèque Nationale.

army and navy. Villoteau became Menou's secretary. Denon was painting Poussielgue's portrait and exploring the surroundings in search of antiquities to sketch. The botanists and zoologists were amongst the busiest members of the group, even though the former complained that there were only twenty different species of flora in the country: it was in fact the dry season during which plants are rare. Geoffroy Saint-Hilaire observed and captured many birds which he either stuffed or prepared as specimens of skeletons.

On 1 August some of the scholars took a trip to the tower of the monastery of Abu Mandur, with its view over Aboukir Bay. They arrived in time to see Nelson's fleet approach, and they watched in agony as the French fleet was destroyed. A few days later the painter Joly was killed in an ambush. These disastrous events so demoralized the colony of scholars at Rosetta that they were relieved to be able to set off at once when a letter from Lancret, summoning them to Cairo, reached them on 18 August.

At that time the great majority of the members of the Commission were still in Alexandria, which was a hive of activity. The architects Norry and Protain had been instructed to prepare plans and estimates for the building of barracks and hospitals, the mineralogists and antiquarians began to explore the area, and a map of the town and its surroundings was being drawn up by the astronomers, civil and military surveyors and civil engineers. Jacques Marie le Père and Pierre Simon Girard, civil engineers-in-chief, devoted themselves to inspecting the many cisterns, almost all of which needed to be dredged. Three of their subordinates, Louis Bodard, Hervé Charles Faye and Gilbert Joseph Chabrol de Volvic, were given the task of repairing the canal running from Alexandria to al Rahmaniya, which the army had followed on its march on Cairo.

By the beginning of September 1798 most of the work undertaken in the province of Alexandria had been completed, and the members of the Commission were able to leave for Cairo where they joined Monge, Berthollet and their colleagues from Rosetta.

THE EGYPTIAN INSTITUTE AND THE SCHOLARS' LIFE IN CAIRO

As soon he was installed in the Egyptian capital, Bonaparte founded the Egyptian Institute, a project no doubt conceived before the departure of the expedition and foreshadowed by the evening gatherings on board the *Orient*. Monge and Berthollet, asked to find premises for the new society, chose a group of mansions in the Nasiriyyah quarter belonging to exiled mamelukes, about 2 km from the palace of Azbakiyyah in the centre of Cairo where general headquarters had been set up. The four adjoining palaces, surrounded by magnificent gardens, were ideal for the vast scientific enclave that the Commission for Arts and Sciences, the Egyptian Institute and their various departments were to become.

Then, on the 21 August 1798, the two friends convened a group appointed by Bonaparte, comprising Brigadier Caffarelli, Geoffroy Saint-Hilaire, the surveyor Louis Costaz, Chief Medical Officer Desgenettes and Brigadier Andréossy, to write the twenty-six articles of a decree, to be signed by Bonaparte the next day, outlining the aims of the new academy down to the last detail:

There will be an Institute dedicated to the sciences and the arts in Egypt, which will be based in Cairo. The principal objectives of this establishment are:
1 the advancement and propagation of learning in Egypt
2 the research, study and publication of the natural, industrial and historical facts about Egypt
3 to advise on the various questions on which it will be consulted by the government.

The rest of the decree divides the Institute into four departments with twelve members each—Mathematics, Physics, Political Economy, Literature and the Arts—and establishes the frequency of the meetings (two per *décade**), the membership of the board, the recording and publishing of minutes and the two annual prizes to be given.

The Institute was thus defined as at once an active agency for the education of the native population, a learned élite based in Cairo responsible for directing the research and work of the members of the Commission dispersed throughout the country, and an instrument of colonization and government which would lend support to the French occupation.

At that same meeting a list of all the members of the Institute was drawn up:

DEPARTMENT OF MATHEMATICS: Brigadier Andréossy, General Bonaparte; Costaz and Fourier, surveyors; Girard and Jacques Marie le Père, both civil engineers-in-chief; le Roy, naval supplies officer; Malus, Engineers officer; Monge; Nouet and Quesnot, astronomers; Horace Say, Engineers officer.

DEPARTMENT OF PHYSICS: Berthollet; Jacques Pierre Champy, chemist; Conté, chief of aerostatics; Alire Delile, botanist; Descotils, mining engineer; Desgenettes; Dolomieu; Antoine Dubois, surgeon; Geoffroy Saint-Hilaire and Savigny, zoologists.

* the Revolutionary ten-day week.

DEPARTMENT OF POLITICAL ECONOMY: Caffarelli; Gloutier, economist; Poussielgue, general financial administrator; Joseph Sulkowski, officer; Sucy, chief supplies officer; Tallien, government representative.

DEPARTMENT OF LITERATURE AND THE ARTS: Denon; Dutertre, draughtsman; Norry, architect; Parseval-Grandmaison, writer; Don Raphael de Monachis, orientalist; Henri Joseph Redouté, painter of natural history; Rigel, pianist; Venture de Paradis, orientalist.

The Institute was originally to have comprised forty-eight members, but in the event only the Mathematics Department reached the full complement of twelve. In the Physics Department two seats remained vacant; in Political Economy there were six; and in Literature and the Arts there were four (this was not for long, for it appears that the painter Rigo joined it almost at once).

Most of the members were culled from the Commission for Arts and Sciences. Its administration was represented by Sucy, Poussielgue and Gloutier; the army by Bonaparte, Caffarelli and Andréossy and officers Horace Say and Joseph Sulkowski; the health service by Desgenettes and Dubois; and last but not least, a member of the Eastern clergy, Dom Raphael de Monachis.

Bonaparte approved the list as it stood, and the first sitting of the Institute took place

Jean Constantin Protain, *View of the interior of one of the great halls in Hasan Kachef's house, used for meetings of the Institute,* 1798-9. Pen and wash heightened with gouache. Paris, Bibliothèque Nationale.

at 7 a.m. on 23 August in the harem drawing-room at Hasan Kachef's palace. Monge was elected president for the first quarter, while Bonaparte contented himself with the vice-presidency. He proposed six subjects for deliberation: improving the baking of bread, the replacement of hops in beer-brewing, the purification of the waters of the Nile, the construction of wind- and watermills, the local manufacture of powder, and improvements in the Egyptian legal and educational systems. Each project was given to a commission of those most qualified to execute it, and the new academicians set to work immediately. They were also to develop projects on their own initiative and to present their results to their colleagues.

The minutes of those early meetings, held between the end of August and the beginning of October, are amazing both for their depth of inquiry and for the number of subjects, both practical and theoretical, that they covered. Monge's report on 'The phenomenon of the mirage' and Berthollet's on 'The formation of ammoniac salts in hitherto unexpected substances' and 'The manufacture of indigo in Egypt' were much applauded of course, and the efforts of many of their colleagues were far from being without merit.

On Monge's advice Bonaparte dropped the idea of personally reading a paper but, endlessly active and persevering, he continued to stimulate his colleagues. Not forgetting that he was a

André Dutertre, *A meeting of the scholars from the Commission for Arts and Sciences in the gardens of the Institute*, 1798-9. Pen and watercolour. Paris, Bibliothèque Nationale.

André Dutertre, *Outskirts of Cairo, water being drawn from the Cairo canal and the festivities held at the opening of the dyke,* 1799. Watercolour. Paris, Bibliothèque Nationale.

member of the National Institute, he promoted a friendly collaboration between Paris and Cairo, though the English fleet unfortunately soon put a stop to that.

In September the scholars from Rosetta and Alexandria reached Cairo and gratefully took up residence in the palaces in the Nasiriyyah suburb, by then dubbed 'the Institute Quarter'. In Hasan Kachef's palace, where Monge and Berthollet lived, there were, besides the Institute Hall, two vast rooms converted into a refectory for the members of the Commission and a laboratory for public experiments. The library and some of the scientific instruments were installed in various other rooms. Elsewhere a museum had been provided for the antiquities that were being gathered in Cairo or would later be brought from the provinces, foremost of which would be the celebrated Rosetta stone, discovered in the summer of 1799 by Engineers Lieutenant Pierre Bouchard, which the scholars immediately recognized as the key to the hieroglyphs even though they did not manage to decipher it. An observatory and a chemical laboratory completed the ensemble, and it was soon possible to tell the time from a sundial installed by the astronomer Nouet.

Now that it was comfortably housed and paid for its services, the colony of scholars became very active, with each member putting his talents to best use. Even the young students from the École Polytechnique, who had left France before their finals, exhumed their schoolbooks from their trunks and prepared for the exams, which they sat on 6 October before a board presided over by Monge, assisted by their professor, Fourier, and the surveyors Louis Costaz and Louis Alexandre Olivier de Corancez.

Bonaparte often gave the scholars various administrative and financial tasks, calling upon them to organize the numerous parties held in Cairo to impress the Egyptians. The staging of the one held on the first day of the Republican year, 22 September (1 Vendémiaire Year VII), was entrusted to Engineers Officer Malus, a member of the Institute, assisted by Lancret and

Jollois, and the military parades of 1 December and 14 January 1799 gave Conté an occasion on which to send up some large hot-air balloons, by which the Egyptian spectators were bemused rather than impressed.

The uprising of 21 October 1798 brutally disrupted the apparent calm of the Egyptian capital and cost the lives of four scholars: chief surveyor Testevuide, civil engineers Léonard Duval and Claude François Thevenot and Bonaparte's Polish aide-de-camp, Joseph Sulkowski, a member of the Institute and a distinguished Arab scholar. Following this brief but violent episode, which at least gave the army a chance to confirm its authority, life quickly returned to normal. The scholars, perched on the little donkeys known as 'Cairo cabs', their legs dangling to the ground and their eyes peeled, recommenced their daily outings through the crowded streets of the handsome Arab town, stopping here and there to admire the spectacles it offered—snake-charmers, soothsayers or the Egyptian dancing girls.

Cairo was quickly becoming Gallicized. French signs appeared over the doors of cafés and restaurants furnished in the European style, where even billiard tables could sometimes be found. Saddlers' shops 'as good as the best workshops in France' making belts, boots and saddles of all kinds, hatters, embroiderers, shops selling European furniture, distillers of liqueurs

Nicolas Jacques Conté, *View of the interior of a weaver's workshop*, 1798-1801. Watercolour. Private collection.

86

André Dutertre, *Woman wearing traditional Egyptian costume*, 1798-1801. Watercolour. Paris, Bibliothèque Nationale.

OPPOSITE: André Dutertre, *Oriental dancing girl's red silk dress*, 1798-1801. Watercolour. Paris, Bibliothèque Nationale.

Nicolas Jacques Conté, *View of the interior of an oil press,* 1798-1801. Watercolour and wash. Private collection.

and cordials, brewers producing beer without hops following the recipe provided by the Egyptian Institute, bakers and a French tobacco factory all flourished. A certain Dargevel even opened an 'Egyptian Tivoli' in the gardens of the exiled Eyub Bey. The establishment included a restaurant, a gaming room, a reading room and an auditorium. It was there that Bonaparte met Pauline Fourès, soon nicknamed 'Cleopatra' by the soldiers.

In the absence of professional actors, which Bonaparte had not succeeded in bringing over from France, the scholars themselves took to the boards, and towards the end of the expedition a number of them formed a dramatic society which put on a quite respectable number of plays.

CONTÉ'S MACHINE SHOP AND THE PRINTING PRESS

During the Cairo revolt many of the scientific instruments in Caffarelli's house were destroyed. When Bonaparte learned of this he exclaimed: 'What are we going to do now? We don't even have any tools!' One of his listeners, Conté, coolly replied: 'In that case, we shall make tools.'

Born in 1755 near Séez in Normandy, Nicolas Jacques Conté first won recognition as a painter but, whilst earning his living with his brushes, he was also busy with chemistry and, above all, physics and mechanics. He settled in Paris in 1785 and set up a laboratory where he conducted experiments which brought him into contact with well-known scientists such as Louis Bernard Guyton de Morveau, Antoine François de Fourcroy, Louis Nicolas Vauquelin and Alexis Vandermonde. The Revolution called upon his extraordinary ingenuity a number of times, and in spring 1794 he produced his most famous invention and the only one still associated with his name—the artificial chalk that replaced the unobtainable English graphite. He also studied the possible military uses of gas and hot-air balloons and was made director of the aerostatic school at Meudon and commander of the Aerostatic Corps four years later.

An explosion in the course of a dangerous experiment cost him an eye, but he went back to work undaunted as soon as he recovered. He was made a brigadier and entrusted, along with Vandermonde and le Roy, with the direction of the recently created Conservatoire des Arts et Métiers. He had just presented a new concept in barometers to the First Class of the National Institute, on 31 March 1798, when he was invited, on Monge's recommendation, to

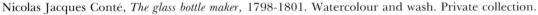

OVERLEAF: Nicolas Jacques Conté, *View of the sundial in one of the courtyards of Hasan Kachef's house,* 1798-1801. Watercolour. Private collection.

Nicolas Jacques Conté, *The glass bottle maker,* 1798-1801. Watercolour and wash. Private collection.

join the Egyptian expedition as chief of the Aerostatic Brigade and a member of the Commission for Arts and Sciences.

It is impossible to convey even briefly the full range of Conté's achievements in Egypt. No sooner had he landed in Alexandria than his restless mind was at work resolving practical problems—constructing furnaces for casting bullets, developing a burnishing process to stop gun barrels from rusting, building flour mills and fire engines, setting up a brewery, and so on. Shortly after his arrival in Cairo on 21 September Caffarelli appointed him director of the machine shops set up in the Institute Quarter.

Despite having lost the best part of his equipment when the *Patriote* ran aground, he dedicated himself to the relentless work that was to be his lot until the end of the expedition, ably assisted by his colleagues in the Aerostatic Corps. By the middle of 1799 the machine shops were fully functioning, a windmill had been built on the island of Rawdah on the Nile and others were being planned for the heights surrounding Cairo and Rosetta. Little by little, machinery followed for the manufacture of powder horns, built by Conté himself and the chemist Champy, for printing and for minting coins. Cardboard, oilskin, steel and topographers', surveyors' and astronomers' instruments were later manufactured to replace those lost during the Cairo revolt, as well as excellent lenses, cannonballs, sword blades and even bugles for the cavalry. During military parades Conté supervised the launching of hot-air balloons.

Later, in 1800, he built lead cisterns to make up for the lack of barrels, and improvised a wool-weaving factory of the capacity required to supply the army with the uniforms it so desperately needed. After Kléber's murder in June 1800 it was he who was given the grisly task of preparing the general's coffin 'in such a manner as for him to be transported back to France'.

In 1801 the Minister of the Interior, Chaptal, sent him official congratulations on the orders of the First Consul. Conté had a brilliant career before him but, aged beyond his years, he died shortly after his return from the expedition. Napoleon immortalized him as 'A Universal

A. Burckhardt, engraved portrait
of Nicolas Jacques Conté.

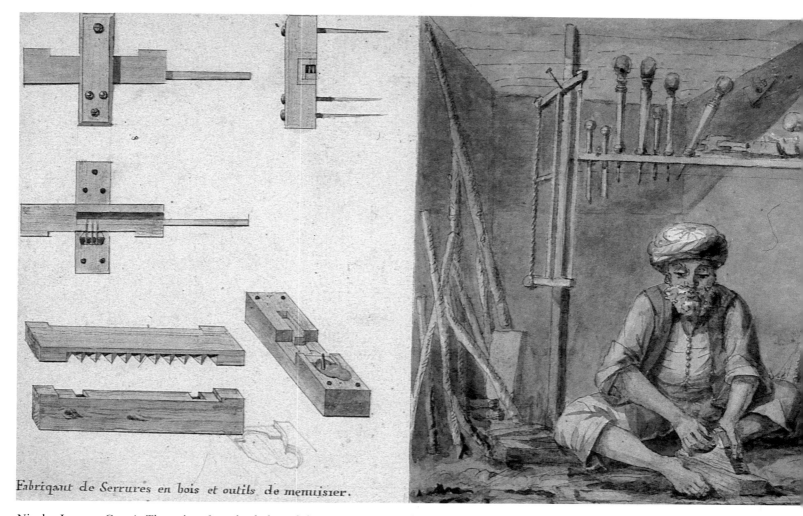

Nicolas Jacques Conté, *The maker of wooden locks and the carpenter's tools*, 1798-1801. Watercolour and wash. Private collection.

Man with the taste, erudition and genius of the artist... who re-created the arts of France in the deserts of Arabia.'

The printing presses brought by Bonaparte to Egypt played an important part in the history of the expedition. The official press, divided into two sections—Oriental and French—and under the direction of Marcel, had a staff of about thirty, comprising a foreman, proofreaders and typesetters along with the interpreters recruited in Rome. The arabist Dom Elias Fatalla was in charge of the Oriental section.

There was, however, another press, which belonged to a member of the Commission for Arts and Sciences, Marc Aurel. The son of a printer and bookseller from Valence who had met Lieutenant Bonaparte and published the second edition of his *Souper de Beaucaire*, Marc Aurel had been in turn the printer for the Army of the Alps and the Army of the Mediterranean, though he joined the Egyptian expedition in a purely private capacity.

Whilst still at sea Marcel's presses had begun working in the holds of the *Orient*. Bonaparte's proclamation and orders to the army of 28 June 1798 and his proclamation to the Egyptians of 2 July 1798, published in Arabic and widely distributed after the landing, were all printed on his presses.

94

OPPOSITE: Charles Louis Balzac, *Cairo, the Citadel, view of the exterior of Joseph's Divan*, 1798-1801. Pen and watercolour. Paris, Bibliothèque Nationale.

André Dutertre, *An Alexandrian child*, 1798-1801. Watercolour heightened with pastel. Paris, Bibliothèque Nationale.

When Marc Aurel, by then appointed Printer to the Army, followed Bonaparte to Cairo, Marcel, against Bonaparte's wishes, remained behind with his presses in the Venetian consul's house in Alexandria and only transferred his equipment to Cairo in October, shortly before the uprising. The Oriental and French presses, set up near Azbakiyyah, then became the State Press. Poussielgue became its director whilst Venture de Paradis and Bourrienne became inspectors of the Arabic and French printshops respectively.

Thus for a while there were two active presses in Cairo until, judging his equipment to be technically inferior, Marc Aurel decided to sell out. The transaction dragged on until it was finally completed by Kléber in September 1799, leaving only Marcel's State Press, which was based in Cairo with a modest branch in Alexandria.

A wide variety of publications came off the French presses in Egypt, including a bilingual edition of the fables of Loqman, an African poet contemporary with Solomon, and an Arabic grammar for the use of French and Arab nationals, both printed by Marcel, as well as an 'Almanac of the French Republic, calculated on the Cairo Meridian, for years VII and IX', several short medical treatises by Desgenettes and the many proclamations, orders of the day and administrative documents ordered by general headquarters, which accounted for the majority of the printing. Of greater interest to the scholars were two important periodicals: the *Courier de l'Égypte* and *La Décade Égyptienne*.

The complete series of the *Courier de l'Égypte* runs to 116 issues, the first of which appeared on 29 August 1798 and the last on 9 June 1801. It was a small-format (22 x 14 cm), four-page

La Décade égyptienne,
journal littéraire et d'économie politique.
The first issue, published on 1 October 1798.

The *Courier de l'Égypte,* a political and military review.
The first issue, published on 29 August 1798.

publication, and was planned to appear twice per *décade*. The first thirty issues were printed by Marc Aurel, the rest by Marcel. The editors were Fourier, then Costaz, and finally Desgenettes.

Devoted to political and military news about Cairo, the provinces and, more rarely, Europe, the *Courier* relieved the monotony of their stay by keeping the army and the scholars abreast of events. The contents were carefully filtered for, throughout its existence, it was the official mouthpiece of the Supreme Command and was used as a vehicle for its policies.

The *Courier* had far too little column space for the work of the scholars, in particular that of the members of the Institute, and since the publication of reports and memoranda was undoubtedly the best way to make them generally and lastingly useful, at its very first meeting the Institute decided to publish its own scientific and literary review. It was baptized *La Décade égyptienne, Journal littéraire et d'économie politique,* in imitation of *La Décade philosophique* then appearing in Paris.

The *Décade* was published in instalments which were later bound into three volumes of about 300 pages each and dedicated respectively to Bonaparte, Kléber and Menou. The first issue was put on sale on 1 October 1798 by Marc Aurel, whose involvement came to an end after the third issue. It was intended to be published every ten days, as the title implies, but from the second volume onwards it was published monthly. The third volume only has three issues, of about a hundred pages each, the last of which left the press on 21 March 1801.

Like the *Courier de l'Égypte, La Décade égyptienne* was widely distributed, copies even being sent to the English on occasion. The editor was Desgenettes until he left to join the Syrian campaign, when Fourier took over. The prospectus, which also served as an introduction, was written by Tallien and declared the review open to voluntary authors who were invited to contribute 'anything concerning the domains of science, art and commerce . . . civil and criminal law, moral and religious institutions'. In fact the Institute's memoranda and reports, printed in full or as extracts, largely sufficed to fill every issue and are more or less the review's sole contents. Of unequal quality, especially in the last volume, the *Décade* nevertheless gives an evocative picture of the work of the scholars in Egypt.

These two periodicals were of course intended for French readers. The local people were kept informed mainly by dual-language posters, leaflets distributed among the chiefs, and proclamations, read out from the minarets, of the news and orders from the commander-in-chief. In order to reach the people more directly, General Menou planned to start a newspaper printed entirely in Arabic, *El Tambyeh,* but the project did not come off.

How did the Egyptians react when they first came in contact with European science and technology? In general, especially at first, the impact was slight. Conté's hot-air balloons, with which the French had hoped to impress the natives, were greeted with universal indifference, and Berthollet tried in vain to amaze the elders with experiments in chemistry and electrostatics. Of all the European innovations, printing was the one that most impressed the Egyptians. Nevertheless it is clear from reading contemporary Egyptian accounts of the expedition—those of al Jabarti, for example, who cannot be suspected of favouring the French—that the educational aims which were among the reasons for the creation of the Institute would have been largely achieved if the French occupation had lasted longer. In any case, this is what Monge believed when he wrote to his wife in the autumn of 1798:

> When this country has been built up, planted and pervaded by French influence for about fifty years, it will become an earthly paradise where landowners will winter to improve their property and then hasten back to Paris in the spring to dine away their profits.

THE SCHOLARS' TRAVELS AND FIELDWORK

At the end of the summer of 1798, the scholars set out on their first tentative forays into the desert, beginning with a few trips to the immediate surroundings of the town—at that time still somewhat unsafe. By the autumn a large number of them had dispersed throughout the country to explore and do fieldwork of all kinds.

On 29 August, Monge, Berthollet, Caffarelli, Andréossy, Villiers du Terrage and several others, riding horses or donkeys and protected by sixty soldiers, set off to visit the ruins of ancient Heliopolis. On 19 September Bonaparte himself visited the pyramids at Giza with Berthier, Caffarelli, Monge, Berthollet, Denon, Fourier, Geoffroy Saint-Hilaire, Costaz and Jollois. Villiers du Terrage and Dubois-Aymé even spent the night on board one of the boats that had been readied for the Nile crossing in order to be sure of being with the party. From then on the pyramids and the sphinx at Giza attracted a constant stream of visitors, both military and civilian.

As soon as the surveyors reached Cairo, in early September, they busied themselves drawing up a map of the town. One of them, Pierre Jacotin, surveyed the immediate surroundings and their chief, Testevuide, began work on a map of the whole of Egypt.

After the Cairo revolt they extended their activities into Lower Egypt and even into Syria, where Jacotin followed the troops as far as Acre. By the time he returned, in June 1799, a great number of maps had been drafted by his colleagues Lecesne, Dulion, Schouani, Simonel, Jomard and Bertre.

Under the direction of their chiefs, le Père and Girard, the civil engineers were rebuilding the canals throughout the delta to regulate the flooding of the Nile and to improve irrigation. Engineers Bodard, Faye and Chabrol, soon joined by Lancret, continued the work begun shortly after the landing on the canal between Alexandria and al Rahmaniya connecting the Mediterranean with the Nile, which was particularly important since it completed the canal that once joined the river to the Red Sea. To the west, Cazals, Théviotte and Pottier were reconnoitring Lake Burullus and, at the opposite end of the delta, Malus and the civil engineer Fèvre were busy with the Moez Canal.

André Dutertre, engraved portrait
of Édouard de Villiers du Terrage.

Alire Delile, *Arabian desert, view of the Gabal Gharib*, 1798-1801. Watercolour and wash. Paris, Bibliothèque Nationale.

Nouet, Méchain and Quesnot, helped by the surveyor Jean Baptiste Corabœuf and the mechanic Paul Lenoir, charted the exact locations of Alexandria, Cairo, Damietta, Salihiyya, Suez and many other towns, villages and ancient monuments.

Desgenettes and his health department studied the symptoms of smallpox and the plague—the latter soon to make its appearance among them.

The naturalists were also busy: Alire Delile and Ernest Coquebert de Montbret were studying the flora of Lower Egypt while Geoffroy Saint-Hilaire explored the eastern part of the delta between Damietta and Salihiyya, and especially Lake Manzalah, the shores of which were inhabited by a multitude of aquatic birds at the time; here he was able to study the habits and anatomy of the flamingo. His best finds, however, were ichthyological: he collected a large number of unknown or little-known fish such as the extraordinary tetrodons or puffer fish, the heterobranchus, which on dissection revealed a pair of organs similar to human lungs, and the rare Nile bichir, equipped with curious fins, like atrophied limbs, which it uses as much to

99

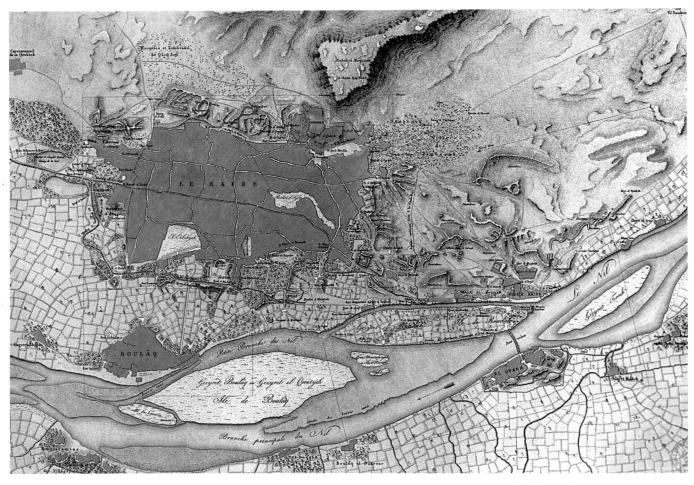

General map of Bulaq, Cairo, the island of Rawdah, Old Cairo and Giza. Drawn by Jacotin, Simonel, Lathuille, Jomard, Bertre and Lecesne. Engraving from the *Description de l'Égypte,* 1809-26.

crawl along the bed of the lake as to swim with. These discoveries, which confirmed Geoffroy Saint-Hilaire's belief that there is a unity in the composition of animal life, sowed the seeds of the great controversies that later broke out between him and Georges Cuvier. Cuvier later said that the discovery of the bichir alone made Bonaparte's expedition worthwhile.

Savigny spent his time amassing a magnificent collection of desert insects. The engineer Pierre Arnollet and the chemist Champy studied and catalogued the minerals of the Red Sea on a journey that took them as far as Qusayr, from which they returned at the end of February 1799. Shortly before this, another group, comprising Jomard and Corabœuf, the mineralogists Victor Dupuis and François Michel de Rozière, had completed a journey through the Fayyum enlivened by attacks from bedouin looters.

Brigadier Andréossy, a member of the Egyptian Institute, conducted two major explorations. On the first he spent most of October 1798 in the company of le Père and Fèvre and Engineers Lieutenant Bouchard making a detailed survey of Lake Manzalah, an immense lagoon on the east side of the Nile delta.

Bonaparte then sent Andréossy to explore the strange area of the Natron Lakes, so called after the salt gathered there, and the Bahr Belama or 'dry river'. Berthollet, Fourier, the painter Henri Joseph Redouté, the civil engineer Duchanoy and the chemist Regnault were part of

100

Antoine Poiteau, *Artemisia monosperma*, 1798-1801.
Wash. Private collection.

Henri Joseph Redouté, *Crucifera thebaica* (*Hyphaene thebaica*
or *dum*, a palm tree from Thebes), 1798-1801. Watercolour.
Paris, Bibliothèque du Muséum National d'Histoire Naturelle.

this expedition, which lasted from 22 to 27 January 1799. Andréossy gathered enough material
to fill a fat report which was read at the Institute and published in *La Décade égyptienne*, while
Berthollet returned with some 'Observations on Natron', also read at the Institute, in which
he explained the formation of the salts.

The two areas visited by Andréossy and his colleagues were soon further explored, Lake
Manzalah by Jacotin and Villiers du Terrage and the Natron Lakes by engineers Gratien le
Père and Levesque.

Bonaparte himself conducted the exploration of the isthmus at Suez. After sending Horace
Say to reconnoitre, he left Cairo on 24 December 1798 with Caffarelli, Monge, Berthollet,
Bourrienne and a privileged few including Jacques Marie le Père, Costaz, Descotils and Dutertre.

They reached Suez on 26 December and began surveying the port and exploring the
Fountains of Moses on the east side of the Gulf. Bonaparte spent 29 December giving last-minute
orders for the fortification of the port and for setting up a new customs office under
Parseval-Grandmaison.

The next day, whilst the bulk of the column returned to Cairo, Bonaparte, the generals
and the scholars went north and explored some 20 km of the remains of the ancient canal that
once carried the waters of the Red Sea to the Bitter Lakes. After spending a further two days

examining the ruins of the next section of the canal, from the Bitter Lakes to the eastern branch of the Nile, they returned to Cairo on the evening of 6 January 1799.

Bonaparte's trip was a prelude to a whole series of technical explorations which he set in motion as soon as he was back in the Egyptian capital. Jacques Marie le Père, who had accompanied him, was put in charge and left Cairo on 16 January with his brother Gratien le Père and Alexandre Saint-Genis.

Between 20 and 31 January the engineers studied the Fountains of Moses and the tide cycle of the Red Sea. Then, joining up with the engineer Dubois-Aymé, who happened to be at Suez, they left the town with an escort of forty men and followed the traces of the old canal as best they could for ten days. At Bilbays they took the road to Cairo, which they reached on 9 February. The Syrian campaign began the next day, so the engineers, left without an escort, were forced to postpone their work until September when the campaign was over.

Dominique Vivant Denon was the first of the scholars to travel up the Nile into Upper Egypt. In November 1798, having received Bonaparte's permission to join a convoy of reinforcements, he embarked with them and, after two days sailing upriver, joined Brigadier Belliard's 21st Regiment, whose life he was to share for the next six months. On 9 December Desaix joined his convoy at Bani Suwayf in the Fayyum and took command of the forces he would launch south in pursuit of Murad Bey.

The journey's brisk pace left little room for archaeology. Denon, a man of great culture and an intelligent traveller, managed nevertheless to bring back many magnificent drawings and copious notes which he later transformed into a lively and attractive account of his journey, *Voyage dans la Basse et la Haute Égypte* (1802).

On 22 December Denon was greatly moved by the celebrated portico at Hermopolis, then the march south continued. On 25 December he was at Asyut; on the 28th we find him studying the architecture of the Red and White Monasteries; after that he was forced to bypass the ruins of Aphroditopolis and Ptolemais and spend three very dull weeks at Girga, the capital of Upper Egypt, which was of no interest to him.

Henri Joseph Redouté, *Tetrodon fahaca*, 1798-1801. Watercolour. Paris, Bibliothèque du Muséum National d'Histoire Naturelle.

OPPOSITE: Jacques Barraband, *Adult haje viper*, 1798-1801. Watercolour. Paris, Bibliothèque du Muséum National d'Histoire Naturelle.

Dominique Vivant Denon,
Self-portrait, *c* 1780. Pastel.
Chalon-sur-Saône, Musée Vivant Denon.

Dominique Vivant Denon, *View of Miqyas,* 1798-9. Pen and wash. London, British Museum.

They set off again on 20 January 1799, and from then on Denon found much to admire and marvel at: first Dendera, then the ruins of Thebes, which were so magnificent that the army stopped and broke into spontaneous applause. Denon sketched feverishly. On the move once more, they saw Hermonthis and Esna, Hieraconpolis, where Denon sketched himself standing before the ruins of the temple, Edfu, Syene, which they reached on 1 February, and finally the island of Philae, just before the first cataract of the Nile, which marked the end of their journey. Denon was exhausted, but after several weeks' rest, during which he made a leisurely inspection of the surrounding monuments, this vigorous fifty-year-old was back on his feet despite the terrible climate.

Meanwhile, Murad Bey had crossed to the right bank of the Nile and was making his way north. Desaix led his cavalry in pursuit, going ahead of the infantry under Belliard's command. A warm friendship had grown up between Desaix and Denon during the campaign, and the two men parted with feeling. They would never meet again.

It was time for Denon also to begin the trek north. He left Syene by boat on 24 February and descended the Nile as far as Esna, stopping for an hour at Kom Ombo to make a quick sketch. From Esna he travelled overland, reaching Thebes, via Hermonthis, on 7 March. The army carried out manœuvres round the town for several weeks, which enabled Denon to visit and make numerous drawings of the temples at Karnak, Luxor, Madinat Habu, the Ramesseum and the colossi of Memnon. He explored the tombs of the Valley of the Kings and one day, to his great excitement, he was brought a mummy holding a papyrus in its hand.

At last it was time to return to Cairo and on 4 July Denon embarked once more and descended the Nile. In Cairo he was welcomed by the scholars with great enthusiasm, and he gave them a résumé of his impressions in a 'Speech to be read at the Cairo Institute' published in *La Décade égyptienne*. On the 25th he witnessed the victory at Aboukir, which he sketched at Bonaparte's request. A few weeks later he embarked secretly for France with Bonaparte, Monge and Berthollet.

Dominique Vivant Denon, *Vivant Denon at the ruins of Hieraconpolis*, 1798-9. Pen and wash. London, British Museum.

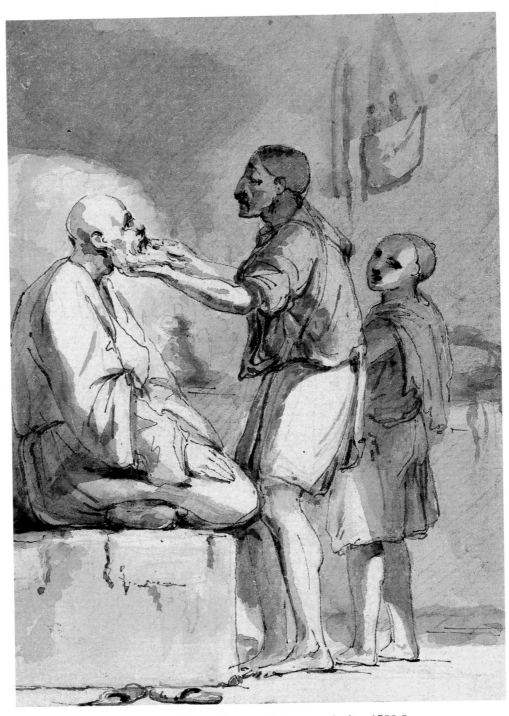

Dominique Vivant Denon, *The Egyptian barber*, 1798-9.
Pen and wash. London, British Museum.

On 4 February 1799 the Egyptian Institute heard Dolomieu's report on the Nilometer on the island of Rawdah, the great Abbasid structure for measuring the level of the Nile, and Andréossy's and Berthollet's reports on their trip to the Natron Lakes. This was to be the Institute's last sitting for several months, when it was disrupted by the Syrian campaign, and it would not meet again until 29 June. Many of the scholars took part in the campaign: from the Institute alone there was Monge, Berthollet, Caffarelli, Andréossy, Horace Say, Costaz, Malus, Venture de Paradis and Savigny, not counting a number of their colleagues from the Commission for Arts and Sciences.

The affair began sombrely, for the devastations of the plague considerably dampened their spirits. One of the surveyors, Bringuier, and the one-time Knight of St John, Saint-Simon, succumbed to the plague at Jaffa. At Acre two young surveyors, Picquet and Charbaud, both from the École Polytechnique, were killed, as was Horace Say. Caffarelli was seriously wounded and died after ten days of fever. In him the scholars lost not only their chief but their staunchest supporter. Then dysentery appeared. Monge only survived it thanks to the devoted care of Desgenettes, Berthollet and Costaz. Worn out by the fatigues of the campaign, Venture de Paradis, doyen of the Commission for Arts and Sciences and the expedition's best orientalist, succumbed to it. During the last days of the siege the plague wreaked havoc despite the heroic

Dominique Vivant Denon, *The Egyptian bath*, 1798-9. Pen and wash. London, British Museum.

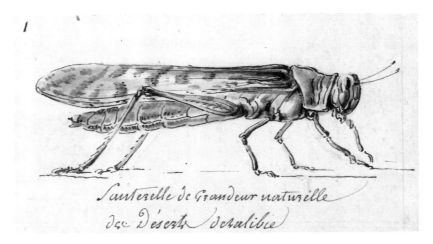

Dominique Vivant Denon, *Arabian desert grasshopper,* 1798-9.
Pen and wash. London, British Museum.

efforts of Desgenettes and the other doctors, amongst whom were Labatte and Desvesvres, members of the Commission. Desvesvres himself fell victim to the infection and died within forty-eight hours.

The siege of Acre was at last abandoned on 20 May, followed by a painful retreat. On 4 June Bonaparte, Monge and Berthollet left the troops at Qatia and set off to explore the ruins of ancient Pelusium. (Much later, in 1808, Napoleon remembered this trip and conferred the title of Count of Pelusium on Monge.) The army reached Cairo on 14 June. The setback at Acre, the many dead and the business with the plague victims at Jaffa had demoralized the army and left everyone with a bitter aftertaste.

Nevertheless it is apparent from the minutes that the Institute diligently continued its work. During the meeting held on 29 July a letter from Lancret was read out announcing the discovery of the celebrated Rosetta stone. This black stone slab with its three inscriptions was immediately recognized as a possible key to the enigma of the hieroglyphs, and the orientalist Marcel at once began to study it.

One of the duties of the Institute was to fill the vacancies in its ranks as they came up, and a certain number of changes in its membership were made between its founding and Bonaparte's departure. On 7 September 1798 the astronomer Pierre Joseph de Beauchamp, who had just arrived in Egypt, was elected to the Physics Department. To counterbalance this, there were soon some empty seats: the surgeon Dubois and the architect Norry, both ill, resigned on 7 October and 21 November respectively, and Sulkowski was killed during the Cairo revolt. On 1 December Norry's chair was given to another architect, Jean Baptiste Lepère.

More members were to leave during the following few months. The first was Sucy, seriously wounded during the march back to Cairo, who embarked on the Genoan transport ship *Liberté* at Alexandria on 16 December. A few days later the ship was forced to put into port at Augusta in Sicily and Sucy and other Frenchmen on board were massacred by the Sicilians. A little later, Beauchamp left on a diplomatic mission to Constantinople: he spent many months in Turkish prisons and died of exhaustion as soon as he got back to France.

Dolomieu, after falling seriously ill, sailed on 7 March 1799 with his friend and colleague Cordier, a member of the Commission for Arts and Sciences, but his ship was blown into the Gulf of Taranto by a storm and he was arrested and transferred to Messina at the instigation

Dominique Vivant Denon, *Study of a head,* 1798-9. Pen and wash. London, British Museum.

of the Order of Malta, which had not forgotten his role as negotiator in the capitulation of the island. He was to suffer twenty-one months of harsh imprisonment and died in 1802, shortly after being set free. Another departure was that of Quesnot, though it is not known when he left or what became of him.

The Syrian campaign having taken the lives of Caffarelli, Horace Say and Venture de Paradis, the scholars proceeded to hold further elections without delay. On 29 June Bourrienne succeeded Sucy, and five days later Lancret, Chief Surgeon Larrey, Louis de Corancez and the Institute's librarian Louis Madelène Ripault took the places of Horace Say, Dubois, Caffarelli

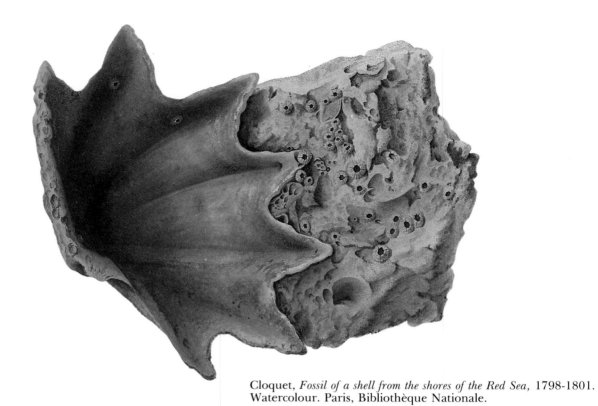

Cloquet, *Fossil of a shell from the shores of the Red Sea,* 1798-1801.
Watercolour. Paris, Bibliothèque Nationale.

Henri Joseph Redouté, *The Polypterus bichir* (Nile bichir), 1798-1801.
Watercolour. Paris, Bibliothèque du Muséum National d'Histoire Naturelle.

Ringuet, *Memnonian puddingstone from the Gabal al Silsilah,* 1798-1801.
Watercolour. Paris, Bibliothèque Nationale.

Henri Joseph Redouté, *Three-clawed emys or Nile tortoise,* 1798-1801.
Watercolour. Paris, Bibliothèque du Muséum National d'Histoire Naturelle.

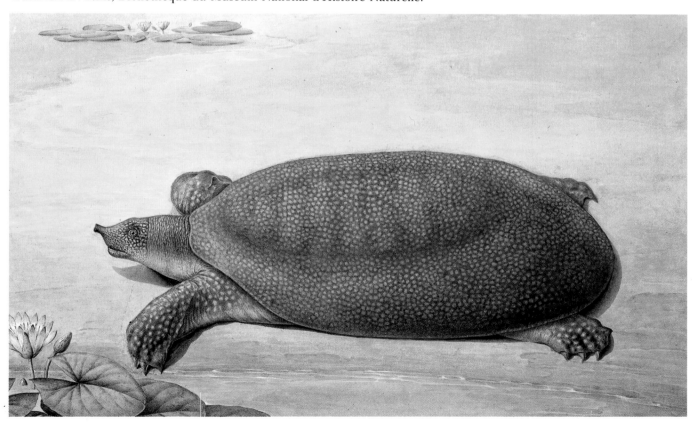

and Venture de Paradis. Concurrently with this, important decisions were taken concerning the Commission for Arts and Sciences and particularly the surveyors and civil engineers, who were placed under the orders of Jacotin and le Père, thus becoming directly answerable to general headquarters.

On 25 July Bonaparte crushed the Ottoman army which had landed on the beaches at Aboukir supported by the English fleet, and flung them back to the sea. A month later he embarked secretly for France with Monge, Berthollet and Denon. Back in Paris on 16 October, Bonaparte took his chair at the National Institute on 23 October to report on the scientific achievements in Egypt, the discovery of the Rosetta stone and the work on the Suez Canal. On 9 November he became First Consul of France.

Denon's journey through Upper Egypt was the preface to a methodical exploration of the area of a kind not possible when travelling with the army, marching or halting in response to military requirements. The expedition, conducted by three field-groups from the Commission for Arts and Sciences and the Egyptian Institute, began in March 1799 even before Denon's return to Cairo and continued without interruption until October.

Following orders left by Bonaparte before his departure for Syria, the first group left Cairo on 19 March under the direction of Girard. Its purpose was to gather as much information as possible on the art, commerce and agriculture of Upper Egypt, and above all to study the tide cycle and irrigation of the Nile between Cairo and the first cataract. The group comprised three mining engineers—Descotils, Rozière and Dupuy—and four civil engineers—Jollois, Villiers du Terrage, Dubois-Aymé and Duchanoy, together with the sculptor Castex.

The group travelled up the Nile in feluccas—Arab boats with triangular sails—as far as the staging post at Asyut, which it reached on 29 March and where the real work began. It continued as far as Qena, opposite the Dendera site, reaching it on 25 May and meeting up with Belliard, who was busy preparing an expedition to Qusayr on the shores of the Red Sea with Denon and Schouani. Girard and Rozière decided to go with them and, shortly afterwards, Dubois-Aymé was forced to join them.

Dominique Vivant Denon, *Study of a dromedary's head*, 1798-9.
Pen and pencil. London, British Museum.

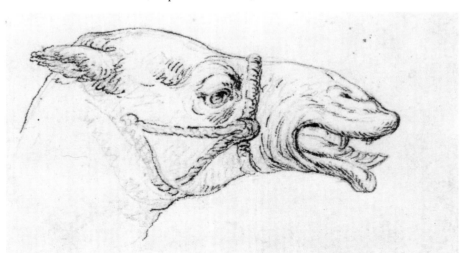

Dominique Vivant Denon, *General headquarters in the tombs near Naqada,* 1798-9. Centre, Brigadier Belliard;
Vivant Denon is seated far right. Pen and wash. London, British Museum.

OVERLEAF: Cécile and Balzac, *Thebes, view of the ruins of Karnak,* 1798-1801.
Watercolour. Paris, Bibliothèque Nationale.

Jollois and Villiers du Terrage took advantage of the absence of their chief, who was more
interested in hydraulics and levelling than in archaeology, to make frequent trips to the temple
at Dendera, spending a great deal of their time studying the renowned zodiac discovered earlier
by Desaix and Denon.

On Girard's return from Qusayr the group set off south. They passed Qift and Qus by,
made a brief stop at Karnak and Luxor and finally halted at Esna, capital of the southernmost
Egyptian province and at that time the largest French military post between Qena and Syene.
There they met up with part of the 21st Regiment with which Denon had campaigned against
the mamelukes. The soldiers had laid down their guns and taken up their respective trades,
fraternizing with the natives and even, on occasion, employing young Egyptian apprentices.

Jollois and Villiers du Terrage, lost in admiration before the temples at Esna, were called
to order by Girard and enjoined to forget about antiquities and get on with the construction
of a nilometer, thus further straining relations between this competent but authoritarian chief
engineer and his young subordinates.

On 9 July, Jollois, Villiers du Terrage, Castex and the rest of the engineers set off, without

André Dutertre,
engraved portrait of Louis Costaz.

Girard, for the first cataract on the border between Egypt and Nubia, travelling via Edfu, Kom Ombo and Syene, where they stayed from 13 to 26 July and executed a great number of drawings despite the oppressive heat. They visited the island of Philae several times, where Castex carved an inscription on the Great Temple commemorating the passage of the French which has remained famous to this day.

They rejoined Girard's group at Esna and set off for Thebes on 7 August. Once there, Descotils, Rozière, Dupuy and Duchanoy left their companions and returned to Cairo, while the inseparable Jollois and Villiers du Terrage began a methodical exploration of the ruins. They were soon joined by Dutertre, the botanist Nectoux and Dubois-Aymé. When these three expressed a desire to travel up the Nile to Syene, Jollois and Villiers du Terrage decided to go with them. Girard, his mission accomplished, went back to Cairo leaving his undisciplined collaborators to 'mess around with hieroglyphs' to their hearts' content. He reported on his journey in a long and remarkable report, read at the Egyptian Institute and published in *La Décade égyptienne*, in which he reviewed the geography and economic status of Upper Egypt as well as its property and tax laws, and concluded with a historical essay on the commercial route to India via the Nile, the desert at Qusayr and the Red Sea.

Having conversed with Denon at length and admired the drawings he had brought back, Bonaparte, on the point of leaving for France, appointed two further field-groups on 14 August to complete the exploration of Upper Egypt, which he placed under Costaz and Fourier respectively. The first consisted of Nouet and Méchain, astronomers; Corabœuf, surveyor; Saint-Genis and Viard, engineers; Charles Louis Balzac and Jean Baptiste Lepère, architects; Coutelle, Conté's deputy at the Aerostatic Corps and the machine shops in Cairo; Savigny, zoologist; Coquebert de Montbret, botanist; Ripault, the Egyptian Institute's librarian; Lenoir, mechanic; and Labatte, health officer. The second, under Fourier, consisted of Cécile, Lancret, Jomard, Chabrol, Arnollet and Vincent, engineers; Geoffroy Saint-Hilaire, zoologist; Delile, botanist; Henri Joseph Redouté, painter; Villoteau, singer and musicologist; Lacipière, health officer; and Rouyer, pharmacist. Both groups left Cairo on 20 August and made their way without incident up the Nile, stopping at the same places along the way as Villiers du Terrage, Jollois and Denon had done before them. Hostility developed between Fourier and Geoffroy Saint-Hilaire, about which the latter complained several times in his letters home.

On 10 September the Costaz group met Jollois and Villiers du Terrage on their way back from Syene with Dutertre, Nectoux and Dubois-Aymé, between Edfu and Gabal al Silsilah. The scholars embraced and exchanged news while Jollois and Villiers du Terrage proudly showed their drawings and notes to the newcomers. Seeing the quantity of work already accomplished, the scholars decided to use it as a base and adopt the methods of the two friends, collaborating with them to continue and complete their studies.

It was now the turn of the recent arrivals to express a wish to see Syene, so Jollois and Villiers du Terrage agreed to wait at Esna and meet up with them on their return. At Syene on 16 September the two groups learned of Bonaparte's departure for France. Their spirits

Caristie, *The Fayyum, view of the Begig obelisk* (now known as the Abgig stele), 1798-1801. Pen and wash. Paris, Bibliothèque Nationale.

dampened by the news, they went back down the Nile and explored the tombs of al Kab with Jollois and Villiers du Terrage, then they all went on to Thebes where Belliard and the 21st Regiment had just been celebrating the anniversary of the Republic in the grand setting of the hypostyle hall at Luxor.

The scholars finished their description and study of the monuments at Thebes, then moved on to explore Madinat Habu, the colossi of Memnon, the Ramesseum, Karnak, Luxor and especially the Valley of the Kings. After this they slowly descended the Nile, stopping at Dendera again, then at Abydos and Antinoe, arriving in Cairo at the end of October.

The scholars' work in Upper Egypt was over. Almost a year separated Denon's departure from Cairo and the return of the two field-groups, during which an enormous amount of documentation had been accumulated. They had also collected a great number of archaeological items together with specimens gathered by the naturalists, including mummified ibis, cats and

Cécile, *Thebes, Karnak, general view of the propylaea and the ruins of the palace seen from the north-east*, 1798-1801. Watercolour. Paris, Musée du Louvre.

118

other animals found in the burial chambers. When Georges Cuvier was asked in 1802 to evaluate the collection brought back by Geoffroy Saint-Hilaire and donated by him to the Muséum d'Histoire Naturelle, his conviction that life on earth was only a few thousand years old was strengthened by his examination of the mummified specimens, leading him to conclude in favour of the immutability of the species:

The collection includes animals of all periods. We have long wanted to know whether species change their forms with the passage of time.... One's heart leaps on seeing an animal preserved with all its smallest bones and hair in a perfectly recognizable form, knowing that two or three thousand years ago it had its own priests and altars in Thebes or Memphis.... It is clear from these items in Citizen Geoffroy's collection that these animals exactly resemble those of today.

Jean Constantin Protain, *Cairo, perspective view of part of the City of the Tombs*, 1798-1801.
Pen and wash. Paris, Bibliothèque Nationale.

A REVERSAL OF FORTUNES

In his instructions to his successor, Kléber, Bonaparte ordered that 'The Commission for Arts will make its way to France after negotiations which you will request to this end, in conformity with the exchange agreement in November [1799], as soon as they have accomplished their mission. At present they are busy with what was still left to do, to wit the exploration of Upper Egypt.'

Supported by the great majority of men of the Army of the Orient, who desired nothing better than to return to France, Kléber duly opened negotiations with the Turks in which the English Commodore Sidney Smith would soon play a part.

Whilst awaiting the results of Kléber's negotiations, the scholars got back to work. The new general-in-chief fully supported their efforts, and one of them, Fourier, became his secretary and an intimate friend. The Egyptian Institute, deprived of seven more of its number since Bonaparte's departure, showed its appreciation of Kléber by making him a member, on 10 November 1799, along with Generals Desaix and Reynier. A little while later, in the course of

120

Jean Constantin Protain, *Elevations of Hasan Kachef's house (the Institute) facing the courtyard and garden*, 1798-1801.
Pen and wash. Paris, Bibliothèque Nationale.

December and January, the Institute added General Dugua, the pharmacist Boudet, Jacotin and Protain to its roster. Very soon, however, diplomatic and military events would force the Institute to suspend its meetings for a period of eight months.

A worthy successor to Bonaparte, Kléber immediately set about coordinating the work of the Institute and the Commission for Arts and Sciences. On 19 November he created a commission 'to gather all information pertaining to the modern Egyptian state', for which a research programme under ten headings was prepared. Many of the scholars were involved in the project, including Fourier, Tallien, the economist Gloutier, Girard, Conté, Marcel, Dutertre, Protain and Redouté. Geography, entrusted to le Père and Jacotin, received special attention.

A short while later Kléber proposed another project of at least equal importance: at a meeting of the Institute on 22 November, Fourier read a letter from Kléber inviting the scholars 'to combine the fruits of their work on Upper Egypt into a single publication'. Very quickly this project expanded to include the whole of Egypt and resulted in the publication, from 1809 to 1826, of the magnificent *Description de l'Égypte*.

In the provinces the travels and fieldwork continued. It was during Kléber's command that the scholars measured the Great Pyramid, established the exact location of ancient Memphis and explored the foothills of the Libyan mountains.

Rozière, back in Upper Egypt once more, took part in a military reconnaissance of the isthmus at Suez. In the same area Alire Delile, Geoffroy Saint-Hilaire and Marie Jules Savigny completed their botanical and zoological collections, while the levelling of the ancient canal running from the Nile to the Red Sea continued under the supervision of Chief Engineer le Père.

Although by this time the plan to reopen the canal had been abandoned, le Père picked up the work interrupted by the Syrian campaign and completed it in two further operations carried out between September and December 1799. He was helped by a great number of engineers including Fèvre, Dubois-Aymé, Favier, Duchanoy, Chabrol, Alibert, Gratien le Père, Saint-Genis and Villiers du Terrage. All this work was later summarized in the *Mémoire sur le canal des deux mers* which le Père presented to Napoleon in 1804.

In fact, despite their zeal, the work of le Père and his collaborators turned out to be useless. Without the spirit-levels destroyed at Caffarelli's house during the Cairo revolt, which Conté for all his inventive genius was only able to replace with rudimentary and less suitable instruments, and harried as they were by the Arabs and frequently short of water and supplies, they were often forced to work too fast and dispense with the usual checks on their findings. All of this resulted in an enormous error on which le Père based his conclusions: he believed the level of the Red Sea to be 9.91 m higher than that of the Mediterranean, a calculation that the opening of Lesseps' canal would prove to be totally false, the level of the two seas being in fact more or less the same.

The engineers, on the other hand, did not work in vain, and Bonaparte's objective, the reestablishment of a canal joining the Red Sea to the Mediterranean, was finally achieved.

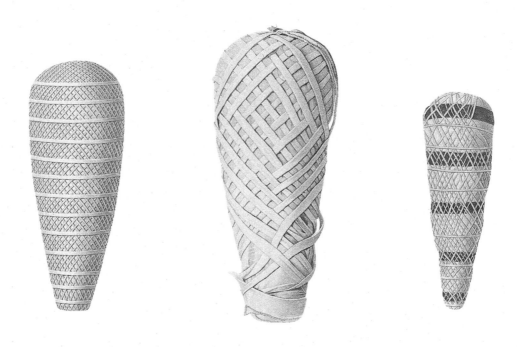

André Dutertre and Edme François Jomard, *Thebes, ibis mummies found in the hypogaea.*
Coloured engraving from the *Description de l'Égypte,* 1809-26.

122

Nicolas Jacques Conté, *View of the pyramids at Giza,* 1798-1801. Watercolour. Private collection.

No sooner was he back in Cairo than Villiers du Terrage was ordered to accompany Girard, whom he disliked, on an itinerary as yet unexplored by the French, leading from Cairo to Suez through the Valley of the Lost. Reaching Suez, Villiers du Terrage met up with Saint-Hilaire, Delile and Savigny. Just as they were on the point of setting off for Mount Sinai, the news of the capture of al Arish by the Grand Vizier's Turkish army reached them. Cut off from Cairo and in danger of being taken prisoner, the scholars were relieved to hear that a peace treaty was about to be signed with the Anglo-Turkish alliance, and immediately seized the opportunity to take the road back to the capital.

Indeed, after long negotiations conducted on the French side by Poussielgue and Desaix, Kléber signed the treaty of al Arish on 24 January 1800, under the terms of which the French army was free to leave Egypt with its arms and baggage, aboard its own men-of-war or those that the Porte might be required to provide. The treaty was well received by everyone. The wounded were to be repatriated without delay together with the scholars from the Commission for Arts and Sciences and the Egyptian Institute, and Kléber ordered Tallien to go to Alexandria to attend to the practical details of their embarkation aboard the brig *Oiseau*. During the negotiations the English gave Kléber news of the *coup d'état* of 18 Brumaire and of Bonaparte's rise to supreme power.

Everything appeared to be going well and, with the exception of the surveyors whom Kléber retained to complete the overall map of Egypt, all the scholars were in Alexandria by 17 March and embarked on the *Oiseau* ten days later. They would remain on board for a month, vexed by the daily expectation of departure in which they were daily disappointed. In a reversal of their original conciliatory attitude, the English had blockaded Alexandria once more, and in contempt of the agreement signed at al Arish, Lord Keith, commander of the British naval forces in the Mediterranean, sent Kléber a haughty letter in which he summoned him to lay down arms in unconditional surrender. We know Kléber's reply: on 20 March he crushed the Grand Vizier's vastly superior army at Heliopolis with a mere 15,000 men. The survivors were chased to the Syrian frontier. As for the English, they prudently stayed on board their ships. Egypt had been reconquered.

Kléber then had to hasten back to Cairo where a new and bloody revolt had broken out. Isolated in the town, a handful of Frenchmen were bravely holding out. Desgenettes and Marcel, trapped with them, were both wounded in the head. Finally, after a siege lasting over fifteen days and fierce fighting in the streets, the town fell.

There was no longer any point in the scholars dreaming of their return home: they were soon recalled to Cairo and invited to get back to work. Under the direction of Jacotin the surveyors, assisted by their colleagues the civil engineers, settled down to their tasks once more. Simonel drew up a map of Lake Burullus and the outskirts of Rosetta and Damietta; Schouani finished mapping the interior of the delta and then went to Upper Egypt to survey the surroundings of Thebes and Qusayr; Legentil busied himself with Lake Manzalah and then he too travelled up the Nile to trace the contours of the surroundings of Esna, Kom Ombo, Edfu and Syene; Jomard was busy in the Fayyum, Bertre and Lecesne in the region of Asyut. Later, under General Menou's period of command, Coutelle and Rozière would go as far as Sinai to draw maps of the area and Martin would complete Jomard's work in the Fayyum.

Very soon came the sombre news of Kléber's murder, which deeply affected soldiers and scholars alike and added to the gloom caused by their thwarted hopes of seeing France again. Kléber was solemnly interred on 17 June and his funeral oration was read by his friend Fourier amidst general sorrow.

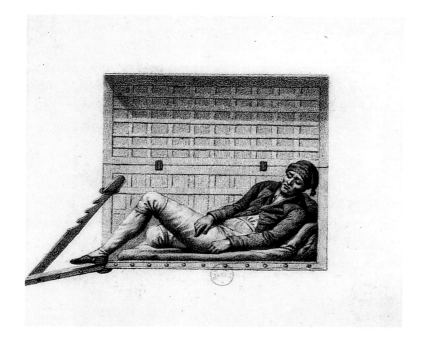

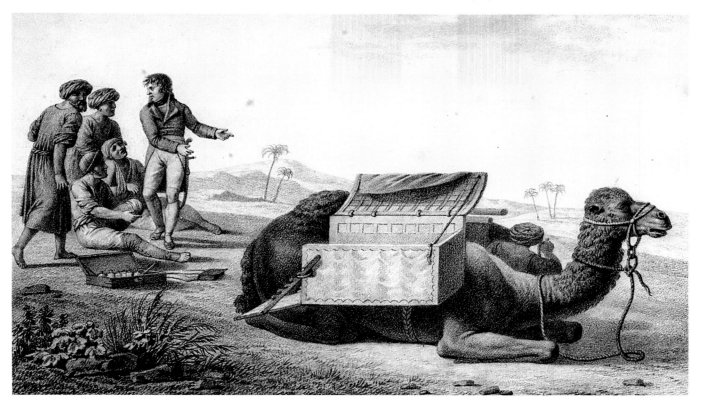

ABOVE AND OPPOSITE: *Portable bed for the wounded invented by the surgeon Dominique Larrey*, 1798-1801. Graphite. Paris, Bibliothèque Nationale.

OVERLEAF: Edme François Jomard, *Night view of the Qasr Qarun temple situated at the western edge of the lake known as Birkat al Qarun*, 1798-1801. Watercolour. Paris, Bibliothèque Nationale.

Kléber was succeeded by General Menou, towards whom the soldiers, scholars and, later, history itself have undoubtedly been somewhat unjust. Envied by the other generals and despised for his conversion to Islam, he was nevertheless one of the few who still believed in the future of the French colony in Egypt. But his pernickety administration and his authoritarian and often tactless measures would finally end up alienating both soldiers and scholars.

On 16 July the new general-in-chief ordered the Institute to resume the meetings interrupted at the end of January, but there was a great feeling of lassitude amongst its members and the Institute did not comply until nearly two months later, on 8 September. A few interesting reports were read, but its activities had generally slowed down and there would be no further elections to fill the seats that fell empty.

Menou, however, was very well intentioned. He was full of praise for the achievements of the scholars and, like Bonaparte and Kléber before him, he called upon many of them for the administrative tasks that arose during his command. His mistake was perhaps his refusal to take into account the exhaustion of the civilians, who were by now virtually obsessed with the forlorn hope of returning to France. Taking an opposite political line to Kléber, he adopted every measure he considered necessary to prolong the French occupation of Egypt. In June and July he asked the scholars to compile inventories of all the scientific instruments held by the Egyptian Institute, the surveyors, civil engineers, machine shops and the State Press. Once in possession of this information, he had a list drawn up of all the requirements of the learned

colony and managed to send it to Paris. He even demanded that further civilian specialists such as doctors, surgeons, engineers and mechanics be sent to Egypt, but the increasingly stringent blockade by the English fleet would prevent most of what was sent from reaching its destination, and many of the crates got no further than Toulon. As for the grand projects envisaged by Menou—the exploration of distant areas, the creation of a land registry, etc.—events would not leave him time to carry them out.

The scholars dragged their heels. A few of them none the less made an excursion to the pyramids at Giza on 4 September, to Dahshur on 5 January 1801 and to Saqqarah on 24 January. During February Coutelle and le Père excavated round the pyramids and Geoffroy Saint-Hilaire dug at Saqqarah. Only a few of the scholars went any distance from Cairo: Rozière and Coutelle when they travelled as far as Sinai at their own risk and without an escort, Martin when he methodically explored the Fayyum, and Lepère, Villiers du Terrage and Chabrol, who made a brief visit to Suez and returned through the Valley of the Lost.

Larrey invented a new kind of portable bed for the sick and wounded. The surveyors continued drawing up the map of the delta in collaboration with the Engineers Corps. Le Père and the civil engineers worked on improvements to the irrigation system, building a road from Cairo to the Nile through Bulaq and surrounding the palace of Azbakiyyah with a walkway planted with trees. But the course of all these operations was much affected by the ill humour and discouragement of the engineers.

On 3 February the frigates *Justice* and *Égyptienne* anchored in the port of Alexandria after an uneventful ten-day passage. Aboard the *Égyptienne* were two shipbuilding engineers, Vincent and Bonjean, sent over at Menou's request, who immediately joined the ranks of the Commission for Arts and Sciences. But they had come too late, for on 1 March the British fleet under Lord Keith appeared before Alexandria. On the 8th the 18,000-strong English army disembarked at a point near Aboukir which General Friant and 1500 Frenchmen vainly tried to hold. On 21 March Menou, who had advanced to face the enemy at Canopus, was defeated and entrenched himself in Alexandria. Communications between the town and Cairo were threatened.

In the Egyptian capital, caught between the English and a Turkish force on the march from Syria, a rebellion was hatching. The French retreated to the forts and the citadel taking the printing presses, general command and administrative documents and all the scholars' papers and collections with them. To make things worse, the plague wreaked havoc despite the heroic efforts of the Medical Corps, and in a few days the scholars lost several of their comrades, notably Coquebert de Montbret and Champy. Malus was twice struck down and the writer Lerouge was already infected by the time he left Cairo.

The majority of the scholars had in fact come to a decision that they would have reason to regret bitterly. Instead of staying in Cairo under the protection of Belliard, who had so often shown his good will towards them, particularly in Upper Egypt, they requested and finally obtained his permission to accompany a convoy of supplies to Alexandria, where Menou would regard them as so many useless mouths to feed. Many tribulations awaited them.

Those who stayed behind, among them Boudet, Desgenettes, Conté, Malus, Dutertre, Girard, Jean Baptiste Lepère and Jacotin, would not regret it. When Belliard, whose troops were being decimated by the plague and famine, decided to deliver the town to the English, he negotiated the scholars' right to leave for France without hindrance and to take their manuscripts, drawings and collections with them. They embarked with the Cairo garrison in August with their private collections, their papers, the library and the scientific instruments from the Institute carefully packed by Girard, as well as the equipment from the State Press got ready by Marcel, and were back in France by the beginning of October.

Their colleagues, on the other hand, having at last reached Alexandria after many vicissitudes—the soldiers' hostility towards the scholars had revived with even greater vigour amidst the general disorder—were extremely ill-received by Menou, who was to become increasingly unpleasant towards them. After weeks of beating about the bush, Menou at last permitted them to embark, and on 5 June 1801 he agreed to allow them a collective passport but obstinately refused to make any kind of approach on their behalf to the English. That evening the scholars embarked on the same brig aboard which they had languished for so long in March and April 1800, the *Oiseau*.

This marks the beginning of a shameful episode. Between 15 and 17 July, in an attempt to weigh anchor, the scholars were caught between the English, who refused to let the ship through, and Menou, who was totally uninterested in their fate and even talked of sinking their ship if they tried to reenter the Alexandrian port, with the result that they understandably felt their last hour had come. Paradoxically it was thanks to Commodore Sidney Smith that they were at last allowed on dry land where, on 31 July, after a final quarantine, they found themselves trapped in besieged Alexandria, under relentless shelling and with a serious lack of supplies.

This lasted for four terrible weeks. Geoffroy Saint-Hilaire, however, hardly noticed it in his absorption in fresh zoological finds: a lucky chance brought him, one after the other, two electric fish that he had long wanted to examine—the Nile catfish and a Mediterranean torpedo ray:

Nicolas Maréchal, *Mongoose*, 1802. Watercolour on vellum. Paris, Bibliothèque du Muséum National d'Histoire Naturelle.

Henri Joseph Redouté, *Nefaschia citharus*, 1798-1801.
Watercolour. Paris, Bibliothèque du Muséum National d'Histoire Naturelle.

OPPOSITE: Edme François Jomard, *Middle Egypt, view of Turah* (detail), 1798-1801.
Watercolour. Paris, Bibliothèque Nationale.

Henri Joseph Redouté, *The Malapterus electricus* (electric catfish), 1798-1801.
Watercolour. Paris, Bibliothèque du Muséum National d'Histoire Naturelle.

131

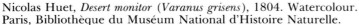

Nicolas Huet, *Desert monitor* (*Varanus grisens*), 1804. Watercolour. Paris, Bibliothèque du Muséum National d'Histoire Naturelle.

Nicolas Huet, *Egyptian hare*, 1806. Watercolour on vellum. Paris, Bibliothèque du Muséum National d'Histoire Naturelle.

> Captivated by the sight of these electrical phenomena, in which I became an assiduous experimenter, I was seized by a feverish activity which held me in its thrall for three whole weeks.... I was unable to sleep for more than an hour or two out of the twenty-four in a day. It was a crisis which went through phases of exaltation ... despair and exhaustion.

He later produced a celebrated treatise, published in 1802, on the comparative anatomy of electric tissue, in which he posited the fertile theory of the non-speciality of nerve activity.

Meanwhile the Army of the Orient was at the end of its tether. On 26 August Menou was forced to ask for an armistice of three days, which was granted. On 2 September he signed the capitulation dictated by Lord Keith, one of the conditions of which was that the scholars should leave all their collections behind. Learning that Menou had accepted such an outrageous clause, the scholars bluntly expressed their indignation and categorically refused to agree to it. Then, after Menou had made a feeble and utterly fruitless approach to the English, they took matters into their own hands. Saint-Hilaire, Delile and Savigny paid a visit to General Hutchinson and informed him that they would destroy all their work and their collections rather than hand them over to the English. Hutchinson was impressed enough to soften his demands, but he did not forgo them completely. The French were permitted to take whatever could be considered their personal possessions, but the already famous Rosetta stone and other beautiful sculptures, sarcophagi and artefacts were seized by the British. However, thanks to their energetic intervention, the scholars had at least managed to rescue all their papers.

Repatriated on a variety of ships, they reached Toulon and Marseilles in October and November. The last to leave Egypt was probably Larrey, who embarked on the English frigate *Diana* on 18 October with Menou, who had contracted the plague, and the general's family.

Bonaparte had no doubt intended that the results of the scholars' work would eventually be published when he founded the Egyptian Institute, though it was Kléber who instigated the compilation of the *Description de l'Égypte*. When the Institute met on 22 November 1799 to hear

132

Kléber's letter to their permanent secretary, Fourier, they convened all the scholars from the Commission for Arts and Sciences to a meeting in order to prepare a reply. The meeting took place two days later and the motion for a major joint publication was adopted enthusiastically, with Fourier being elected almost unanimously as its coordinator. Kléber immediately approved their choice.

The decision had been taken, but everything still remained to be done, foremost of which was deciding on the necessary means and equipment. During a second full assembly of the scholars, held on 24 December, they planned to form a company, with twenty-four shares to be owned by its members, for the publication of a book of which 2000 copies would be printed. They even went so far as to choose these members: Fourier and the businessman Hamelin would be the editors; Ripault would be their deputy; André Dutertre would oversee the engravings.

The rupture of the al Arish negotiations, followed by the renewal of the fighting and Kléber's murder, prevented them from getting any further. And Menou, the new commander-in-chief, had other ideas which he unveiled to Napoleon in a letter dated 24 September 1800. In his view it was the Republic and the Republic alone that should publish the proposed major work, and on 5 February he wrote to the Egyptian Institute expressing his wish to see all the work of the scholars collected together. But it was too late: military events overtook the project and dispensed the scholars from having to obey.

The great project was not abandoned, however. As soon as Fourier was back in Paris he was received by the First Consul and instructed to confer with Monge, Berthollet and Laplace

Léon de Wailly, *Ram with a thick tail,* 1805. Watercolour on vellum. Paris, Bibliothèque du Muséum National d'Histoire Naturelle.

Cécile, *Mameluke dagger,* 1798-1801. Gouached watercolour. Paris, Bibliothèque Nationale.

about the immediate publication of the *Description de l'Égypte,* since it was essential to forestall individual publications. Denon—always the individualist—went ahead and had his *Voyage dans la Basse et la Haute Égypte* published by Didot, in 1802. To prevent others from imitating him, Chaptal, the Minister of the Interior, convened the community of Egyptian scholars to a meeting on 18 February 1802 in order to select eight members to form a publishing committee. Those inseparable friends Berthollet and Monge became part of it, along with Conté, Desgenettes, Fourier, Costaz, Girard and Lancret, all of whom were members of the Egyptian Institute and almost all of whom were or would become members of the National Institute. Berthollet became their president, Costaz was vice-president, Conté was appointed government commissioner in charge of engraving and printing and Fourier, despite having been called upon for the prefecture of Isère, was asked to write the historical introduction.

In March 1802 Chaptal decided that the scholars were to present a summary of the drawings and other material intended for publication. The subjects to be treated were Geography, the Modern State and Natural History. Jacotin had already handed Brigadier Andréossy all the material for the great map of Egypt which is one of the most brilliant achievements of the expedition.

Once a week the committee of the *Ouvrage sur l'Égypte,* as it was described on their letterhead, met to select the material to be included, to report on the progress of the texts and to approve the illustrations for engraving. The actual printing of the work was given to the State Press—soon to become the Imperial Press—which Jean Jacques Marcel was put in charge of on 1 January 1803. Several technical innovations were devised expressly for the publication, foremost among them being an engraving machine invented by Conté which produced astonishingly beautiful results, as well as improvements in the manufacture of vellum, a new system for printing colour and the construction of larger presses. Already an intellectual landmark, the *Description de l'Égypte* was also a great leap forward in the development of French book production.

Begun in 1803, the work would take twenty-three years to complete. In 1805 Conté died, a victim of his relentless activity, and was succeeded by Lancret as government commissioner; Lancret also died, and was replaced by another Egyptian veteran, Edme François Jomard, who requested a dispensation from active service. The work of printing and engraving went on at such a pace that by 1 January 1808 a delegation was able to present to the emperor a volume of engravings and a substantial section of the text. A mere twenty-one years old when he left Egypt, Jomard would see the enterprise through to completion and survive all his companions, living just long enough to see the re-formation, in 1862 under the designation Institut Égyptien, of the learned society founded in Cairo by Bonaparte in 1798.

The first volumes of the book began to appear in 1809, containing pieces from all three parts of the work, covering Antiquities, the Modern State and Natural History. The structure of the work and the rate of publication were decided upon in a decree dated 4 December 1809 and explained both in the foreword and in a prospectus published in 1810. That same year Jollois and Villiers du Terrage, who did so much in Upper Egypt, were added to the commission of eight editors, reduced to six by the deaths of Conté and Lancret. Jollois became its secretary.

The years went by, the Empire collapsed, and in 1814 the new king, Louis XVIII, gave his patronage to the project and ordered the inclusion of a map suppressed by Napoleon for military reasons. On 1 January 1815 Marcel was removed from the direction of the Royal Press and the Minister of the Interior received orders to economize. Jomard multiplied his efforts in vain: the work, begun with such enthusiasm, was completed in an atmosphere of lassitude. From 1823 the Chamber of Deputies no longer voted any funds for the enterprise. On 6 January 1826 Jomard presented Charles X with the final plates from the colossal work he had been in charge of for eighteen years.

Despite all the restrictions, and despite a number of unfinished sections and the complete lack of a table of contents, the book is a spectacular achievement. It is made up of nine small folio volumes of text, one large volume containing Fourier's introduction and foreword, a further ten large volumes of plates and three very large volumes containing the atlas and yet more plates. The whole set was housed in a cleverly constructed cabinet specially designed by Jomard to occupy a minimum of space.

In 1820 the bookseller Charles Louis Panckoucke was authorized by Louis XVIII's government to publish a new edition of lesser quality, which was finished in 1826 at the same time as the original.

The passing of time has confirmed the *Description de l'Égypte* as one of the greatest achievements of French publishing and a particularly evocative reminder of that extraordinary adventure, the French expedition to Egypt. As Geoffroy Saint-Hilaire so rightly concluded,

The work of the Commission for Arts will one day lead posterity to forgive the levity with which our nation, in a manner of speaking, plunged into the East. While deploring the fate of the many brave warriors who perished in Egypt after so many glorious exploits, there is some consolation to be derived from the existence of such a precious work.

Edme François Jomard, *Abyssinian tray made out of dum leaves,* 1798-1801.
Gouached watercolour. Paris, Bibliothèque Nationale.

Jean Baptiste Lepère, *Thebes, Memnonium, perspective view of the painted interior of the western temple*.
Coloured engraving from the *Description de l'Égypte*, 1809-26.

THE ARCHAEOLOGICAL
CONQUEST

Although he had been sent to Egypt by the Directoire to conquer it, Bonaparte was to complement his military project with a scientific enterprise in the course of which a number of eminent scholars joined him in the Nile valley and studied the many aspects of the country. Thanks to him the complete architectural survey of the ancient monuments and the discovery of the Rosetta stone, which was to enable Jean François Champollion to decipher the hieroglyphs in 1822, brought back to life the civilization of the pharaohs and the heritage of the Nile valley, then under the domination of the mamelukes for whom those 'heaps of stones' had lost all meaning.

In his foreword to the *Description de l'Égypte*, Jean Joseph Fourier justly noted that the publication was the first step in a new science—Egyptology:

> Before the French expedition we had only a very limited knowledge of the monuments that have immortalized Egypt; indeed it could be said that they were totally unknown. The present work will give an exact description of them.... It is clear that the ruins in Thebes, Apollinopolis, Abydos and Latopolis are those of the palaces inhabited by the kings or of the more important temples, and that they are the very monuments described by Hecataeus, Diodorus and Strabo; there can be nothing more valuable for the history of the arts than a knowledge of the great models that fired the imagination of the Greeks and helped develop their genius.[1]

The first known description of a journey through Egypt was written in the middle of the fifth century BC by Herodotus, who explored the Nile valley as far as Syene and described the journey in the second book of his *Histories*. A mixture of fact and fable, the book is a distant ancestor of the *Description de l'Égypte*. The river interested him, the customs of the population intrigued him, and he learned from the priests themselves the genealogy of the kings and their religious beliefs.

Manetho, Diodorus Siculus and Strabo complete our knowledge of this dying civilization. The Greeks and Romans, both of whom conquered the Nile valley, were fascinated by the colossal architecture and paid it frequent visits. They came to admire the pyramids and the sphinx at Giza, the labyrinth of the Fayyum and the colossi of Memnon, one of which, according to legend, emitted a vibration—the 'song of Memnon'—caused by the sun rising over the fissured stone. Several obelisks, the earliest pharaonic artefacts to be brought to Europe, were

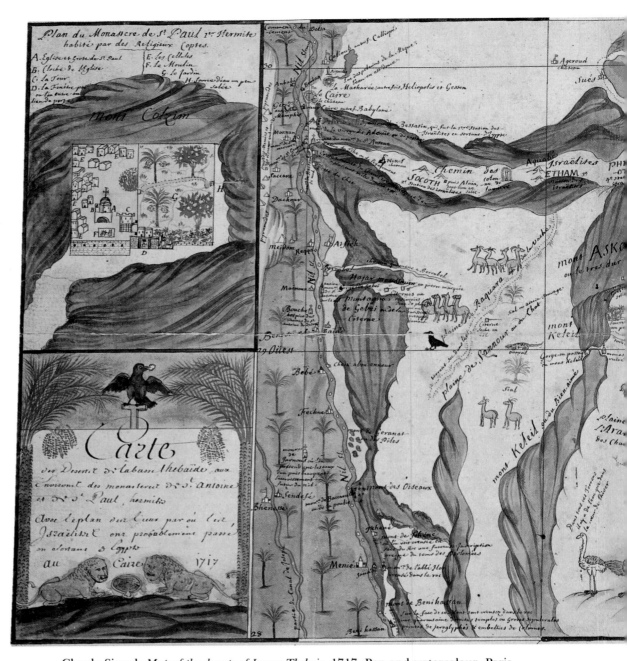

Claude Sicard, *Map of the deserts of Lower Thebais*, 1717. Pen and watercolour. Paris, Bibliothèque Nationale.

transported to Rome, though only one of them—in the Vatican—was erected at the time. It was not until the sixteenth century that the remaining seven would ornament the Italian capital.

In the early centuries AD a religious exchange developed in which Eastern cults spread throughout the Mediterranean. Isis, to whom a sanctuary was dedicated at Pompeii, was worshipped as far away as Gaul, and during the Middle Ages her influence extended even to Paris. The emperor Hadrian, whose favourite Antinous drowned himself in the Nile, erected authentic Egyptian statues and copies of others around a sanctuary to Serapis in the Canope Gardens in Tivoli. A few centuries later, however, the last remaining centre of the cult was closed in the land of the pharoahs itself, when Justinian converted the temple at Philae into a church.

138

It was then that the meaning of the hieroglyphs was lost. 'Pagan' paintings and texts were chiselled away and the abandoned monuments were gradually covered by the sands or, worse, raided for their stone to build new villages, such as the one at Edfu. The pharaohs' tombs and cemeteries were still visited, but only for the gathering of *mummia*, the bitumen used in embalming. This powder, recognized since the Middle Ages for its medicinal properties, became the object of a busy trade which was still going on when Vivant Denon travelled through the country in 1798 and 1799:

They brought me fragments of mummies: I promised to give them anything they asked for complete or intact ones, but the greed of the Arabs deprived me of this satisfaction, for they can sell the resin which they find in the entrails and skulls of the mummies in Cairo, and nothing will prevent them from removing it.[2]

Under the successive domination of Byzantium, Arabia and Turkey, Egypt lost all memory of its glorious past. During the Middle Ages Christian make-believe gradually appropriated the ruins of the pharaohs, and pilgrims stopping at Giza on the road to Jerusalem believed the pyramids to be the 'Joseph's granaries' described in the Bible, while Heliopolis became the fountain at which the Virgin Mary stopped to draw water during the flight into Egypt.

During the Renaissance the French established trading interests in Egypt and, thanks to treaties negotiated by Francis I, the commercial ports of the Levant, with their own consulates and permanent settlers, grew up in Cairo, Alexandria and elsewhere. Although their fortunes fluctuated according to the political tribulations of the moment, these trading posts were to foster the development of a taste for the exotic as the more intrepid Europeans ventured to the land of the pharaohs and brought the first Egyptian mummies and papyri back to Europe. Among those who took these first tentative steps towards the rediscovery of antiquity were Pietro della Valle (1586-1652), Paul Lucas (1664-1737), Claude Sicard (1677-1726) and Richard Pococke (1704-65).

From the seventeenth century on there was more than just commercial interest and curiosity as scholars began the search for the key to this lost civilization, laying the foundations for the task that Bonaparte's expedition, and later Jean François Champollion, was to complete. As more and more journeys and field studies took place, many new monuments were uncovered and identified, and the quest for the key to the hieroglyphs began. John Greaves, professor of geometry at Oxford, visited Egypt in 1638-9 and wrote the first scientific study of the pyramids. Athanasius Kircher (1602-80) unfortunately attributed to the hieroglyphs an occult, mystical significance which resulted in a current of esoteric belief which is still thriving today. Basing

John Greaves, *The first pyramid.* Engraving from *Pyramidographia, or a description of the pyramids in Aegypt,* 1646.

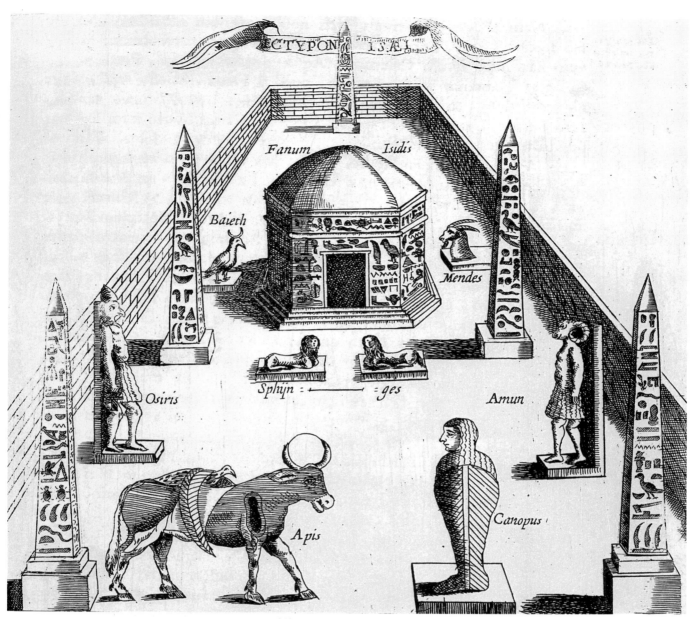

Athanasius Kircher, *The temple of Isis Campensis in Rome.* Engraving from *Obelisci aegyptiaci,* 1666.

his study of hieroglyphic texts on Horapollo's research, he allowed his imagination to run away with him and translated the royal names carved on the obelisks in Rome on the principle that each sign had a symbolic meaning. His error was widely accepted and for a long time prevented any progress in the deciphering of ancient Egyptian. He did however guess correctly that Coptic was not a language but merely a transliteration into the Greek alphabet, to which a number of symbols representing Egyptian idioms had been added. This was to be of great use to Champollion.

Up to the seventeenth century travellers rarely strayed from the pilgrim's route which ran through Alexandria, Cairo, Rosetta and Sinai to Jerusalem. Then, in the latter half of the century, a greater penetration of Upper Egypt by Europeans began. In 1672 Vansleb reached the Fayyum; Lucas went to Hermonthis in 1701 and Sicard got as far as Syene, where he had been sent in 1721 by the French regent, Philip of Orleans, to survey and make drawings of the monuments he visited. He was to discover the site of Thebes, Homer's 'city of a hundred gates', and bring back descriptions of the temples at Kom Ombo, Elephantine and Philae. Sicard, head of the Jesuit mission in Cairo, combined a great scientific interest in the country with his missionary work. Shortly afterwards Dr Granger, from Dijon, was to discover the magnificent temple of Seti I at Abydos which, deeply buried in the sand, would not be uncovered until Auguste Mariette excavated it in 1859.

Two eighteenth-century travellers further advanced our knowledge of Egypt. The Revd Richard Pococke described in minute detail the monuments he saw, some of which had disappeared a century and a half later when Bonaparte's scholars began their systematic inventory of the ancient architecture. He saw the zodiac at Dendera and, more astute than the scholars, who wrongly thought it to be older, he ascribed it to Greek workmanship.

At the request of the king of Denmark, Friderik Norden travelled throughout Egypt to write a complete report on the country. His *Travels*, published in 1751 and illustrated by his drawings, aroused widespread interest.

Egypt thus became less mysterious and most of its sites were identified. Unfortunately the still-undeciphered hieroglyphs remained a major obstacle to the understanding of pharaonic history, as was the tendency to judge the monuments by the criteria of the Hellenic civilization:

André Dutertre, *Karnak, view of a colossus at the entrance of the hypostyle hall of the palace,* 1798-1801. Pen and wash. Paris, Bibliothèque Nationale.

Greek art, synonymous with beauty, surpassed Egyptian genius, deemed barbarian.

The writings of two Frenchmen, who travelled in the Nile valley in the second half of the eighteenth century, served as manuals for the scholars in Bonaparte's expedition. Claude Étienne Savary undertook his journey in 1776 and published his *Lettres sur l'Égypte* in 1785-6, and Constantin François de Chassebœuf Volney, who set off in 1782, published his *Voyages en Syrie et en Égypte* in 1789. These two books, utterly different from each other, were extremely popular.

Savary was an erudite tourist, always ready with a reference to the authors of antiquity. His Arabic was fluent (we are indebted to him for a translation of the Koran), which made his stay a pleasant one and enabled him to truly appreciate the country. There is some doubt as to whether he got as far as Upper Egypt, as he claims, but he nevertheless enthusiastically summed up the existing knowledge about it. He was equally inspired by the beauty of the countryside and the customs of the people, and his interest in archaeology was vast.

Volney painted a quite different and highly critical picture of a country in which everything seems to have disappointed him. Here the traveller's tale becomes a geographical and political treatise in which he allowed himself not the smallest anecdote. More at home in a library than on a camel, he seems to have found very little to interest him in ancient monuments and barely

Cécile, *Thebes, Madinat Habu, view of the propylaea of the temple and of the pavilion taken from the south side*, 1798-1801. Watercolour. Paris, Musée du Louvre.

Friderik Norden, *View of the main gate of the antiquities at Luxor.*
Engraving from his *Travels*, 1751.

mentions even the pyramids. The value of his book, which Bonaparte was to take with him to Egypt, lies instead in the very detailed description he gave of Ottoman Egypt at the end of the eighteenth century.

A summary of the literary knowledge of ancient Egypt of the members of the French expedition is given by Gaspard Antoine Chalbrand, one of Bonaparte's officers:

> I took advantage of the little time left to me before my departure to reread all the ancient and modern authors who had written about Egypt and Palestine. Herodotus, Strabo, Homer, Diodorus Siculus, Pliny the Elder were in turn the object of my nightly reading; but first and foremost I reread the Bible and the naïve and touching tales of Genesis and Exodus, from Abraham's journey into Egypt and the fascinating history of Joseph up to the exodus of the Hebrews from that country under the leadership of Moses. Later I was frequently able, as will be seen, to confirm the truthfulness of the sacred author and the correctness of his descriptions. I also read the historians of the Crusades, especially the anthology entitled *Gesta Dei per Francos,* and the curious chronicles of Lord Joinville; then I finished this study by reading two modern travellers, Savary and Volney.[3]

By then most of the ancient monuments were known and a reasonably precise map of the country had been established. What remained to be undertaken was a systematic survey of the ancient architecture—the indispensable basis for any study of the pharaonic civilization. This was one of the missions that Bonaparte was to entrust to the Commission for Arts and Sciences, that scholarly army which accompanied the troops to Egypt.

THE FIRST ARCHAEOLOGISTS

Bonaparte wanted his expedition to follow in the tradition of the great explorations of the eighteenth century. Journeys such as those of Louis Antoine de Bougainville (1766-9), James

144

Cook (1768-71 and 1772) and Jean François de la Pérouse (1758), sometimes undertaken for commercial ends although they rarely included plans for colonization, all contributed to the stock of knowledge of distant lands. Taking astronomers, naturalists or painters with them, these intrepid seafarers brought back rich harvests of documents and artefacts. Bonaparte clearly hoped to achieve something similar in Egypt, but did he really intend to study the ancient monuments? Nothing is less certain.

The idea, of course, was not new. Benoît de Maillet, consul-general of France under Louis XIV and purveyor of antiquities to the king himself and to the Comte de Caylus, stressed the value of such an entreprise; and in 1697 Bossuet expounded the same idea in his *Discours sur l'histoire universelle à Monseigneur le Dauphin*:

Now that the name of our King is spread across the lesser known areas of the world, and that said Prince extends the quests undertaken on his behalf for the most beautiful works of Nature and Art equally far, would it not be a noble aim that such curiosity be bent on the beauties that Thebais encloses in its deserts and that our architecture be enriched by the inventions of the Egyptians? Think of the immense power and great art that made such a country into the wonder of the Universe! It was surely not intended that Egypt alone build monuments for posterity.[4]

It is not proven that Bonaparte had this ambition right from the moment that the Commission for Arts and Sciences was formed. It is more likely that he intended to send the major works of art he might find back to France, as had been done under the Convention and the Directoire during the European conquests. In Italy, as in Egypt, a commission had been entrusted with

Charles Louis Balzac, *Thebes, Madinat Habu, view of the interior of the palace peristyle*, 1798-1801.
Pen and wash. Paris, Bibliothèque Nationale.

advancing science and the arts, but it appears that the conqueror's plans for the East may have been more comprehensive. He hoped in fact to initiate the Egyptians into European civilization and, in order to achieve this, gathered together technicians and intellectuals capable of transforming a military conquest into a civilizing mission.

Amongst the 167 scholars, engineers and draughtsmen he recruited were many who were to play a decisive role in the beginnings of Egyptology. The work of the cartographers and topographers was particularly important.

André Dutertre, a draughtsman, engraver and lithographer, played a major part in the archaeological surveys. He is the author of many drawings and it was he who drew the portraits of the members of the expedition that are now preserved at Versailles and in the Bibliothèque Nationale.

Charles Louis Balzac was an architect and painter who had exhibited his work in the salons of the revolutionary period. During his stay he made numerous drawings of Philae and the temple at Karnak. Jean Baptiste Prosper Jollois, accepted into the École Polytechnique at the age of eighteen, joined the Civil Engineering Corps. Recruited as an engineer, he was to work extensively on the sites at Philae, Thebes and Dendera with his colleague Édouard de Villiers du Terrage, who became an engineer after his arrival in Egypt, where he sat his finals before a board presided over by Gaspard Monge. Fascinated by the pharaonic ruins, he made numerous drawings of them together with Jollois. This is how Edme François Jomard describes their collaboration:

> While he was in Dendera, at the same time as M. Jollois, there arose between these two men, so perfectly suited to each other, a friendship that only ended with the latter's death. It was there that, struck by the importance of Dendera's famous zodiac, they would disobey Brigadier Belliard's orders and slip out of the encampment at night to note the details of that celebrated monument, writing a description of it with drawings the absolute accuracy of which was proved when it was taken to Paris.

Advancing with the outposts of the army in the course of the same journey, they

OPPOSITE: Edme François Jomard, *Elephantine, view of a granite rock with traces of quarrying* (detail), 1798-1801. Watercolour. Paris, Bibliothèque Nationale.

Henri Joseph Redouté, *Thebes, Karnak, bas-relief carved in the corridor round the granite apartments of the palace*, 1798-1801. Wash. Paris, Bibliothèque Nationale.

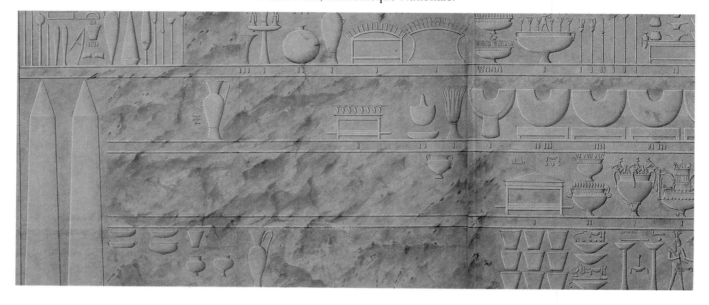

Dominique Vivant Denon, *Elevation of the portico at Dendera*, 1798-9.
Pen and wash. London, British Museum.

visited the antiquities at Philae, Koptos, Esna, etc., and were able to bring back detailed descriptions of them.

On their return to Thebes, they ventured some fifteen leagues from the French posts under the protection of a platoon of ten men, and single-handedly constructed a map of this ancient city and all its palaces and temples, which extends over an area greater than the city of Paris.[5]

Edme François Jomard, a surveyor and one of the first students to be accepted at the École Polytechnique, did fieldwork all over Upper Egypt and especially at Philae and Thebes (the temple at Karnak and the Valley of the Kings). His stay on the banks of the Nile affected him so deeply that he spent the rest of his life studying this lost civilization and closely collaborated on the decipherment of the hieroglyphs.

Lastly there is Dominique Vivant Denon, a diplomat and courtier but also a painter and engraver, who was to succeed in persuading Bonaparte of the vital importance of a study of the ancient monuments. It was thanks to Joséphine de Beauharnais, whose salon he frequented, that he was introduced to Bonaparte. After some hesitation Bonaparte agreed to include him among the members of the expedition. He was to prove of considerable value.

A few weeks after the Battle of the Pyramids the army entered Cairo and Bonaparte founded the Egyptian Institute, after which he ordered all the civilians to come to the capital. Always at the mercy of military requirements, a wide variety of fieldwork was carried out on his orders. Explorers from this 'general headquarters of the arts and sciences' criss-crossed the land, along with many scientists who had joined the expedition but were not part of the newly formed Institute. Apart from Dutertre, none of the main illustrators and authors of the Antiquities section of the *Description de l'Égypte*—Jollois, Villiers du Terrage and Jomard, for example—were members of this élite, while the architect Jean Baptiste Lepère only joined it later on.

Bonaparte was clearly not yet interested in Egyptology. In his letters he wrote little about archaeology. At the very most he listed the main sites:

The antiquities in this first zone are those of the island of Philae, Elephantine, Ombos, Apollinopolis Magna, Eileithyaspolis, Hieraconpolis and Latopolis.... Thebes and Dendera contain ruins which have aroused the admiration of mankind for many centuries.[6]

At no other time in history was military glory so closely allied to historical and artistic discovery. Everyone, from the humblest soldier to the highest generals, whether learned or not, was bewitched by what they saw.

Learning that the scholars were longing to see the pyramids, Bonaparte decided to visit them himself, perhaps with a view to using the event to enhance his prestige. In those days this jaunt, so easy today, was quite an expedition because of the presence of the bedouin, as Geoffroy Saint-Hilaire recounted in his *Recollections*. With an escort of sixty guides on foot and horseback, plus several generals and various members of the Institute, Bonaparte set off for Giza. He spent the night in the palace belonging to Murad Bey, who had fled into Upper Egypt. At dawn the escort reached the Cheops pyramid by boat up a Nile in full spate. He then invited scholars and soldiers to climb the stone mountain, declining to enter the monument himself. This one expedition was as far as his archaeological curiosity went.

Everyone else on the expedition was fascinated by the antiquities. François Bernoyer, head of the clothing workshop, wrote very little about the scholars in his correspondence, taking their presence entirely for granted. Despite his lack of education, he described the pharaonic monuments accurately:

> We directed our march towards the pyramids; at dawn we were at the foot of the largest one. We had neither scholars nor surveyors to tell the history or give us the dimensions of these ancient monuments; nevertheless we were enraptured by these enormous masses of gigantic stones piled one upon the other, without either mortar or cement. They have stood there for centuries and yet they still arouse astonishment and admiration. The sight of them leaves one at a loss to imagine the existence of men mad, vain and powerful enough to create such gigantic and costly buildings to no practical end. Reason can only ascribe the building of such colossal constructions to the folly of proud tyrants. Wishing to be eternally remembered, they had themselves buried in these monuments, which became oppressive tombs from that day on.[7]

The officer Chalbrand, fascinated by the country through which he was travelling, became a 'soldier-archaeologist'. After much lobbying to become part of the reinforcements sent up the Nile to General Desaix, he met up with Denon who, like himself, had just reached Upper

Edme François Jomard and Michel Ange Lancret, *Island of Philae, bas-relief carved under the gallery of the western temple*, 1798-1801. Pen and wash. Paris, Bibliothèque Nationale.

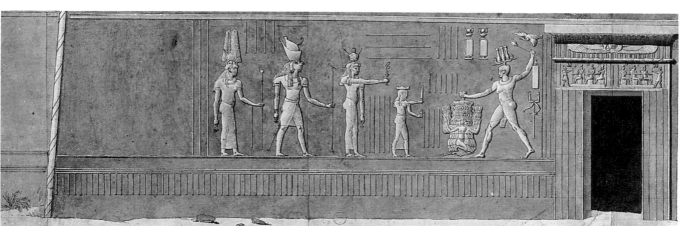

Egypt. His memoirs are full of his admiration for ancient architecture and he was to take a great many artefacts from the Theban tombs and Arab works of art back to France with him.

When Noël Dejuine, an officer in the 20th Dragoons, became part of the scholars' escort, he too began sketching. He drew several landscapes, but above all he sketched the pyramids, the gates of the temples at Karnak, Esna and Dendera and made detailed drawings of several bas-reliefs. He also attempted, though somewhat cursorily, to transcribe the hieroglyphs.[8]

Although the antiquities aroused everyone's curiosity, it was Denon who was to produce the first true reference work on archaeology. His self-portrait, preserved at the museum of Chalon-sur-Saône, is a typical late-eighteenth-century pastel showing a smiling young man at the start of his career, sporting a wig and a wide-brimmed black hat, with his arm stretched out towards his easel, looking at himself in a mirror.

Baron Vivant Denon (1747-1825), a pupil of Noël Halle and perhaps of Boucher, learnt drawing and engraving and became the Marquise de Pompadour's master engraver. In the diplomatic service from 1772 to 1785, he lived successively in St Petersburg, Sweden and Italy. It was while he was in Naples that he began to collect paintings and then antiquities, taking part in the excavations of Herculaneum and Pompeii. He explored palaces and churches and increased his knowledge of art history, purchasing canvases by the masters for the royal collections or Etruscan vases for the Sèvres porcelain factories to copy. Returning to France, he enrolled at the Académie de Peinture. During the Revolution he was branded an émigré, his possessions were confiscated and he would have gone to the scaffold had not the painter David come to his rescue. Denon was to become director-general of the museums of France

OPPOSITE: Dominique Vivant Denon, *Alexandria, Vivant Denon measuring Pompey's pillar,* July 1798. Watercolour. London, Victoria and Albert Museum.

Benjamin Zix, *Allegorical portrait of Vivant Denon,* 1811. Pen and brown ink. Paris, Musée du Louvre.

151

and to create the Napoleon Museum at the Louvre, directing it until 1815, when the restitution of the collections requisitioned during the revolutionary wars brought about his resignation.

This brilliant man played a crucial role in the Egyptian expedition, and although he returned to France at the same time as Bonaparte, long before the rest of the scholars, the thirteen months he spent in the East, between July 1798 and August 1799, were decisive ones for Egyptology.

On reaching Alexandria he examined Pompey's pillar, finding it far inferior to its reputation. With the geologist Dolomieu he visited the church of St Athanasius, which had been converted into a mosque, and to his great joy discovered his first example of the pharaonic age—a sarcophagus covered in hieroglyphs which had been reused. He then left Alexandria for Rosetta in the company of General Menou and became totally absorbed in the study of the ancient sites of the delta where he unsuccessfully attempted to identify the geographical siting of Canopus and ancient Saïs. His nomination to the Egyptian Institute obliged him to go to Cairo, but he took a back seat in its proceedings, preferring the dangers of exploration to the peaceful work of the Institute. In any case his stay in the city was too brief for him to take a really active part in the Institute's studies.

A man of many talents and interests, on being asked to examine the columns discovered near the Cairo aqueduct he took advantage of the occasion to demonstrate, in a concise report on his findings, the need to study Egyptian history from antiquity to the Ottoman domination; and he even turns up on a commission formed for the observation of snakes.

DENON AND THE EXPLORATION OF UPPER EGYPT

In November 1798, when General Desaix's army was in Upper Egypt in pursuit of Murad Bey's troops, Denon was authorized to join it. As Bonaparte recorded: 'Some artists and scholars wished to follow Desaix. This was doubly inconvenient, for it would have exposed valuable men to the dangers of war and caused delays in military operations. Denon alone was given permission to follow the senior command as a volunteer'.[9]

Denon acknowledged the help given him by the army in the preface to his *Voyage dans la Basse et Haute Égypte*:

If my zeal employed all the ability I might possess to the full, it was powerfully seconded

Dominique Vivant Denon, *Temple of Dendera*, 1798-9. Pen and wash. London, British Museum.

Cécile, *Dendera, view of the façade of the Great Temple*, 1798-1801. Watercolour. Paris, Musée du Louvre.

by the commander-in-chief, who never forgets a single detail even in the vastest of projects. As he knew that my ambition was to visit the monuments of Upper Egypt, he allowed me to accompany the division that was to conquer it. In General Desaix I found a scholar, an inquiring mind and a friend of the arts; I obtained from him every assistance that circumstances permitted. In Brigadier Belliard I found an even temper, friendship and unfailing attentions; the officers behaved graciously towards me, and the soldiers of the 21st Regiment were friendly and obliging. In truth I so identified myself with the battalion they formed, in the midst of which I had, if I may so express it, established my abode, that I forgot more often than not that I was at war, and that war was a stranger to my own pursuit.[10]

Denon explored pharaonic, Coptic and Muslim sites with equal interest, and was the first European to travel up the Nile as far as Syene with the sole aim of surveying the monuments.

Desaix's pursuit of Murad Bey occasionally led him to change direction, frequently causing the French troops to retrace their steps. This was very much to Denon's taste, especially when it entailed stopping in the region of Edfu or Dendera once more. He was none the less short of time, and complained that often he was only able to see monuments from afar, and thus could not study them:

It had been twenty-one days days since we had been fatigued by anything other than our own uselessness; I knew I was close to Abydos, where Osymandias had built a temple, where Memnon had his abode; I tormented Desaix with requests that he push a reconnaissance as far as al Araba, where I was daily informed ruins were to be found, and every day Desaix would reply: I wish to take you there myself; Murad Bey is only two days' march away, he will come the day after tomorrow, there will be a battle, we shall

153

André Dutertre, *Thebes, Memnonium, view of the two colossi,* 1798-1801. Pen and wash. Paris, Bibliothèque Nationale.

defeat his army and, on the day after, we shall think of nothing but antiquities which I shall help you to measure myself. He was right, our good Desaix; but had he been wrong I would have had to make the best of it in any case. At last, on 2 Nivôse [20 January 1799], we left Girga at nightfall. We passed the antiquities by. Desaix dared not look me in the eye: Tremble, said I: if I am killed tomorrow my shadow will haunt you, and you will hear it all around you ceaselessly repeating—al Araba. He remembered my threat, for five months later he sent an order from Asyut that I should be given a detachment to accompany me there.[11]

And on the left bank of Thebes

... well ahead of the troops although pressed by their march, I ran to the two colossi and sketched them, using as an effect the sun rising at the same hour at which they used to come to hear the voice of Memnon; afterwards that I went to that isolated palace called the Memnonium, which I also drew. Whilst I forgot myself in my absorption, they forgot to call me, and I discovered that the detachment was already half a league ahead; I set off at a gallop once more to catch up with them. The troops were tired, and it was a question of whether the expedition to the tombs would take place after all: I silently swallowed the rage that consumed me; and I believe my silence achieved far more than could have been dictated by the discontent I was prey to, for at last they set off without further discussion.[12]

Conditions were extremely difficult. Badly lodged, driven by the army, never able to find a quiet place to work, Denon nevertheless managed, in the thick of a military campaign, to bring back a multitude of drawings from this trip to Upper Egypt. This is how he describes his discomfort:

... drawings that I do for the most part on my knee, or standing up or even on horseback: I was never able to finish a single one as I had wished, since throughout that entire year I never found a table well enough set up for a ruler to be placed upon it.[13]

He was to visit—or catch a glimpse of—Saqqarah, Meydum, Illahun, Asyut, Dendera, Thebes, Esna, Edfu, Elephantine, Philae and then, on the road back to Cairo, Kom Ombo and Gabal al Silsilah where, leaving the Nile valley for the Red Sea, he travelled as far as Qusayr.

Returning to Qena he met Girard's group of engineers on a hydrographic survey of Upper Egypt. Their fascination with hieroglyphs led them to add the drawing of ancient monuments to their work on the level of the Nile. Among them were Jollois and Villiers du Terrage whom Denon decided to join, thus revisiting Karnak, Luxor, Esna and Edfu. He went to Thebes once more and visited Madinat Habu and the Valley of the Kings, then set off at last for Cairo.

Denon had been so impatient to discover Egypt that one might have expected him to have been disappointed by the monuments he so ardently desired to see. Far from it. His enthusiasm was limitless, as for instance on first discovering Dendera:

The first thing I saw was a little temple, on the left of our path, so ill-conceived and badly proportioned that I judged it from afar to be merely the ruin of a mosque. On turning towards the right, I discovered a door built of enormous blocks covered in hieroglyphs pitifully buried in rubble, and through that door I saw the temple. I wish it were possible to make the reader share in my emotion. I was too amazed to judge it, for everything that

OVERLEAF: Cécile, *Thebes, Luxor, view of the palace gates*, 1798-1801. Watercolour. Paris, Musée du Louvre.

Dominique Vivant Denon, *Elephantine, ruins of a temple*, 1798-9. Pen and wash. London, British Museum.

I had seen in architecture so far was useless as a guide to my admiration. The monument appeared to be a very early one and could be nothing other than a temple for, despite the rubble in which it stood, the feeling of silent respect it inspired in me seemed to prove it and, although there could be no great partiality for the antique amongst their ranks, it similarly overawed the entire army.[14]

As for his reaction to Philae, he apologizes for being so carried away:

The enthusiasm that was so constantly felt by the present traveller at the sight of the monuments of Upper Egypt may seem perpetually emphatic to the reader, an exaggeration carried to the limits of monotony, whereas it is simply the naïve expression of feelings that arose before their sublime nature, and the suspicion that my drawings give an inadequate idea of their grandeur, which led me to attempt to put into words the extent of the amazement these buildings inspire and the admiration which is their due.[15]

Denon was to take a great number of artefacts back to Europe from this fantastic journey, including a papyrus found on a mummy. (Some of these works are now preserved in the museum at Angers.) On his return to Cairo he showed his drawings to Bonaparte, who immediately recognized their import, and on 14 of August 1799 the general decided to send

André Dutertre, *Memphis, view of the second pyramid taken from the east side*, 1798-1801. Pen and wash. Paris, Bibliothèque Nationale.

Cécile, *Memphis, views of the high gallery in the Great Pyramid taken from the upper and lower landings.* Engraving from the *Description de l'Égypte,* 1809-26.

Nicolas Jacques Conté, *Memphis, view of the sphinx and the Great Pyramid taken from the south-east,* 1798-1801. Watercolour. Private collection.

two field-groups into Upper Egypt to make a systematic survey of all the ancient works to be found there.

On 20 August, shortly before Bonaparte, accompanied by Denon, left for Paris, these two groups—one directed by Costaz and the other by Fourier—left Cairo. In the eyes of the Commission for Arts and Sciences, archaeology had suddenly acquired an importance that it had not had up to then. The study of antiquity became a priority, and it was due to Denon that this great enterprise took place.

The studies undertaken by the Commission for Arts and Sciences and the Institute had frequently concerned archaeology. The architect Balzac had studied the ancient monuments of Alexandria. Geoffroy Saint-Hilaire was naturally interested in all the mummified animals, especially ibis. In a report listing the fieldwork to be done in ancient Memphis he showed great insight in a discipline that was not his own. Quoting Pausanias, he emphasized the need to locate the Serapeum, and it is in fact thanks to this classical text that Mariette was at last to find the cemetery of the bulls of Apis some forty years later.

Bonaparte had requested that the scholars explore the country as well as working at the Institute itself:

> Several trips were organized. Occasions presented themselves for journeys to Upper and Lower Egypt and the Natron Lakes. The commander-in-chief expressed a wish to see the members of the Institute and the various members of the Commission go to different locations in Egypt to study the curiosities that might be found there.
>
> A wish on the part of the commander constituted an order. Brigadier Caffarelli seized this opportunity to lay his hands on several people who had escaped him up to then, making out lists and giving destinations of his own choosing. It was truly painful to watch the officers of his staff giving orders to the various members of the Institute and the Commission as the fancy took them. Castex, Jomard, Victor Dupuis, Rozière, etc., were sent to Upper Egypt. Brigadier Andréossy, accompanied by Citizens Berthollet, Fourier, etc., went to the Natron Lakes; Fèvre and Malus explored the delta.[16]

Whether military campaigns in which they had a part to play or purely scientific outings, everything served as a pretext for sending the scholars out and about, both at their own request and under orders. They reached the Red Sea at Qusayr, Sinai was explored, and teams set out to reconnoitre Wadi Natrun with its Coptic monasteries, Middle Egypt, the Fayyum, and even as far afield as Acre. Others stayed closer to Cairo and scoured the delta, while Bonaparte himself presided over the exploration of the pharaonic canal in the Suez isthmus. Accounts of these journeys regularly lightened the ordinary business at the meetings of the Institute.

There seems to have been no overall plan defining the surveys to be carried out. Each draughtsman worked on a day-to-day basis according to circumstances, and yet there were few places not investigated or monuments left unsketched. Scientific missions proliferated in every direction.

Henri Joseph Redouté, *Thebes, Madinat Habu, painted bas-relief carved in the southern gallery of the palace peristyle,* 1798-1801. Watercolour and wash. Paris, Bibliothèque Nationale.

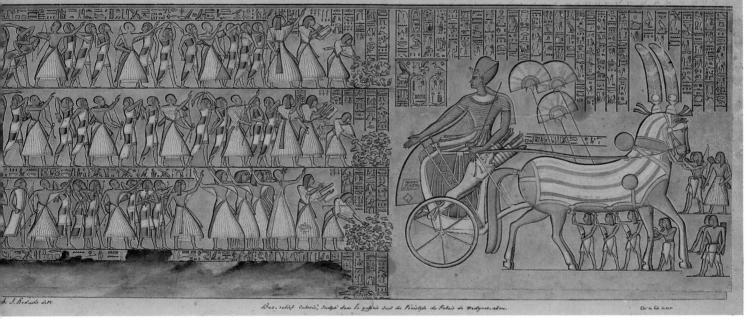

In March 1799 Dugua sent a group of engineers to Upper Egypt on Bonaparte's orders. The team, directed by Pierre Simon Girard, comprised Aimé Dubois-Aymé, Louis Duchanoy, Hippolyte Victor Descotils, François Michel de Rozière, Jean Baptiste Prosper Jollois and Édouard de Villiers du Terrage, all civil or mining engineers, accompanied by the sculptor Jean Jacques Castex. Although their principal task was to examine the tidal flow of the river from the first cataract and to design an irrigation system to increase the land under cultivation, Jollois and Villiers du Terrage were above all attracted by the temples and the hypogaea. They visited and studied Antaeopolis, Asyut, Hermopolis, Luxor, Karnak, Esna, Edfu, Dendera, Hermonthis, Antinoe, the islands of Elephantine and Philae, Syene and Kom Ombo.

Villiers du Terrage was greatly interested in the Egypt of the pharaohs, and Jollois even went so far as to do his own excavations:

> Yesterday I went to see Heliopolis with Monge, Berthollet, etc. This one-time school for Egyptian priests is about a league and a half away from Cairo, not far from the road to Bilbays. On the way there one can see the obelisk I am about to describe from quite far away. It measures 18 m 73 cm from the ground to its tip, 1 m 87 cm across the width of its lower section, and 1 m 21 cm at the top. Our excavation of three or four feet has still not revealed the base of this superb piece of red granite. Its four sides are covered in hieroglyphs which are almost identical on each side, being well preserved near the top but a little worn nearer the bottom.[17]

The passion for antiquities that these two men shared was not to the taste of Girard. On 8 July Villiers du Terrage gave an account of his troubles with him to Louis Madelène Ripault, the Institute's librarian:

André Dutertre, *View of the island of Philae and of the surrounding granite mountains*, 1798-1801. Pen and wash. Paris, Bibliothèque Nationale.

Edme François Jomard, *View of a brick pyramid east of the Fayyum*, 1798-1801. Watercolour. Paris, Bibliothèque Nationale.

We are leaving for Syene tomorrow, my dear friend; our trip will last twelve days, after which we shall be back in Esna. We have to take enough supplies to cover the journey.... I cannot tell you how delighted I am to be going.... Our trip would have been a thousand times more pleasant without Girard.... I declare he does not like antiquities, for of the four hours he spent at Dendera he slept for three.[18]

On the same day he complained to Dubois-Aymé:

We informed Denon this morning of Girard's behaviour towards you. Brigadier Belliard told me and then Jollois that he had no need to give us orders for we were well aware of what we had to do.... Girard had told the brigadier that we were drawing hieroglyphs and that that was not our business, so we challenged him to deny we had done all he had asked, which he could not do.[19]

Nothing could interfere with the enthusiasm with which they studied the monuments. Educated with a taste for the classical and used to Graeco-Roman art, they were sometimes surprised by what they saw. The lack of symmetry confused them:

Faced with these ruins, one regrets once again that the rules of symmetry have been disregarded. The piers ... are not at all parallel nor do their openings match. The handsome door in front of one of the oldest buildings in Karnak is not on the axis of the temple. It is very possible that this door was once flanked by two piers, or should have been, if one judges by the disposition of the walls, flush with the earth, on either side.

However that may be, it cannot be denied that the door's isolation emphasizes all the

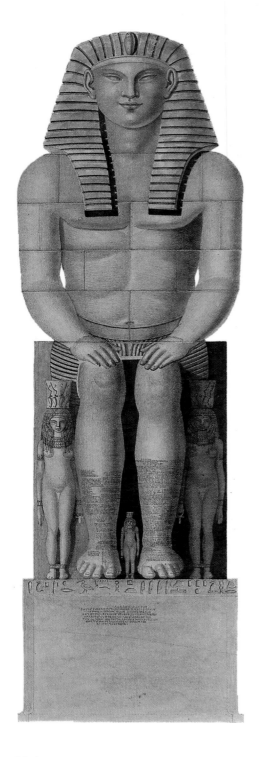

RIGHT: Henri Joseph Redouté, *Esna, Latopolis, interior decorations on a wall between the pillars of the portico*, 1798-1801. Wash. Paris, Bibliothèque Nationale.

BELOW: Prosper Jollois and Édouard de Villiers du Terrage, *Thebes, Memnonium, detail of the colossal statue of Memnon*, 1798-1801. Watercolour and pen. Paris, Bibliothèque Nationale.

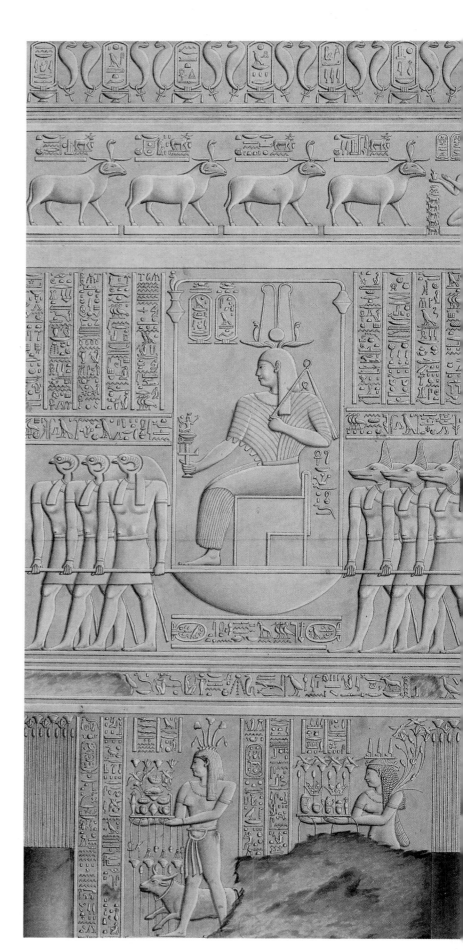

Prosper Jollois and Édouard de Villiers du Terrage,
*Thebes, Biban al Maluk, lid of a vase
found in the hypogaea,* 1798-1801.
Gouached watercolour.
Paris, Bibliothèque Nationale.

elegance of its proportions. The avenues of sphinxes are not at all parallel nor do they cross each other at right angles, and their courtyards are of unequal size.[20]

Nevertheless, little by little both men fell under Egypt's spell and, as always, it was the temple at Dendera that was most admired:

On 18 Prairial Year VII [29 May 1799] we visited the temple at Dendera for the first time. Since then we have made ten trips there. In the beginning Brigadier Belliard allowed us an escort, but these early visits, far from satisfying our curiosity, merely served to excite it further. As it would have been more than indiscreet to ask for an escort whenever we desired to visit it, or, to put it another way, needed to do so, we decided to go alone unbeknownst to the general, who had expressly forbidden us to do so since we were in danger of coming across bedouin Arabs or ill-intentioned fellahin. Every day at around eleven o'clock or midday we went to the right bank of the Nile, facing the ruins of Dendera.[21]

It was there that they found the zodiac later purchased by the Louvre:

Apart from its beauty, the temple at Dendera contains a monument of vital interest: by this I mean the famous circular zodiac discovered by Desaix and Denon. It is not the only one there, incidentally, for Jollois and I have found one on the ceiling of the great portico.

Denon had not had time to make a sketch; we wished for a faithful rendition in order to study the knowledge of astronomy possessed by the ancient Egyptians with precision.

The task was long and painful for, set in a little room built on top of the great temple, the zodiac is in almost complete darkness. We had to copy it in very bad light most of the time and, because the ceiling was much blackened by a sort of smoke, we frequently had to stare at it for a long time and from an uncomfortable position before being able to see a sign clearly.[22]

Prosper Jollois and Édouard de Villiers du Terrage, *Thebes, Memnonium, bas-relief carved in the hypostyle hall,*
1798-1801. Pen and wash. Paris, Bibliothèque Nationale.

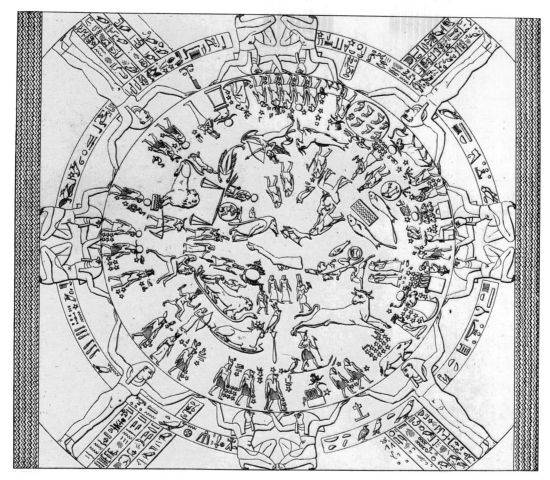

Dominique Vivant Denon, *Zodiac in the small apartment in the temple at Dendera.*
Engraving from *Voyage dans la Basse et la Haute Égypte*, 1802.

OVERLEAF: Cécile, *Thebes, Luxor, characteristic view of the palace taken from the south,*
1798-1801. Watercolour. Paris, Musée du Louvre.

Everywhere they went they made detailed studies of the monuments as well as general views and diagrams of the decorations. They catalogued the iconography into scenes of offerings, ritual massacres of prisoners and so on, and copied the hieroglyphic texts. Despite not being able to understand what they were copying, their transcripts are accurate. Denon did the drawings and Jollois and Villiers du Terrage, both surveyors, took measurements and made precise copies of the reliefs. When they joined up with the two official field-groups at Esna, the draughtsmen compared their work and harmonized their methods.

No detail was too insignificant for Bonaparte's attention. Because of its distance from Cairo and because the war had lasted longer there than elsewhere, Upper Egypt had been visited by only a very few scholars and artists, such as M. Denon and others of equal courage. Nevertheless this region, which contains so many superb ruins, offered, perhaps even more than Lower or Middle Egypt, a wonderful field for exploration and study by the scholars. Bonaparte made it a point of honour to allow no one else to open up such a fertile ground to science and the arts. He set up a commission to do so, dividing it into two sections of which the first had the secretary of the Egyptian Institute, Fourier, for president and the second the surveyor Costaz. He wrote a series of questions for each of them on agricultural methods, industrial products and the history and traditions of the country. A circular sent

167

to Desaix and his principal officers ordered them to give immediate protection by every means in their power to the lives and researches of the members of the said commission.[23]

Thanks to the abundance of his drawings, Denon had convinced Bonaparte of the interest of a historical mission to Upper Egypt. All the monuments are to be found in his portfolio, but only in hastily done—albeit excellent—sketches, since he lacked the time to make more precise surveys. Unaware that Jollois and Villiers du Terrage had already made a large number of engravings and observations, Bonaparte sent Costaz and Fourier out at the head of two separate teams. All the disciplines were represented—botanists, zoologists, astronomers and engineers—and the most prolific among them—Balzac, Lepère, Redouté, Cécile and above all Jomard—produced endless amounts of drawings.

A sensational discovery awaited them in the Valley of the Kings. Eleven tombs had been

André Dutertre, *Thebes, bronze statuette found in the hypogaea,* 1798-1801.
Watercolour. Paris, Bibliothèque Nationale.

known since the days of Strabo. Now they discovered a twelfth, belonging to Amenophis III.

The scholars met up with Villiers du Terrage and Jollois on the river between Edfu and the Gabal al Silsilah. There, after seeing how much work had already been accomplished, they adopted a common standard.

During the two months spent in Upper Egypt (August and September 1799) they covered more or less the same itinerary as Denon. Taking advantage of the seasonal north wind, they quickly reached the first cataract after short halts at Asyut and Antinoe. After visiting the granite quarries of Syene, from which the Egyptians once extracted colossi and obelisks, they lingered on the islands of Elephantine and, especially, Philae, which enthralled them with its special charm. It was there that Castex carved on the temple pylon the famous inscription celebrating Desaix's victory. They then made their way downriver. At al Kab they were amazed

Cécile, Thebes, Karnak, view of the gate and the southern temples, 1798-1801. Pen, wash and pencil. Paris, Bibliothèque Nationale.

Cécile, *Al Kab, view of an ancient quarry.*
Engraving from the *Description de l'Égypte,* 1809-26.

by the decorations in the tombs carved in the mountainside. Having only visited temples up to then, their knowledge was limited to religious and battle scenes, whereas the hypogaea depicted daily life and proliferated in evocations of hunting, fishing, agricultural pursuits and seafaring.

They visited Edfu, Madamud, Abydos and of course Thebes, where they stayed for some time. Back in Cairo, an article in the *Courier de l'Égypte* summed up their achievements. The course of the Nile had been charted with precision along with the locations of the pharaonic monuments. The topographical maps of Philae, Thebes, Dendera and Antinoe were up to date. General views and details of decorations appear side by side with copies of texts. Architects, painters and surveyors 'were not limited, as those who preceded them had been, to making isolated drawings of subjects which offered some singularity; they set themselves instead to present complete series, by drawing all the paintings ornamenting a single room, or the entire façade of a wall or a ceiling.'[24] The scholars did not merely observe or reproduce what they saw; where necessary they organized excavations and other searches.

Chalbrand, commander of the group's escort, has left us his impression of the Karnak site. At the time the site was in confusion:

172

Charles Louis Balzac, *Gabal al Silsilah, view of the grottoes cut at the entrances to the ancient quarries,* 1798-1801. Watercolour. Paris, Bibliothèque Nationale.

One comes across a huge pylon (a kind of doorway peculiar to Egyptian architecture), as wide as half the façade of the Invalides and as tall as the column in the Place Vendôme. It was never finished. One enters through this pylon into a vast peristyle in the middle of which stand twelve columns. All but one have been felled by an earthquake and their drums lie next to one another like an overturned pile of draughts. Opposite there is a second pylon placed before that wonderful pillared hall that is called the Hypostyle Hall of Karnak. Here one begins to get a feeling of the gigantic. The earthquake brought down a mass of masonry from the second pylon, and it now has the appearance of a mountain rock fall. A colossal mutilated statue of Sesostris or Rameses III stands on the threshold of the great hall. When I entered it I stood stock still in admiration; never had my eyes feasted on a more magnificent spectacle. One would think oneself in a forest of towers before those 134 columns each of the thickness of the column in the Place Vendôme.[25]

The study of the sites was very detailed. Fourier's travel notes describing this or that site include digressions which show how perceptively he worked. He pondered over the general characteristics of the decorations, categorized each temple's iconography according to subject and noted the similarity between the drawings and the hieroglyphs. Their scale was the only

173

The Rosetta stone (detail). London, British Museum.

difference. The colours of the symbols also intrigued him, for they changed from text to text.

Costaz, Fourier and most of the other scholars returned to Cairo in the autumn of 1799. They were not to be repatriated to France until two years later.

Between them Denon and the three scientific missions to Upper Egypt brought back a huge number of drawings, maps, notes and ancient artefacts. A section of the Institute was set aside for an archaeological collection—forerunner of the present Cairo museum—and the geologist Dolomieu was put in charge of selecting and transporting the finds, mainly stone objects. Geoffroy Saint-Hilaire included everything that bore on embalming in his zoological collection, even adding sarcophagi containing human mummies to those of crocodiles, snakes and birds.

When General Menou surrendered to the English in September 1801 a quarrel arose over the documents and collections belonging to the Institute. The scholars fought with unparalleled bitterness to keep the fruits of their work. To the following item in Menou's capitulation: 'The members of the Commission for Arts and Sciences have the right to take all the results of their work in Egypt with them, as well as the artistic monuments that they have had sent to Alexandria,'[26] General Hutchinson replied: 'As for the Commission for Arts and Sciences, it will not remove any public monuments, Arab manuscripts, maps, drawings, memoirs or collections; it will place them at the disposal of the English generals and commanders,'[27] which led Geoffroy Saint-Hilaire to declare: 'We will personally burn our acquisitions. You are after the glory—well, you will just have to rely on History's memory, for you will have burned a second Library of Alexandria.'

The scholars nevertheless managed to keep the documents and artefacts that they had personally collected, but several important pieces, stored in Alexandria at the time, were seized by the English. Fourier's inventory mentions two obelisks from Cairo, two sarcophagi, a ram's head from a Theban dromos and the celebrated granite fist of the colossus of Memphis, all now in the British Museum in London. The prize among them is incontestably item 8 in Fourier's inventory—the Rosetta stone. Aware of its value, the French had hidden it in a boat in the hope of keeping it despite the clauses in the capitulation, but Hutchinson found them out.

The stone, discovered in the summer of 1799 at Fort Julien near the town of Rosetta, is a decree by Ptolemy V, dating from 196 BC, carved on a basalt stele 1.1 m high. It is a late work of the pharaonic civilization, but despite its fragmentary state it was to be of crucial importance. On it the same text is reproduced three times, once in Greek and twice in Egyptian (hieroglyphics and demotic). Announcing the lucky find to the Institute, Michel Ange Lancret underlined its importance. The block was sent to Cairo in August 1799, where Jean Jacques Marcel and Nicolas Jacques Conté immediately made copies using the stone as a printing block.

Henri Joseph Redouté, *Rosetta and its outskirts, view of the hill known as Tell Abu Mina,* 1798-1801. Watercolour. Paris, Bibliothèque Nationale.

Henri Joseph Redouté, *Island of Philae, collection of stained, carved and painted vases in the Great Temple,* 1798-1801. Watercolour. Paris, Bibliothèque Nationale.

OPPOSITE: Henri Joseph Redouté, *Thebes, Biban al Maluk, paintings in the fifth tomb of the kings to the east and bas-reliefs at the entrance of the same tomb,* 1798-1801. Watercolour and wash. Paris, Bibliothèque Nationale.

André Dutertre, *Thebes, Karnak, bas-reliefs carved on the stelae and walls of the granite apartments of the palace* (detail), 1798-1801. Watercolour. Paris, Bibliothèque Nationale.

After the capitulation the French were allowed to make some final casts of it before it left for England.

The epigraphists thus had all they needed to enable the hieroglyphs to be deciphered, and they knew it. In France, as in England and the rest of Europe, the work began: Silvestre de Sacy, Johan David Akerblad and Thomas Young settled down to the task.

THE EARLY PUBLICATIONS

The dawn of Egyptology was accompanied by the publication of an enormous number of travel books, memoirs, soldiers' tales and academic studies. Bonaparte, well aware of the fashion for

178

the Orient then reigning in Europe and wishing to take advantage of it to enhance the prestige of his expedition, decided to ensure that scholars published everything they could while they were still in Egypt.

In Cairo Marcel had already been printing the two French journals that Bonaparte had initiated: the *Courier de l'Égypte,* covering the anecdotal side of the scientific expeditions, and *La Décade égyptienne,* in which the Commission for Arts and Sciences recorded its work. Marcel, knowing Arabic, took advantage of his stay in Cairo to make friends with local academics. He mainly visited Arab monuments and discovered the Cufic characters unknown to orientalists at the time, who thought them to be merely architectural decorations. An author and translator, he published many works on the study of Arabic and copied a number of inscriptions. Back in France in 1801, Bonaparte asked him to take part in the publication of the *Description de l'Égypte,* on which he was to work as both writer and printer.

As soon as the Army of the Orient returned to France, individual works—travel notes, journals and memoirs by scholars and soldiers—began to appear. Jean François Grobert, an artillery brigadier, writing about the Giza pyramids, gives us a good example of this genre:

> Norden is . . . mistaken in believing that the stones are joined without lime. He thinks that Cheops was never cladded, whereas this cladding was still intact towards the middle of Augustus's reign. Fragments of it, albeit in small amounts, are to be found around it; I have given some samples of it to the Jardin des Plantes. In any case, how could they have not cladded Cheops when Mycerinus was entirely so and the greater part of this cladding is at present worked around the base?
>
> Also, there is probably a printers' error in the assertion of Norden's that the entrance to the Great Pyramid is east-south-east of Giza; it should have said west-south-west. The speed of their visits and the difficulties in measuring are the main causes of the mistakes which are to be found fairly frequently in the works of the most erudite travellers. Remarks such as these cannot diminish our recognition of their work nor the praise that their talents deserved.
>
> I have spoken of the extravagant buildings I saw. On more than one occasion, with the help of some keen officers, I checked otherwise known measurements with all the precision that the nature of the site and circumstances allowed. These were in my favour during the time that I was in command at Giza. Had they been given the same facilities, the scholars and admirable artists now in Egypt might doubtless have obtained more interesting results—perhaps further studies will perfect the results that I have consigned to the present work. . . . Philosophers do not share the enthusiasm of some travellers about these monuments. Their opinion is confirmed by the intimate conviction of many of the Frenchmen who have visited Egypt recently. The description that follows may captivate the attention of the learned and the curious, but it offers no fruits for morality other than the following remark—that the great of this world should not accumulate all their magnificence in a single place! . . . If one traverses lands that are poor and afflicted in search of an edifice that could be defined by that variable concept called majesty, such a system will disclose the barbarism as much as the weakness of its author.[28]

Dated 1801, this account demonstrates through its references to earlier writers—in this case Norden—the erudition of many of those who took part in the Egyptian campaign and the desire of both civilians and soldiers to understand the civilization of the pharaohs.

Vivant Denon's book, *Voyage dans la Basse et la Haute Égypte pendant les campagnes du général Bonaparte,* published in 1802, is in the same vein. Denon only spent thirteen months in Egypt,

Hand of the statue of Rameses II found at Memphis.
Granite. London, British Museum.

OPPOSITE: André Dutertre, *Memphis, view of the ruins taken from the south-east*,
1798-1801. In the foreground, scholars measure the hand of the statue of Rameses II.
Watercolour and pastel. Paris, Bibliothèque Nationale.

Charles Louis Balzac, *Fist (and its measurements) of a colossus at Memphis*,
1798-1801. Pencil and wash. Paris, Bibliothèque Nationale.

181

returning to France before the majority of the members of the Commission for Arts and Sciences, and at the time of writing he did not know whether they had managed to leave for Upper Egypt or whether circumstances would permit them to bring the fruits of their labour back to France.

Believing himself to be perhaps the only one in possession of certain scientific information, he began including it in his account of his stay, but as soon as he learned that Costaz and Fourier had been to Upper Egypt and brought back a large haul of material intended for publication he went back to his introductory role and included no further academic material in his book.

A volume of plates accompanied the text, containing sketches of battles, views of modern Egypt (daily life, portraits, costume), exquisite landscapes, drawings of antiquities and a plethora of general views, maps and details of reliefs of the pharaonic monuments, all with captions giving precise descriptions of what he personally observed. The engravings of the temples at Edfu and Dendera, which were to become justly famous, clearly show their author's admiration.

The drawings, far less accurate than those in the *Description de l'Égypte,* make up for that

Dominique Vivant Denon, *Egyptian heads* (detail).
Engraving from *Voyage dans la Basse et la Haute Égypte*, 1802.

in charm as stormy skies follow on glorious sunsets—a quality totally absent from the monumental publication produced by the Commission for Arts and Sciences. Under constant pressure from the army, Denon rarely had time to work as he pleased and what we see is the work of an artist rather than a draughtsman. His superb drawings of the temple at Elephantine, for example, are far less precise that the plates in the *Description de l'Égypte* or the later watercolours by Nicolas Huyot.

Denon was interested in all the ancient cultures and was just as fascinated by Arab and Coptic Egypt as he was by the pharaonic civilization. His book is a mixture of anecdote and descriptions of sites and monuments. After a picturesque narrative of the journey, he describes his stay in the delta and the pursuit of Murad Bey into Upper Egypt by Desaix's troops. He gives a day-by-day account of the destitution and exhaustion of the soldiers, but he also describes the lighter moments and the surrounding countryside. The Nile interests him, as do the flora and fauna. The pages given over to descriptions of the pyramids and the sphinx at Giza, of Dendera and Hermopolis, are celebrated for their eloquence. His enthusiasm broke all bounds when he found a papyrus:

The famous Thoth was therefore a book, and not panels of inscriptions carved on the

BELOW AND OPPOSITE: Michel Rigo, *Egyptian costume.*
Engraving from Vivant Denon, *Voyage dans la Basse et la Haute Égypte,* 1802.

walls as had been suspected. I could not resist feeling flattered by the thought that I was the first to make such an important discovery. I was even more flattered when I was provided with proof of my discovery in the form of an actual manuscript, which I found in the hand of a superb mummy brought to me a few hours later. You must needs be of an inquiring mind, an amateur and a traveller, to fully understand the pleasure of such an emotion. I felt myself go pale. I was about to chide those who had violated the integrity of the mummy despite my insistences, when—in its right hand tucked under its left arm—I perceived a roll of papyrus which I might never have discovered without this violation. I was at a loss for words. I blessed the greed of the Arabs and above all the accident that had brought about my good fortune. So great were my fears of destroying it that I knew not what to do with my treasure and dared not lay my hands upon the book—the most ancient of any known to this day. I feared to entrust it to the keeping of any person or place of storage; the entire cotton coverings from my bed seemed insufficiently soft to wrap it in. Did it contain an account of its owner? Were the period and the reign of the sovereign under which he lived inscribed upon it or did it perhaps contain some dogma, prayers or the consecration of some discovery?[29]

Denon's studies of the monuments are shorter than those in the *Description de l'Égypte* but, thanks to his lively intelligence, he instinctively found the right approach to pharaonic civilization and defined its criteria. The arts are frequently discussed:

OPPOSITE: Dominique Vivant Denon, *Egyptian baker's oven near Naqada,* 1798-9. Pen and wash. London, British Museum.

Michel Rigo, *The sphinx near the pyramids.* Vivant Denon climbs the sphinx and measures it. Engraving from Vivant Denon, *Voyage dans la Basse et la Haute Égypte,* 1802.

185

Charles Louis Balzac, *Island of Elephantine, view of the south temple,*
1798-1801. Pen and wash. Paris, Bibliothèque Nationale.

Being linked to architecture, sculpture was circumscribed in its principles, methods and fashion: a figure expressed no sentiments; it had to take a specific pose to express a specific concept; the sculptor had the pouncing pattern and was not permitted to make any alteration that might change its fundamental meaning. These figures can be compared to our playing cards, the imperfections of which we accept for the ease with which we can recognize them. The perfection of [the sculptors'] treatment of animals proves that they recognized style, for they expressed their characteristics in a few simple lines of great fundamental merit, tending towards sobriety and the ideal of beauty.[30]

He also attempted to define the chronology of Egypt, which had barely begun to be elucidated at the time:

I sought to determine if the arts had had epochs and a continuity in Thebes: if a palace

Prosper Jollois and Édouard de Villiers du Terrage, *Thebes, Biban al Maluk, cover of vase found in the hypogaea,*
1798-1801. Gouached watercolour. Paris, Bibliothèque Nationale.

186

had ever existed in Egypt, its remains had to be sought in Thebes, since Thebes was once the capital; and if there had been epochs in the arts, [the evidence of earlier periods] should also have been in the capital, for luxury and magnificence spread progressively elsewhere only after having been established there.[31]

In Hermopolis he abandoned the idea of the supremacy of Greek art, which was a great innovation at the time:

I sighed with pleasure: it could be said that this was the first result of all the advances I had made—the first fruit of my labours. Except for the pyramids, this was the first monument that appeared to me to be typical of ancient Egyptian architecture, the first stones that had retained their initial purpose and had awaited me four thousand years without additions or alterations to give me an idea of the immensity and perfection of the arts in this area. A peasant taken from the hovels of his hamlet and placed before such a building would at first think that there had been a great lapse of time 'twixt himself and its builder, and knowing nothing of architecture he would say: 'This is a house belonging

André Dutertre, *Qaw al Kabir, view of the temple taken from the west side,* 1798-1801. Pen and wash. Paris, Bibliothèque Nationale.

to a God, for no man would dare inhabit it.' Was it the Egyptians who invented and perfected so great and beautiful an art? It is hard to say, but upon first seeing this edifice I no longer had any doubts about one thing: the Greeks invented nothing, nor have they produced anything of greater value.[32]

Denon's book, the first to reveal the pharaonic civilization to France and the rest of Europe, was a tremendous success. There were no fewer than forty editions, translations and adaptations. The first three editions appeared in 1802, the fourth in 1803 and, despite the costliness of the work, they were all rapidly exhausted. A total of seven French editions, ten English translations with four adaptations, six German translations and two adaptations, as well as Dutch, Italian and Danish translations appeared in the quarter of a century that followed.[33]

The book further fuelled the general public's taste for the East and for Egypt in particular, and was without doubt one of the contributing factors to the fashion in Paris known as the *style retour d'Égypte* or Egyptian Revival.

THE DESCRIPTION DE L'ÉGYPTE

The idea of publishing this encyclopaedic work on the Egyptian monuments first surfaced in 1799. Villiers du Terrage gives us the broad outlines of it in his journal:

Cécile, frontispiece of the *Description de l'Égypte*, 1809-26. Engraving.

Title-page of the *Description de l'Égypte*.

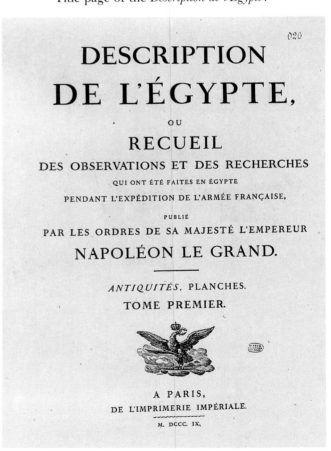

André Dutertre, *Thebes, Biban al Maluk, painting in the Hall of Harps in the fifth tomb of the kings to the east,* 1798-1801. Watercolour. Paris, Bibliothèque Nationale.

One of us ... has had news of the Institute's sitting of 1 Frimaire [22 November]. Fourier read out a letter that the president had just received from Kléber.

In that letter it is said that the government would be happy to see all French citizens, whatever their field, combine their work on Upper Egypt into a common publication.

The Institute has decided that, in order to give this work the greatest unity and perfection possible, Fourier is to gather together the Commission for Arts and all those who have written useful reports for a discussion on the subject.[34]

Possibly prompted by Costaz and Fourier, Kléber issued a decree ordering the combined publication of the works of all the scholars. This was the point of departure for the monumental task that eventually resulted in the publication of the *Description de l'Égypte*.

The scholars set to work as soon as they returned to France:

> Immediately after the return of the Army of the Orient, the government ordered that all reports, maps, drawings and field studies concerning the sciences and arts carried out in the course of the expedition be gathered into a general publication at the expense of the public treasury. Those who had taken part in the fieldwork were invited to provide the texts and illustrations of which the collection would be formed. The direction of the publication was entrusted to a commission of eight people selected by the Minister of the Interior from a list of the proposed authors.[35]

The division of the text into three parts—Antiquities, the Modern State and the Natural Sciences—demonstrates the supremacy eventually achieved by archaeology, to which five of the volumes are exclusively devoted.

The frontispiece is a tableau containing almost all of the monuments studied, with the following description:

Jean Baptiste Lepère, *Thebes, Madinat Habu, plan and longitudinal section of the temple, its propylaea, the palace and the pavilion.* Engraving from the *Description de l'Égypte*, 1809-26.

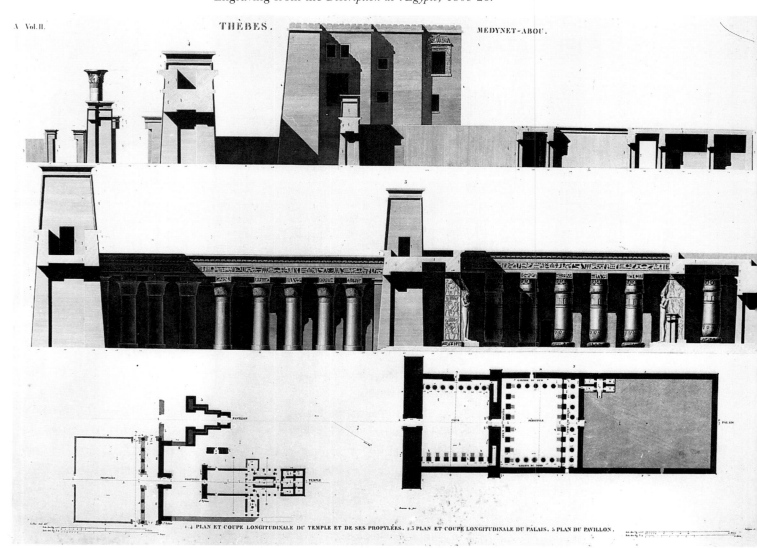

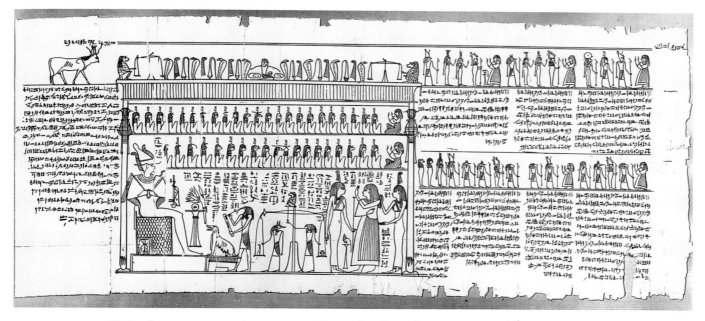

Thebes, hypogaea, manuscript on papyrus. Engraving from the *Description de l'Égypte*, 1809-26.

OVERLEAF: Jean Baptiste Lepère, *Island of Philae, perspective view of the painted interior of the Great Temple taken from the portico.* Engraving from the *Description de l'Égypte*, 1809-26.

It presents a perspective view of Egypt comprising the principal monuments to be found between the sea and the cataracts of the Nile.

Border: the cornice is decorated with the winged globe, onto which a symbolic star has been placed. In the centre of the frieze, the Hero conquering Egypt is depicted on his chariot; before it, the eagle—emblem of the army—crushes the mamelukes as they flee towards the pyramids, while a personification of the Nile looks on. The Arts and Sciences follow the Hero as he leads them back to a land from which they have long been exiled. The two vertical borders show military trophies and standards on which the names of the principal battlefields of Egypt and Syria are inscribed. In the middle of the lower border the Emperor's initial, encircled by a serpent, symbol of immortality, appears. On either side the conquered laying down their arms form varied groups. At each end Egyptian scarabs enclose a bee and a star, a sort of personal symbol of the Emperor's.

Centrepiece: in the foreground by the sea, Pompey's pillar, Cleopatra's needle and the most valuable of the remains collected in Upper Egypt such as the Dendera planisphere, the Rosetta stone, a papyrus, a tent made from date-palm leaves, one of the Theban sphinxes, and some paintings from royal tombs. Beyond them is the Nile, the island of Philae (granite mountains surrounding it), the island of Elephantine (below the cataracts). On the left bank are Edfu, Hermonthis, Esna, Madinat Habu, the colossi from the Theban plains, the tomb of Osymandias, Dendera, Ashmunayn and the pyramids. On the right bank one can see Ombos, the grottoes of Eileithyia, Luxor, Karnak and other remains of Thebes, Antaeopolis, Antinoe and Heliopolis.[36]

The grandiloquence of the writing shows how successfully Bonaparte, identified with the classical Hero, had been able to link his military campaign to the glorious discovery of pharaonic civilization, and underlines the preponderance of archaeological research in what was at first a very diverse scientific enterprise.

André Dutertre, *Edfu, view of the Great Temple*. Engraving from the *Description de l'Égypte*, 1809-26.

In the foreword to the first volume Fourier summarized the whole of the history of Egypt from antiquity to the end of the eighteenth century and then described the French expedition. Finally he defined the aims and methodology of this imposing publication:

In the interests of the fine arts and literature it was essential to provide a complete and faithful description of the monuments that have ornamented the banks of the Nile for so many centuries, making this country the richest museum in the Universe. We measured all the sections of the buildings with rigorous care and, to go with the architectural drawings, we have included topographical maps of the sites where these ancient cities were situated. In individual drawings we have reproduced the religious, astronomical and historical sculptures that decorate the monuments. To accompany the topographical maps, picturesque views, architectural plates, sketches of bas-reliefs, we have provided an extensive description in which any observations that could not be illustrated by a drawing have been assembled. These descriptions are the result of a prolonged and, as it were, corroborated examination throughout which many of those who were there have collaborated to the end of publicizing the present condition of the monuments, the dilapidation caused by the passage of time, the types of materials used to build them and many other facts worthy of attention, such as a variety of comments on the architecture, the building techniques, the colours, the forms and the uses of the objects reproduced.[37]

The text is in the form of a series of essays rather than accounts of journeys. The volumes

194

entitled 'Descriptions of Antiquities' present the sites and note the observations gathered *in situ*. Occasional historical or geographical digressions complete the account. The essays mainly cover everything connected with astronomy, metric systems, the flooding of the Nile and, more generally, the geography of the country. Girard did a study of the nilometers. Villoteau largely covered music. Costaz was more interested in the daily life and religious practices of the ancient Egyptians.

Since no one could read the hieroglyphs the only understanding of the ancient civilization came from depictions of events. The scholars examined and summarized everything that was figurative, but nothing else. This explains the gap between present-day researches in Egyptology and the preoccupations of the scholars during the expedition. Nevertheless Jomard, realizing the immense lacuna caused by the incomprehensibility of the texts, took the trouble whilst in Egypt to draw up a list of hieroglyphs by category: human figures, animals, inanimate objects (furniture, vases, tools), plants and geometric forms. He correctly identified the numbers used by the Egyptians, and then established a list of the hieroglyphs used in counting. Basing his

Prosper Jollois and Édouard de Villiers du Terrage, *Dendera, perspective view of the interior of the portico of the Great Temple,* 1798-1801.
Engraving from the *Description de l'Égypte*, 1809-26.

studies on the text of the Rosetta stone, drawings made at Karnak and ancient authors such as Horapollo, he finally demonstrated that

$$\mathfrak{l} = 1 \qquad\qquad \mathfrak{c} = 100$$
$$\mathfrak{n} = 10 \qquad\qquad \mathfrak{l} = 1000$$

The unlocking of the hieroglyphs was to become, for him as for so many other scholars throughout Europe, the great preoccupation of the new century.

In these volumes Jomard, Jollois and Villiers du Terrage annotated most of their own plates and wrote the texts accompanying Lepère's and Dutertre's drawings. The plates form the core of this beautiful book. It is an encyclopaedia of all the pharaonic monuments which is unsurpassed even today. The principal draughtsmen were Jollois, Villiers du Terrage, Jomard and Dutertre. Dutertre also contributed a considerable body of work on modern Egypt, though he did not write any of the texts. Dutertre was fond of general views, Jollois and Villiers du Terrage specialized in maps, elevations and sections, and, like Jomard, they produced many perspectives and architectural details.

All the drawings—executed by engineers, surveyors and architects rather than artists—are exact reproductions of what they saw. Thanks to this, they are still used by Egyptologists today and their reliability is rarely questioned. This is particularly true of their copies of hieroglyphic inscriptions—a great feat at a time when not even the shapes of the hieroglyphs they copied were understood. Each site was thoroughly analysed: views of the monuments as they stood are followed by maps and topographical surveys, then come plans, sections and elevations of complete monuments with details of the architecture, bas-reliefs, inscriptions and statues.

The authors occasionally indulged in reconstructions, such as Jollois's and Villiers du Terrage's recreation of the temple of Seti I at Qurnah ('Antiquities', vol. II, plate 43). Many of the plates contain the figures of Egyptians or Frenchmen in order to give an idea of the scale of the monuments. The artists frequently portrayed themselves, which lends an anecdotal character to the surveys. Sometimes they got carried away—into the Graeco-Roman era, for

André Dutertre, *Thebes, hypogaea,*
paintings of mummy cases (detail), 1798-1801.
Watercolour. Paris, Bibliothèque Nationale.

OPPOSITE: André Dutertre, *Details of a tunic*
found in one of the tombs of Saqqarah, 1798-1801.
Watercolour. Paris, Bibliothèque Nationale.

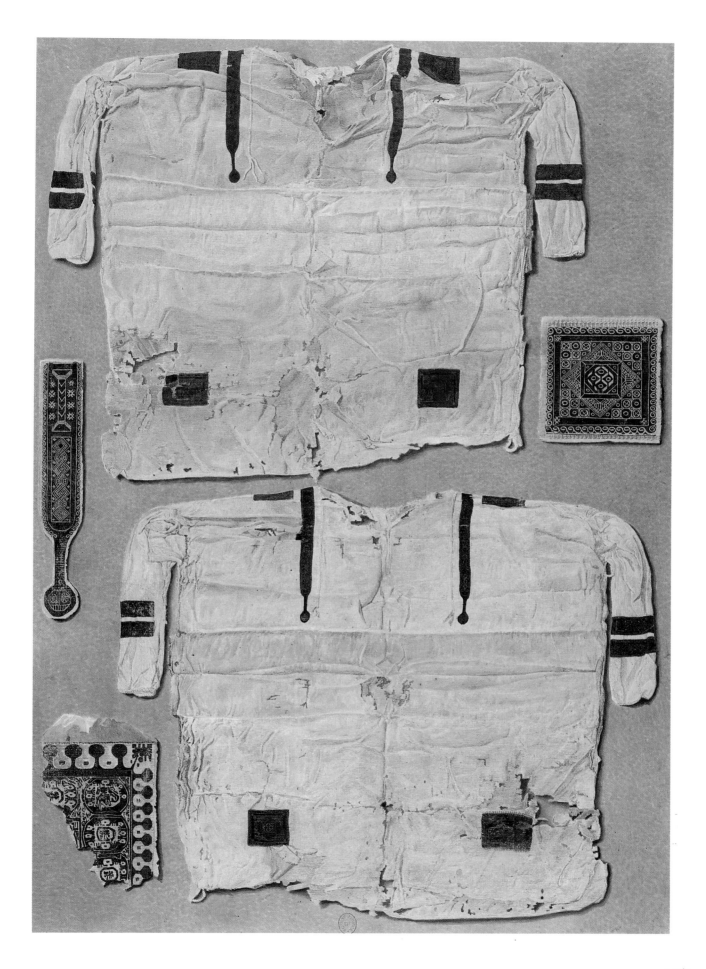

The Rosetta stone. Fragment of a black basalt stele found in 1799 by Engineers
Lieutenant Bouchard in Rosetta
in the western delta of the Nile. London, British Museum.

instance, or when, in a reconstruction of the interior of a hypostyle hall such as the one at Dendera, they included a procession of priests, some of whom are wearing togas whilst others appear to have donned costumes from an Egyptian operetta. The commentary on this particular plate ('Antiquities', vol. IV, plate 30) solemnly states that the authors have restored the bases of the columns but on no account must it be thought that this was a reconstruction, for excavations had enabled them to define their exact proportions and decorations: to dig in order to discover the exact measurements of a monument buried in the sand so as to reproduce it exactly and then to encumber it with a light-opera parade!

Today many of the monuments have disappeared. During the nineteenth century thousands of stones were removed to build lime kilns or factories. The plates in the *Description de l'Égypte* and the drawings by Vivant Denon and other artists have therefore become the only

198

record of these buildings. Because of this they are extremely precious. By 1828, at Antinoe, Jean François Champollion would only find rubble where major ruins previously existed. The same applies to the two peripteral temples at Elephantine, dating from Tuthmosis III and Amenophis III, and to the papyriform portico at Hermopolis, which have all disappeared. The hypostyle hall of Antaeopolis, which so inspired Dutertre, collapsed under the pressure of the Nile in 1821, and there is hardly anything left of the Ptolemaic temple at Armant, plundered of its stone to build a sugar refinery. Even when monuments are still standing, the plates are of great interest because the appearance of many of the buildings has changed since the beginning of the nineteenth century. Most have been dug out of the sand which buried them and others, such as the temple at Karnak, have been restored.

Lastly, the colour plates give an idea of the polychromy used as architectural decoration under the pharaohs, for at many sites much of the painting has now either disappeared completely or is almost invisible.

All of this makes the *Description de l'Égypte* of vital importance even today, a century and a half after its publication.

One of those whose great tenacity was instrumental in bringing this immense enterprise to fruition was Edme François Jomard. Recruited by Bonaparte as a surveyor, he developed a passion for Egyptian archaeology and his collaboration on the publication of the *Description de l'Égypte* is first rate. He was made secretary and then 'government commissioner in charge of printing and engraving'. His own writings in this monumental work and in specialized reviews were extensive, and it was as an Egyptologist that he was elected to the Académie des Inscriptions et Belles-Lettres on 2 October 1818. His copy of the Rosetta stone was faultless, and he was to spend many years searching for the key to the hieroglyphs.

Jomard was fully aware of how much was still unknown of the civilization of ancient Egypt. Although the geography of the country had been widely studied and the Egyptian section of the Nile at least had been extensively explored, even the names and the succession of the

Edme François Jomard, *Copy of the Rosetta stone, detail of the hieroglyphic section*, 1799-1801. Pen and wash. Paris, Bibliothèque Nationale.

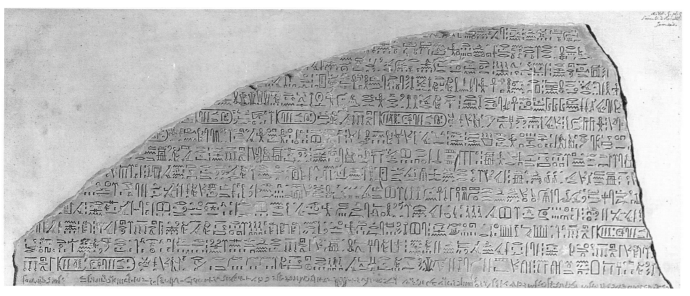

André Dutertre, *Thebes, Biban al Maluk, various chairs and armchairs painted in the fifth tomb of the kings to the east*, 1798-1801. Watercolour. Paris, Bibliothèque Nationale.

pharaohs were still scarcely known. The relationship between the Bible and pharaonic history was of great interest to the scientific world, for at the time it seemed important to know the life of the Hebrews in Egypt, to define the part played by Moses and to place him in his historical context. The ancient religion and its abundant mythology were intriguing.

Jomard illustrated this when he defined the scientific material at the disposal of researchers and existing knowledge in 1819:

Egypt ... is a new subject: its antiquities are truly historical. They bring an imperfectly known people completely to life; they unveil the condition of science and the arts in a very distant era. They are therefore of great interest. Instead of scattered fragments which we have to use our imagination to restore, as so often happens for the works of the Greeks and the Romans, we have works that forty centuries have respected and handed down to us almost intact, and varied and instructive paintings that make a mockery of everything published about Egypt up to now.... The advantage that we had over modern travellers during the French expedition also obtains for ancient ones: the latter may indeed have seen better-preserved monuments, but the religion was not yet entirely extinct and the temples, although violated by Cambyses, were not abandoned. It was therefore impossible for them to penetrate the interior of the sanctuaries and study them at their leisure.... Judging by just the traditions that they have handed down to us, what a multitude of examples we could give of the little light that those very Greeks could shed on the Egyptian monuments! At the beginning of this century we discovered—and are still discovering

200

daily—characteristic features of the ancient Egyptian civilization about which all the early writers have remained absolutely silent.... When a happy accident led to the discovery of those fragile manuscripts enclosed inside embalmed bodies, did we have the least suspicion of their import? What did historians know or teach us about the disposition and decoration of architecture, about the proportions of the monuments and about a thousand other curious facts, demonstrated by the immense labours on what were once mountains and became the largest and most beautiful quarries in the world; the cutting of stones, the techniques used in the arts—everything in fact that proves the exactness of their judgement and their assiduous observation of nature? What did we learn from authors about the forms, taste and richness of the furniture, armour, costumes and fabrics of those peoples, the indubitable proof of a very advanced state of civilization?[38]

Jomard rejected the classical writers, which was unusual at the time, in favour of the studies that began with the accounts of the first European travellers. This was a very real step forward. Nevertheless, before any further advances could be made the hieroglyphic texts had to be deciphered.

Edme François Jomard and Gilbert Joseph Chabrol de Volvic, *Dendera, perspective view of the north gate.* Reconstruction. Engraving from the *Description de l'Égypte,* 1809-26.

David Roberts, *The ruins of Karnak.* Coloured lithograph from *Egypt and Nubia,* 1846-50.

THE BIRTH OF EGYPTOLOGY

THE EGYPTIAN REVIVAL

The taste for ancient Egypt did not begin with Bonaparte's expedition. Earlier we saw the spread of the cults of Isis throughout the Mediterranean in Roman times and the rise of exoticism derived from the civilization of the Nile that followed in their wake, while the first pharaonic works such as obelisks and statues were brought from Egypt to Rome.

Although there are no parallels during the Middle Ages, it can be said that Egypt was always present in the Christian West through biblical references. The many representations of the flight into Egypt, although they did not include any pharaonic iconography, made that distant land familiar to Europeans.

From the end of the fifteenth century there is fresh proof of the resurgence of this taste for the antique. In the Borgia apartments at the Vatican Pinturiccio used the bull Apis to symbolize the fabulous rise of Alexander VI. In France the first decorations with an Egyptian influence appeared in the sixteenth century, when they imitated the Egyptian-style works of the Roman period. This fashion spread throughout the seventeenth and eighteenth centuries with a notable taste for follies in the Anglo-Chinese parks, such as the pyramid still standing in the Parc Monceau in Paris, built by Carmontelle in 1773 and once complemented by an obelisk covered in hieroglyphs.

During the reign of Louis XVI the return to Egypt manifested itself in firedogs, clocks and console-tables, made at Versailles for Marie-Antoinette, sporting numerous '*turqueries*'. This exoticism distanced itself somewhat from the Neoclassical, giving Egypt pride of place.

The Revolution developed this new style, especially in the settings for the great public festivities. The *Fontaine de la regénération* built on the ruins of the Bastille on 10 August 1793 included a large plaster statue of the goddess Isis from whose breast the purifying waters sprang. Assuming the iconography proper to statues of the pharoahs, she was seated on a block stool wearing a *shendyit* loin cloth and a *nemset* headdress. She also wore a crown of Isis.

France was not the only place affected by this return to the antique. During the eighteenth century a British scholar attributed an Egyptian origin to Megalithic monuments. In 1769 Piranesi, inspired by the Egyptian or Egyptian-style statues in Rome, published a collection of prints suggesting various styles of mantlepieces.

Giovanni Battista Piranesi, chimneypiece. Engraving from
Différentes Manières d'orner les cheminées, 1769.

Up to this time Europe knew the pharaonic civilization only from secondhand sources, mainly Roman works containing ill-understood Egyptian iconography. Bonaparte's expedition was to provide precise documentation.

The Egyptian Revival, a fashion that was to last throughout the nineteenth century, is defined by Jean Humbert as 'a re-use of decorative elements borrowed from ancient Egypt in a variety of forms and mediums'.[39] Architecture and the decorative arts were the most influenced, though literature and music were also affected. Pyramids, obelisks, sphinxes, palm-leaf capitals, lotus flowers, winged scarabs and people or animals wearing *nemset* headdresses appeared in every conceivable context.

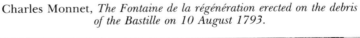

Charles Monnet, *The Fontaine de la régénération erected on the debris
of the Bastille on 10 August 1793.*

The sources of inspiration were numerous. First were the Roman copies, Egyptian-style works in which the pharaonic canon was frequently deformed to fit a more classical style. Examples of these are the pyramid of Caius Cestius and the Canope Gardens in Tivoli. Genuine Egyptian works such as the obelisks erected in the Roman squares also played a major role: the actual shape of the obelisk inspired many artists, but the hieroglyphs covering these stones—the first authentic texts to reach Europe—also appeared frequently.

The accounts and drawings by travellers such as Richard Pococke and Friderik Norden fired people's imaginations, and Bonaparte's expedition, followed by the publication of Vivant Denon's book in 1802 and the *Description de l'Égypte* from 1809 to 1826, fuelled the fire. Documentary sources became more accurate and authoritative, although they still left plenty of room for the imagination to roam free.

In architecture the Egyptian style spread over façades, fountains and funeral monuments such as those of Jean François Champollion, Monge and Fourier in the Père-Lachaise cemetery. Sphinxes multiplied throughout Paris. Unfinished projects, such as the obelisk which was supposed to be erected on the west of the Île de la Cité, would have given the capital an even more exotic air. Some of the surviving monuments are quite surprising enough. The Egyptian house at 2 place du Caire dates from 1799. It has three heads of Hathor and an Egyptian-style frieze in which the Pharaoh is surrounded by bound prisoners. But, for the upper floors, the architect drew upon the troubadour style and put in a plethora of neo-Gothic windows!

OVERLEAF: Jean Julien Deltil, *The Battle of Heliopolis.*
Wallpaper. Rixheim, Musée du Papier Peint.

Auguste Hibon (1780-1857), *Place du Châtelet, Paris.*
Watercolour. Paris, Musée Carnavalet.

T. H. Stepherd, *The Egyptian Hall, Piccadilly,* 1812. Engraving. London, British Museum.

RIGHT: Bralle and Beauvallet, *The Fountain of the Fellah,* 1806-9. Paris, 42 rue de Sèvres.

For the Hôtel de Beauharnais at 78 rue de Lille, once the Hôtel de Torcy and now the German ambassador's residence, Prince Eugène de Beauharnais commissioned his personal architects, Bataille and Calmelet, to add a monumental entrance to the Louis XV façade. They proceeded to build a structure above the perron which was reminiscent of a temple pylon, with toric cornerstones and 'Egyptian' cornices decorated with a winged disc and a fancifully designed uraeus. This pseudo-pylon is opened up by a portico, a façade and two columns with palm-leaf capitals. The whole is completed by portraits of two female divinities whose iconography mixes a few 'curiosities' with its Egyptian components.

Architectural treatises followed this trend. Durand, a pupil of Boullée, was not a great admirer of the antique, and yet he chose two Egyptian forms (the pyramid and the obelisk) for the four styles of commemorative monuments, fountains and tombs he defined. Ledoux and Boullée both let themselves be carried away by chimerical projects from which Egypt was far from absent.

An imperial decree of 2 May 1806 provided for the building of fifteen fountains in Paris, three of which were inspired by Egypt. The *Fountain of the Fellah* (1806-9) at 42 rue de Sèvres includes a copy of the statue by Beauvallet based on the Antinous found in 1738 in Hadrian's Villa at Tivoli which was held as a spoil of war by the Louvre at the time. The upright figure stands in a naos with toric cornerstones and a gorge cornice. The sculptor has added a jug to each of the fellah's hands from which runs a trickle of water.

The *Fountain of Victory* built by Bralle in the Place du Châtelet originally comprised only the central column, which is why it is known as the *Fountain of the Palm*.

Paris was not the only city to build fountains in the Egyptian style. Renaux designed two projects for Bordeaux, both decorated with sphinxes and one with an obelisk covered in hieroglyphs.

The Egyptian style spread rapidly to Russia, the United States and above all England. The Egyptian Hall in Piccadilly, built in 1812 to display the William Bullock Collection, had a façade designed by Peter Frederick Robinson who mostly used Vivant Denon's drawings as his source, but although most of the components were pharaonic in inspiration the overall result was a pastiche far removed from actual Egyptian architecture. The building was imitated in Devonport and Penzance shortly afterwards.

If architecture made extensive use of Egyptian motifs, the decorative arts gave them pride of place. The *Recueil des décorations intérieures,* published in 1812 by Percier and Fontaine, the leaders of Napoleonic architecture, includes two plates permeated by the Egyptian Revival. The caption of plate VIII, 'Clock in the Egyptian manner manufactured by Spain', reads:

> The satiety resulting from the great number of works of this kind, and the desire to possess an object that does not resemble any other, has resulted in this one being in the Egyptian taste without denaturing the shape necessary to the mechanism of a standard clock. The makers have limited themselves to covering the faces and contours with symbols and ornaments from Egyptian works.[40]

Although Percier and Fontaine favoured a return to classical antiquity and, by the same token, to pharaonic Egypt, they feared its abuse:

Thomas Hope, armchair designed for the Egyptian room in his house, 1804. London, H. Blairman & Sons Collection.

RIGHT: Jacob Desmalter, armchair, 1803-5. Mahogany and gilded bronze. Paris, Musée des Arts Décoratifs.

209

Charles Morel, cabinet designed to hold
the volumes of the *Description de l'Égypte*, 1813-36.
The top of the cabinet becomes a lectern
for consulting the volumes.
Carved walnut. Paris, Bibliothèque du Sénat.

If, for example, by the purity of their shapes and their allegorical meaning, sphinxes and Egyptian-style termini are suitable for this or that use in architecture or furniture, we shall shortly be flooded with Egyptian shop signs and door lintels.[41]

The case designed for the *Description de l'Égypte* is the archetype of this kind of ornament. Designed by Jomard, it was built by the cabinet-maker Morel and decorated by the sculptor Dantan. It has fourteen horizontal shelves for the plates and vertical compartments for the volumes of texts. The Egyptian-style decoration is a mass of lotus flowers and temple components.

The decorative repertoire of the revolutionary period had already integrated the finds at Herculaneum and Pompeii, and after the Egyptian expedition new elements were added. The

Jacob Desmalter and Guillaume Biennais,
Dominique Vivant Denon's medal cabinet.
Mahogany and silver. New York,
Metropolitan Museum of Art.

resulting syncretism became a style in itself, which is illustrated by a complete set of furniture created by the cabinet-maker Jacob for Vivant Denon. The medal cabinet, which according to certain sources was intended for Napoleon I, was made by Biennais of ebony encrusted with silver in 1806 and is now in the Metropolitan Museum in New York. It is in the shape of a pylon with a gorge cornice, toric mouldings and a winged disc.

In furniture it was tables and chairs that were most affected by the Egyptian Revival. A desk in the Musée Carnavalet—a 'neo-antique monument' topped by golden sphinxes—shows that the marriage of classical antiquity with ancient Egypt was still *de rigueur* in the 1820s.

In England Egypt was also all the rage for interiors. In 1804 Thomas Hope designed a complete set of furniture for the Egyptian bedroom in his house, including a bed decorated among other things with a 'meeting of two lands', a typical pharaonic scene in which the

211

Sugar bowl from the second
Sèvres Egyptian service, 1812. Porcelain.
London, Victoria and Albert Museum.

divinities bind together plants from the north and south of the country. An armchair decorated with canopic jars, the bull Apis and figures dressed in pharaonic costumes indicates that the Egyptian repertoire was even wider and perhaps more accurate in England than in France.

Lamps were an important feature. Those in the Hôtel de Beauharnais perfectly illustrate the exotic tastes of the time: Nubian women holding candelabras kneel on naoi decorated with scenes of the meeting of the two lands. The large candelabra executed by the most celebrated bronze-worker of the day, Thomire, is in the form of an Egyptian-style caryatid from Graeco-Roman Egypt.

The Sèvres porcelain factory administered at the time by Alexandre Brogniart, was put under the authority of Vivant Denon, director of Arts and Manufacture. The drawings in his *Voyage dans la Basse et la Haute Égypte* had a considerable influence on the production at Sèvres during the Napoleonic era, and the work sold out as soon as it appeared. Historical scenes such as the Cairo uprising or others depicting Muslim Egypt inspired artists like Pierre Nolasque Bergeret and Swebach right from the start. Swebach created two Medici vases for the Trianon, one of them illustrating a superb mosque near Rosetta. They were included in the Trianon inventory of 1809. Another pair onto which he copied four views of Upper Egypt by Denon was delivered in 1811.

A Sèvres Egyptian dinner service, begun in 1804, includes tea and coffee services on which there is a multiplicity of Egyptian scenes, often framed by very accurately reproduced lines of hieroglyphs. A centrepiece, now in the ceramics museum at Kustovo near Moscow, completed the set. Made of white biscuitware and four metres long, it depicts Philae, Edfu, Dendera and the colossi of Memnon. A second Egyptian service was produced in 1811-12. The vase known

212

as the 'Champollion', created in 1832, proves that this exotic series lasted at Sèvres for quite some time.

In England Wedgwood increased the production of Egyptian-style ware from 1770, a style that was copied throughout the nineteenth century.

At first only architecture and the decorative arts were affected by this great fashion for the exotic. It was not until later in the nineteenth century that painters and writers were to take an interest in Egypt.

EGYPT AND THE ARTS IN THE 1830s

In the 1830 artists of all kinds turned to Egypt for inspiration, and biblical stories, scenes from daily life and exotic landscapes became the subjects of more and more paintings as the century advanced. Long before that, however, Hubert Robert (1733-1808) and Jean Michel Moreau *le Jeune* (1741-1814) were perhaps the first to employ Egyptian settings in their paintings.

Hubert Robert discovered Egypt very early in his career from books and a trip to Rome in 1754, where he had sketched the obelisks, sculptures and sphinxes brought back by the Romans. In 1798, the year the Egyptian campaign began, this 'painter of architecture and

Ice-bucket from the second Sèvres
Egyptian service, 1812. Porcelain.
London, Victoria and Albert Museum.

213

214

ruins' produced a *Ronde de jeunes filles autour d'un obélisque brisé devant les pyramides et le Sphinx de Gizeh* ('Young girls dancing round a broken obelisk in front of the pyramids and the sphinx at Giza', Musée des Beaux-Arts, Montreal) which testifies to the painter's continued interest in Egyptian archaeology.

In 1792, a few years before the Egyptian campaign, Jean Michel Moreau *le Jeune* produced an Egyptian-style work of a totally different kind, *Scène d'initiation chez les Égyptiens* ('Egyptian initiation scene'). This astonishing drawing depicts the trials, known as 'the first grade', undergone by future Freemasons, which correspond to the trials by fire, water and air undergone by initiates in Memphis.

In 1827 two rooms in the Musée Charles X destined for the Egyptian antiquities were inaugurated in the Louvre to great public acclaim. The painted decoration of both was inspired by Egypt. François Édouard Picot (1786-1868) painted *L'Étude et le génie dévoilant à Athènes l'Antique Égypte* ('Learning and Genius unveiling Ancient Egypt in Athens') on the ceiling of the Rameses period room, and Abel Pujol (1787-1861) painted a biblical scene, *L'Égypte sauvée par Joseph* ('Egypt saved by Joseph'), on the ceiling of the 18th Dynasty room.

Many painters actually went to Egypt in search of more authentic decors and brought back studies of monuments, landscapes and daily life. Foremost among them were David Roberts (1796-1864), Adrien Dauzats (1808-69) and Prosper Marilhat (1811-47).

OPPOSITE: Adrien Dauzats, *The mosque of al Azhar*, 1831. Oil on canvas. Paris, Assemblée Nationale.

Prosper Marilhat, *The Nile valley with the ruins of the temple of Seti I*, 1844.
Watercolour heightened with gouache. Paris, Musée du Louvre.

215

Adrien Dauzats accompanied the dramatist, traveller and archaeologist Baron Taylor to the East in 1830. He stayed in Cairo and in the Nile valley where he worked every day to produce the hundreds of drawings he would later use over the years in his definitive works. In the words of Théophile Gautier:

> Most certainly, he loved the bitter and ferocious landscapes, the savage and grandiose skylines, the implacably blue sea, the crude white light of the Nile, but what he loved even better were the monuments, the temples, the council chambers, the fortresses, the gates of cities and ruins with magnificent or picturesque traces of the past; for in this painter there was an architect and in the architect there was a decorative artist. He knew his business.... He conveyed with equal power the solid Egyptian temple, the soaring grace of the cathedral and the mysterious elegance of the mosque.[42]

Prosper Marilhat left for the East in April 1831, hired as a draughtsman on a scientific expedition led by the German naturalist Baron von Hügel. He returned to France on 1 May 1833 on board the *Sphinx*, the ship that was to tow the *Luxor* and its obelisk. Having fallen under the spell of Egypt, he brought back numerous sketches and canvases, including studies for his *Ruines de la mosquée el-Hakem au Caire* (1840, Louvre).

David Roberts's Egyptian work is without a doubt amongst the most important of the nineteenth century, especially his first historical painting, *The Departure of the Israelites*, exhibited in 1829. Roberts, who specialized in precise architectural and landscape paintings, was one of the first artists to go independently to Egypt and the Holy Land in order to make surveys and sketches to be adapted into studio works later on. During his stay there from August 1838 to February 1839 he drew, wrote letters and kept a journal. His landscapes and his imposing and theatrical ruins, mainly the sites at Dendera, Karnak, Edfu and Philae, by which he was especially attracted, bear witness to the condition of the monuments when he visited them.

The archaeological discoveries of the Egyptian expedition, the tales brought back by the numerous travellers to the country, the orientalist painting and, later, Champollion's work, would all influence the writers of the nineteenth century. A great number of them, notably Chateaubriand, Gérard de Nerval, Gustave Flaubert, Maxime du Camp and Théophile Gautier,

LEFT: Jean Michel Moreau *le Jeune*, *Egyptian initiation scene*, 1792. Pen and wash. Quimper, Musée des Beaux-Arts.

OPPOSITE: David Roberts, *Great Entrance of the temple at Luxor* (detail). Coloured lithograph from *Egypt and Nubia*, 1846-50.

OVERLEAF: David Roberts, *Temple of Philae, known as the Pharaoh's Bed*. Coloured lithograph from *Egypt and Nubia*, 1846-50.

216

217

would go there in search of the unusual, the exotic and the picturesque and draw their inspiration from it. Others, not being able to visit the country, would nevertheless manage to conjure it up, as Victor Hugo did in *Les Orientales* (1829).

Chateaubriand's visit to Egypt in 1806 resulted in his *Martyrs* (1809), a prose epic on early Christianity, and *Itinéraire de Paris à Jérusalem* (1811), in which he merely skimmed over the land of the pharaohs and concentrated on the ruins of Athens and especially on Jerusalem, the main objective of his journey. In his opinion the accounts of travellers like Volney, and Denon's drawings and the plates in the *Description de l'Égypte*, had made Egypt sufficiently well known: 'I myself have said everything I have to say about Egypt elsewhere. My book *Martyrs*, in which I wrote about that ancient land, covers antiquity more comprehensively than other books of the same kind.'[43]

Gérard de Nerval visited the East and Egypt between December 1842 and December 1843. The definitive version of his book *Voyage en Orient*, a mixture of truth and fiction with the picturesque and symbolism, was published in 1851.

Gustave Flaubert and Maxime du Camp spent over eight months in Egypt in 1849. Flaubert was more attracted by the realities of the life and manners of the people than by archaeology, monuments, history or geography:

> In a word, here is how I sum up what I feel so far: not as much struck by nature as by landscape, sky and desert (except for the mirage), and astonished at the cities and the people.... But there is a new element which I did not expect to find and which is immense here—the grotesque, all the old-fashioned comedy of the belaboured slave, the churlish seller of women and the swindling merchant, is very fresh, very true here, charming [*sic*].[44]

OPPOSITE: David Roberts, *Edfu* (detail).
Coloured lithograph
from *Egypt and Nubia*, 1846-50.

Maxime du Camp, *Flaubert in Cairo, 9 January 1850*.
Photograph. Paris, Bibliothèque de l'Institut.

221

Frederick Schinkel, backdrop for Mozart's *The Magic Flute*, act II, scene vii, Berlin, 1815. Aquatint. Paris, Bibliothèque de l'Opéra.

Théophile Gautier was only able to get to know Egypt in 1869, three years before his death, but he was very much attracted by the exotic and the picturesque and, through his reading and his dreams, works such as *Une nuit de Cléopatre* (1842), *Le Pied de la momie* (1840), *La Mille et deuxième nuit* (1842), *La Péri* (1843), *La Sélam* (1850), *Nostalgies d'obélisques* (1851) and *Le Roman de la momie* (1857) were all inspired by ancient or Muslim Egypt long before this journey.

In opera similar evocations of Egypt began to appear in the mid eighteenth century and flourished during the revolutionary era. One of the most typical examples is Mozart's *Magic Flute*, first performed on 30 September 1791 in Vienna. Using an Egyptian setting—the theme is the initiation of a prince and princess—the opera is concerned with current philosophical preoccupations and especially Freemasonry, which derived all its rituals from ancient Egypt. The libretto was inspired by a Hindu tale and a story by the Abbé Terrasson, *Sethos, histoire et vie tirée des monuments et anecdotes de l'ancienne égypte* ('Seti, history and life drawn from ancient Egyptian monuments and anecdotes'). The costumes and sets, the descendants of a long tradition, mixed Egypt with classical antiquity and India. Mozart's music, however, was entirely European.

The Magic Flute had to wait until 1815 for a completely Egyptian set. Designed by Frederick Schinkel, it incorporated the Nile, a sphinx reclining on a temple and a statue of Osiris with all his trappings in the foreground. Mozart almost disappeared under all this *égypterie*.

Many more examples followed. At the zenith is the most Egyptian opera of them all, Verdi's *Aida*, based on a plot by the Egyptologist Auguste Mariette. First performed in Cairo in 1871, the action takes place at the gates of Thebes, on the banks of the Nile, in the Temple of Vulcan and in the Pharaoh's palace. The sets were also based on Mariette's data.

THE SCRAMBLE FOR ANTIQUITIES

Mohammed Ali was governor and viceroy of Egypt from 1811 to 1849. During his reign he called upon the services of many foreigners to help in the modernization of his country. He modelled the army on European lines, introduced new crops and encouraged commerce and industry. Travellers of all nationalities flooded into the country: merchants, soldiers, engineers, doctors, agronomists and teachers all came in the hope of participating in this development. A number of these foreigners became dealers in antiquities, a trade that had become very lucrative as thousands of artefacts and even monuments left Egyptian soil for Europe.

Foreign consuls played an important part in the antiquities trade. Having obtained a firman or authorization for legal excavations using local labour from Mohammed Ali, they would recruit agents from amongst the adventurers to carry out the work and remove antiquities or purchase objects found in unauthorized digs by the local people. In this way the consuls gradually built up sometimes very large collections which they later resold. These collections form the basis of those owned today by major museums such as the British Museum in London, the Louvre in Paris and the Museo Egizio in Turin.

One of these prospectors was Bernardino Drovetti, a naturalized Frenchman of Italian origin who had been a colonel in Bonaparte's expedition. In 1810 he became consul-general of the country, though on the accession of Louis XVIII he lost the job. He had however earned the esteem of Mohammed Ali and stayed on in Egypt, where he continued to dig for antiquities. In 1821 his job as consul-general was given back to him, and he was to keep the post until 1829.

Drovetti directed some major excavations, notably in Thebes, for which he employed extremely talented agents such as Jean Jacques Rifaud. He built up three collections in all, offering the first to Louis XVIII who turned it down, finding it too expensive. Drovetti finally sold it for 400,000 lire in 1824 to the king of Sardinia, Charles Felix, for the Turin museum,

Goblet given to General Thoutii
by Tuthmosis III, 18th
Dynasty. Gold repoussé.
Paris, Musée du Louvre,
Drovetti Collection.

Amenophis I. Turin, Museo Egizio,
Drovetti Collection.

Funeral urn of Rameses III,
20th Dynasty. Pink granite. Paris,
Musée du Louvre, Salt Collection.

M. Nicolosino, *A hall in the Egyptian Museum in Turin.*
First showing of the Drovetti Collection in the hall in the right wing
of the Palazzo dell' Accademia. Pen and sepia. Turin, private collection.

224

one of the first to own such a valuable Egyptian collection. Amongst other items it includes the famous large seated statue of Rameses II. Meanwhile Drovetti continued collecting. In 1827, on Champollion's advice, Charles X bought his equally prestigious second collection for the Louvre. Drovetti's third and last collection, smaller than the previous one, was bought by the Berlin Ägyptisches Museum, at the instigation of the Egyptologist Lepsius, for 30,000 francs.

Originally a sculptor, Jean Jacques Rifaud spent over forty years in Egypt. He carried out many of Drovetti's excavations and sometimes carved his name on the sculptures he found. The black granite statue of Tuthmosis III (1490-36 BC) in the Turin museum, for example, bears the inscription 'Discovered by Rifaud, sculptor in the service of M. Drovetti in Thebes, 1818'. His drawings, done very rapidly, are of little scientific value. He also wrote several books about Egypt.

Another of the consuls was Henry Salt. In 1797 he came to London to become a portrait painter, and from 1802 he travelled to India, Ceylon, Abyssinia and Egypt with Lord Valentia as his secretary and draughtsman. On his return to England he published an illustrated account of this journey. He spent 1809 to 1811 on a mission to Abyssinia for the British government, and back in London once more he wrote and published *Voyage to Abyssinia*. In 1815 he was appointed British consul in Egypt. He reached Alexandria on 27 March 1816 and was to stay in Egypt until his death on 30 October 1827.

Before Salt left for Egypt, the explorer Sir Joseph Banks had advised him to take advantage of his official position to procure antiquities for the British Museum. Salt settled down to the task as soon as he arrived, recruiting a highly active team to help him in his enterprise. Among them were the very efficient Giovanni Battista Belzoni, Captain Caviglia, his secretary Henry Beechey and Giovanni d'Athanasi. With their help he managed to put together extremely interesting collections for both the British Museum and himself for a mere £2,000. The trustees of the museum refused the finest piece—the alabaster sarcophagus of Seti I—out of parsimony and it was finally sold to a private collector, Sir John Soane. Between 1819 and 1824 Salt formed a second collection of 4014 pieces which was bought by the king of France, Charles X, for 10,000 francs. It included the sarcophagus of Rameses III, two sphinxes and the naos of

The large Egyptian gallery in the British Museum. 1854. Paris, Bibliothèque des Arts Décoratifs.

A. Reagis, *Egyptian Room in the Musée Charles X*. Engraving from *Paris illustré, nouveau guide de l'étranger et du Parisien*, 1863.

Henry Salt, *The pyramids seen from Cairo*. Lithograph from *Twenty-four Views Taken in St. Helena, the Cape, India, Ceylon, Abyssinia and Egypt*, 1809.

Philae, and is now part of the Louvre collection. His third collection, of 1083 pieces, was auctioned off after his death.

Giovanni Battista Belzoni, born in Padua in 1778, settled in England in 1803 and worked first as an acrobat. In 1811 he left England for Portugal and Spain. In Malta in 1814 an agent of Mohammed Ali's, sent to recruit European engineers, suggested that he go to Egypt where he could profit from his knowledge of hydraulics. A short while later Belzoni disembarked at Alexandria with his wife Sarah and an Irish servant. In the hope of an official appointment Belzoni built a hydraulic machine but, alas, Mohammed Ali refused to buy it. Lacking the wherewithal to survive, he turned to his friend the Swiss traveller Jean Louis Burckhardt, who presented him to Henry Salt. Salt gave him the first of his great archaeological tasks, the removal of the colossal bust of Rameses II from the Ramesseum in Thebes to the banks of the river, where it had to be hoisted on to the boat that was to take it to Cairo—a feat the French had failed to achieve:

The fellahin of Qurnah, who knew the Caphany, as they called the colossus, had always believed it could never be moved from where it lay, and when they saw it move they let

Jean Pierre Granger, *Bernardino Drovetti and his entourage measuring a fragment of a colossus in Upper Egypt.*
Black chalk on buff-coloured paper. Paris, Musée du Louvre.

out a cry of surprise.... By means of four levers I had the bust lifted up to a point where a portion of the car could be slipped under it, and once the block was resting on it I had the front of the car itself lifted so that one of the rollers could be put underneath. The same operation was performed at the rear, and when the colossus was in the centre of the car I had it securely tied down, disposing the ropes in such a manner as to spread evenly the weight to be pulled. I placed men with levers on each side of the car who were to use brute force if the statue slipped, thus ensuring that it could not fall. Finally I set workmen to pull the ropes at the front while others were given the task of changing the rollers. By these means I managed to move the block several yards from where it had been found.[45]

On 17 November 1816 Belzoni assembled 130 men to transfer the bust to the boat that was to take it to Cairo. The bust was later donated to the British Museum and sent to England.

After the success of this first assignment Belzoni continued to work for Salt, who financed his expeditions and the purchasing of antiquities. Belzoni's achievements were immense and his discoveries were exceptional. Nicknamed 'the Padua giant' by the Europeans in Cairo, he was an unusual man and passionate about everything he undertook. He got to know the Arabs

227

Amenophis III, 18th Dynasty.
Black granite. London, British Museum,
Salt Collection.

and learned their language, their dress and their mentality so well that they gave him everything he asked for, obtaining workmen for his excavations and antiquities to buy. On 1 August 1817 he managed to get inside the temple at Abu Simbel with two English captains, Charles Irby and James Mangles, and Henry Beechey:

> After enlarging the tunnel we had dug, we had the pleasure of being the first to descend into the largest and most magnificent underground chamber in Nubia and see a monument which is equal to the most beautiful Egyptian ones, apart from the tomb that has recently been discovered at Biban al Maluk. We were amazed first by the immense size of the chamber, but our astonishment broke all bounds when we saw the magnificent works of art of all kinds, paintings, sculptures, colossal figures, etc., which surrounded us.[46]

In October 1817 he discovered several royal tombs in the Valley of the Kings, notably those of Rameses I and Seti I, whose funeral chamber contained a magnificent alabaster sarcophagus. We also owe to him the discovery of the entrance to the second pyramid at Giza—Chephren—and the removal of the obelisk at Philae on behalf of William Bankes.

When he returned to England in 1819 he prepared an exhibition of his drawings and casts which opened to great public acclaim in the Egyptian Hall in Piccadilly on 1 May 1821. He also worked on his account of his travels, *Narrative of the Operations and Recent Discoveries within the Pyramids, Temples, Tombs and Excavations, in Egypt and Nubia . . .*, published in London in 1820. He then set off on an expedition to Timbuktoo but died of dysentery at Gato, near Benin, on 3 December 1823. On his death Sarah Belzoni commissioned a memorial engraving in which Belzoni is surrounded by his major discoveries: the bust of Rameses II, Seti I's sarcophagus, the obelisk at Philae and the arms and head of a pharaoh now in the British Museum.

A Swiss adventurer and explorer, Jean Louis Burckhardt offered his services to the African Society in London in 1808, went to Malta where he converted to Islam then spent two and a half years in Syria. He arrived in Egypt on 4 September 1812 where he was to remain until his death on 15 October 1817. He travelled in the Sudan and Arabia and became involved with the British consul-generals and with Belzoni. It was Burckhardt who discovered the temple of Abu Simbel still buried in the sand in 1813. In 1822 his *Travels in Nubia* was published posthumously.

The great number of travellers who stayed in Egypt during the nineteenth century enabled museums that were less important than the Louvre, the British Museum or the Egyptian Museum in Turin to acquire their first Egyptian pieces and even to form quite interesting Egyptian collections. In 1812 the city of Marseilles bought the collection of antiquities belonging to Antoine Barthélmy Clot, known as 'Clot Bey', for 50,000 francs. It now constitutes the basis of an important collection in the Egyptian department of the archaeological museum at Château Borély. Clot Bey, a doctor from Grenoble living in Marseilles, had embarked on the *Bonne Émilie* on 21 January 1825 to become a doctor in Mohammed Ali's army. Once in Egypt he organized the military health service and in 1827 started a medical school in Abu Zabal (transferred to Cairo in 1833) and founded the first hospitals. Exhausted by the climate and his work, he returned to France in 1849. Fascinated by Egypt, in 1840 Clot Bey published *Un aperçu général*, a comprehensive survey of the history, geography, zoology, botany, customs, as well as monuments and ruins, of the country that interested him so much.

The Rouenese painter Eustache Hyacinthe Langlois, a collaborator of Achille Deville, the first director of the Musée des Antiquités de Seine-Maritime, bought a Graeco-Roman simpulum and some canopic jars from the commander of the *Luxor*, Verninac de Saint-Maur, and his officers, which were added to the few Egyptian pieces then owned by the museum after the painter's death in 1835. In 1889 another Rouenese, Gaston le Breton, director of the Musée

Giovanni Battista Belzoni, *Transporting the bust of Memnon* (now in the British Museum). Engraving from *Narrative of the Operations and Recent Discoveries...in Egypt and Nubia...*,1820.

Giovanni Battista Belzoni, *View of the interior of the temple of Abu Simbel*. Engraving from *Narrative of the Operations and Recent Discoveries...in Egypt and Nubia...*, 1820.

Prosper Jollois and Édouard de Villiers du Terrage, *Dendera, zodiac carved
on the ceiling of one of the upper halls in the Great Temple.*
Engraving from the *Description de l'Égypte,* 1809-26.

de la Céramique, went to Egypt where he made some clandestine excavations around Akhmim. On his return to Rouen he donated several pieces relating to the art of Coptic tapestry and three mummies to the antiquities museum. His best pieces were not added to the museum's collection until after his death in 1920.[47]

During the Restoration the French went to a great deal of expense to bring the zodiac from the temple at Dendera to Paris. This piece, measuring 2.5 m square by 1 m thick, was detached from the ceiling by Jean Baptiste le Lorrain, a master mason, on the instructions and at the expense of Sébastien Saulnier, the son of a member of the Chamber of Deputies. In 1822 Louis XVIII bought it for the huge sum of 150,000 francs, believing it to be a prestigious piece dating from pharaonic times. When it was later found to be a mediocre Graeco-Roman piece, Louis XVIII lost interest in any further purchases.

Nevertheless, the arrival of the Dendera zodiac in Paris excited much interest amongst scholars. It had been found by General Desaix and Vivant Denon in 1799, and others had since been found in Esna. A lively controversy ensued amongst scholars as to the origins and dating of zodiacs. Were they Egyptian or more recent? For Charles François Dupuis (1742-1849), a professor and lawyer who had studied mathematics and antiquity, the zodiac was 'an Egyptian invention' and he dated it to '13,000 years before our era'[48]—i.e., 13,000 BC. In 1800 *Le Moniteur* 'gave official credence to the theory that zodiacs contained a date of five to six thousand years in the order of their signs, and that the temples that housed these artefacts were amongst the most modern in Egypt'.

232

The zodiac from Dendera. Paris, Musée du Louvre.

The Abbé Testa, secretary to the Roman Chancellery, brought the zodiacs up to the third century BC, while Visconti, curator of antiquities at the Louvre, dated them from the beginning of the Roman Empire. 'On the one hand it was a matter of ageing the world at any cost in the hope of contradicting the Scriptures.... On the other it seemed necessary to defend what at the time was rather vaguely termed the foundations of the common faith of all the Christian groups, the early headings in the Book of Revelations and the sacred chronology. By this we mean the chronology of the Hebrew text of the Bible which, under the influence of the Protestant Joseph Scaliger, had prevailed since the end of the sixteenth century.'[49] This controversy slowly died away, and in 1824 Jean Antoine Letronne tried to establish their date once and for all: 'It has been demonstrated that all of the known zodiacs are post-Tiberian, and were all made during a period of less than a century, between the years 57 and 150 of our era.'[50] Champollion, who discovered the key to the hieroglyphs in 1822, went to Egypt in 1828-9 and visited the temple at Dendera, writing: 'Its decorations are entirely Graeco-Roman and the bas-reliefs are hideous.'[51]

In 1839 Mohammed Ali donated the Luxor obelisk to France:

I have done nothing for France that France has not done for me. If I give her the debris of an ancient civilization it is in exchange for the new civilization which she has planted in the East. May the Theban obelisk reach Paris safely and serve as a bond between these two cities for all eternity.[52]

233

Nicolas Huyot, *Erecting an obelisk*. Watercolour. Paris, Bibliothèque de l'École Nationale Supérieure des Beaux-Arts.

Prosper Jollois and Édouard de Villiers du Terrage, *Thebes, Luxor, elevation of the palace façade*, 1798-1801. Graphite, pen and wash. Paris, Bibliothèque Nationale.

Léon de Joannis, *Luxor, view of the eastern section of the route to the ship taken by the obelisk.*
Engraving from *Campagne pittoresque du Luxor*, 1835.

François Dubois, *Erection of the Luxor obelisk, 25 October 1836.* Oil on canvas. Paris, Musée Carnavalet.

David Roberts, *Great Entrance of the temple at Luxor.*
Coloured lithograph from *Egypt and Nubia*, 1846-50.

The ship *Luxor*, specially built to transport the 230,000 kg monolith from Egypt to Paris, left Toulon in March 1831 under the command of Verninac de Saint-Maur and with the engineer Lebas on board. They reached Luxor five months later, on 15 August 1831. The obelisk, enclosed in a wood casing to protects its hieroglyphs, was brought down on 31 October 1831 and transported to the ship, which then waited seven months for the waters to rise before leaving for France in August 1832. It reached Toulon on 11 May 1833, two years after its departure, and finally moored below the Concorde bridge on 23 December where the obelisk was to wait almost three years before being landed. At last, on 25 October 1836, it was put up in the Place de la Concorde before an immense crowd of about 200,000 people.

THE KEY TO THE HIEROGLYPHS

Hieroglyphic writing had long fascinated scientists such as Athanasius Kircher in the seventeenth century and Georg Zoëga in the eighteenth, as well as the scholars in Bonaparte's expedition. The scholars, Jomard in particular, made accurate drawings of texts from papyri and carvings such as the Rosetta stone but they never managed to understand them. Bonaparte was fully aware of their importance: 'If we had the key to the hieroglyphs with which [the monuments] are covered, we would learn new facts about the first ages of society.'[53]

As early as 1802, the Frenchman Silvestre de Sacy (1758-1838) and the Swede Johan David Akerblad (1763-1813) tried to penetrate the secret of the Rosetta stone. Both began with the middle text written in demotic script, a form of writing that was hardly known at the time. Sacy spotted and translated several proper names including Ptolemy, Arsinoe, Alexander and Alexandria. Akerblad deciphered other words and established a short phonetic alphabet which he tried in vain to apply to the rest of the text, believing that the Egyptian inscription was purely phonetic.

Between 1814 and 1818 the celebrated English polymath Thomas Young (1773-1829) from Milverton in Somerset studied the hieroglyphic section. Already very much drawn to linguistics by the age of fourteen, he had a knowledge of Latin, Greek, Hebrew, Persian, Arabic, French, Italian, Spanish, Syrian and Chaldean. After studying in London, Edinburgh, Göttingen and Cambridge, Young became an eminent doctor and physician. He was particularly interested in optics and, through studying the mechanism of the eye, he discovered the phenomenon of light interference. In June 1814 a friend of his, Sir Rouse Boughton, knowing his taste for ancient Oriental languages, gave him a papyrus written in demotic script. From that day Young threw himself into the study of Egyptian writing and attempted to decipher the demotic and hieroglyphic texts on the Rosetta stone. The Austrian Egyptologist Ernest Doblhofer has described how he went about it:

> He divided not just the demotic text but also the hieroglyphic text in such a manner as to make the isolated words correspond to the same words in Greek, and published both the texts treated in this fashion in *Archeologia*. . . . By collating the texts and making mathematical adjustments he achieved truly astonishing results considering the insufficiency of the means at his disposal.[54]

It was thus that Young was able to identify a number of groups of hieroglyphs for the first time. His research led him to the conclusion that demotic writing derived from hieroglyphic writing, and he drew attention to the fact that the names of the gods and the kings were

Jean François Champollion, *Luxor, inscription engraved on the southern wall of one of the palace halls.* Engraving from *Monuments de l'Égypte et de la Nubie...*, 1835-45.

Jean François Champollion, *Lettre à M. Dacier...* Title-page, 1822.

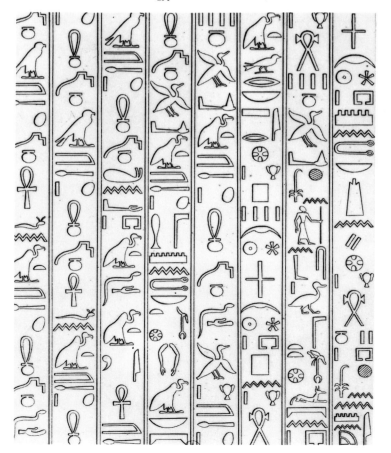

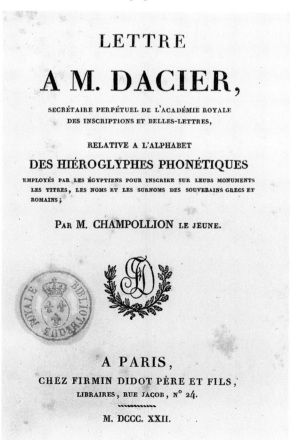

surrounded by a cartouche. He managed to read part of the two cartouches enclosing the names of Ptolemy and Berenice, but he got no further:

> Apart from a few inspired guesses, the man who discovered the phonetic content of the hieroglyphs was satisfied with the results he had already achieved and never took the final step across the threshold of the door he had himself opened. . . . When, for example, he came across the name of the god of the dead, Anubis, clearly written in phonetic signs, he did not recognize it and gave it the name of the Greek guardian of hell, the dog Cerberus.[55]

Jean François Champollion (1790-1832) had been fascinated by the problem of hieroglyphics from early youth and had dedicated himself to the study of Oriental languages such as Hebrew, Arabic, Syrian, Persian and above all Coptic to help him solve it. Like his rivals, he obtained a copy of the cast of the Rosetta stone and tried to decipher it. For a long time he believed that, apart from foreign names, hieroglyphic writing was purely symbolic and figurative, but when he compared the two cartouches on the Philae obelisk he realized that four of the signs were phonetic. Then, on 14 September 1822, his friend the architect Nicolas Huyot (1780-1840) presented him with copies of the inscriptions on the temple at Abu Simbel. (Huyot, who had been to Egypt, brought back many other drawings which he put at Champollion's disposal.)

Léon Cogniet, *Portrait of Jean François Champollion,* 1831.
Oil on canvas. Paris, Musée du Louvre.

Stele of the scribe Harmon found at al Kab, 18th Dynasty. White limestone. Florence, Museo archeologico, Rosellini Collection.

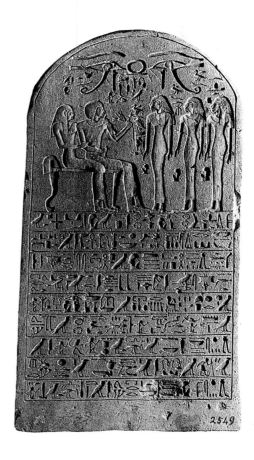

ABOVE: The divine worshipper Karomama, 22nd Dynasty. Bronze inlaid with gold and silver. Paris, Musée du Louvre.

LEFT: Seti I receiving the magic necklace of the goddess Hathor, 19th Dynasty. Painted limestone bas-relief. Paris, Musée du Louvre.

239

Champollion found a cartouche in which he managed to decipher the name of the pharaoh Rameses, part of whose name was written phonetically and the other part ideographically. He then translated another name—Tuthmosis—and the mystery of the hieroglyphs was unveiled at last. He posited the principle of a hieroglyphic writing that was at once 'figurative, symbolic and phonetic' in a letter, the celebrated *Lettre à M. Dacier ... relative à l'alphabet des hiéroglyphes phonétiques employés par les égyptiens* ('Letter to M. Dacier ... on the alphabet of the phonetic hieroglyphs employed by the Egyptians'), which was read out before the Academy on 27 September 1822:

> I am convinced that the same hieroglyphic-phonetic signs used to represent the sound of Greek and Roman proper names were used in hieroglyphic texts carved long before the

Guiseppe Angelelli, *Thebes, picture painted in the tombs of the Valley of the Queens, Amonmai.*
Paris, Bibliothèque Nationale.

Alexandre Duchesne, *Bani Hasan al Qadim, painting on the north partition of the tomb of Rotei (Baquet III).* Watercolour heightened with white. Paris, Bibliothèque Nationale.

Greeks came to Egypt, and that these already reproduced sounds or articulations in the same way as the cartouches carved under the Greeks and Romans. The discovery of this precious and decisive fact is due to my work on pure hieroglyphic script. It would be impossible to prove it in the present letter without going into lengthy detail.[56]

Next he wrote a *Précis du système hiéroglyphique des anciens Égyptiens ...* ('A summary of the hieroglyphic system of the ancient Egyptians'), which he published in 1824. He continued to work on authentic documents and attempted to understand the ancient Egyptian civilization. In 1824 he travelled to Turin to study the collection Drovetti had sold to the king of Sardinia:

It was only at the Royal Museum in Turin, when I was surrounded by such a varied mass of debris from that ancient civilization, that it occurred to me that the history of Egyptian art is still to be written. Everything there shows that we have been too precipitate in judging its procedures, determining its means and above all in defining its perimeters.[57]

Amongst the better-known items was the royal papyrus, the pieces of which he reassembled for the first time. He published the results of this work between 1824 and 1826 in his *Lettres à M. le duc de Blacas d'Aulps....* Still looking for original sources, he visited Milan, Rome, Naples and Florence. In Rome he studied the obelisks and the papyri in the Vatican library. In Leghorn he examined Henry Salt's Egyptian collection which he would later persuade Charles X to acquire for the Louvre. Back in France, he was appointed curator of the Egyptian section of the Louvre which he opened in 1827, writing a *Notice descriptive des monuments égyptiens du musée Charles X.*

241

Nestor l'Hôte, *Nubia, temple of
al Dakkah,* 1828-9. Watercolour.
Paris, Bibliothèque Nationale.

Le Temple de Dake.

Nicolas Huyot, *Abu Simbel*. Watercolour. Paris, Bibliothèque de l'École Nationale Supérieure des Beaux-Arts.

When he visited Egypt in 1828-9 he brought back a collection of antiquities to enrich the Louvre's brand-new Egyptian department. This expedition, which he organized with the help of his friend and disciple the Italian Egyptologist Ippolito Rosellini, was a Franco-Tuscan venture subsidized by the French government and the Grand Duke of Tuscany, Leopold II, in order to complete the archaeological section of the *Description de l'Égypte* with reproductions and studies of writings and monuments. It comprised a group of French scholars under the direction of Champollion and an Italian group headed by Rosellini. Among the French who accompanied Champollion was Nestor l'Hôte (1804-41). Officially employed by the customs

244

Nicolas Huyot, *Temple of Hathor*. Watercolour. Paris, Bibliothèque de l'École Nationale Supérieure des Beaux-Arts.

services, l'Hôte had been fascinated by Egyptology since his youth and had written a treatise on Egyptian archaeology which he had shown to Champollion. Champollion had advised him to continue his researches and a friendly relationship had started up between them. When l'Hôte wanted to become a part of the Franco-Tuscan expedition, Champollion took him along as a draughtsman. After his return from Egypt some of his drawings would illustrate the large volumes produced by Champollion and Rosellini, *Monuments de l'Égypte et de la Nubie*.

The two teams landed at Alexandria in August 1828 and explored Egypt and Nubia as far as the second cataract, stopping at archaeological sites where they copied and deciphered

inscriptions. Champollion wrote to Dacier, the secretary of the Academy, from Wadi Halfa on 1 January 1829:

> I am proud to be able to announce, now that I have followed the course of the Nile from its mouth to the second cataract, that we need change nothing in our Letter on the hieroglyphical alphabet. Our alphabet is good: it can be successfully applied to the Egyptian monuments dating from Roman and Ptolemaic times, and then, which is of far greater importance, to the inscriptions on all the temples, palaces and tombs of the pharaonic era. All of this vindicates the encouragement you were so kind as to give my work on the hieroglyphs at a time when they were far from being favourably received.[58]

After his return to Paris he was made a member of the Académie des Inscriptions et Belles-Lettres in 1830, and in 1831 he was appointed to a professorship at the Collège de France. Alas, shortly afterwards, he died, aged forty-two, worn out by his work.

Despite the shortness of his life, the achievements of this illustrious researcher were prodigious. His great discovery in 1822, his various journeys during which he checked and increased his knowledge and his many publications on the subject were a major contribution to the reconstruction of the greater part of Egyptian civilization. Through him a new science

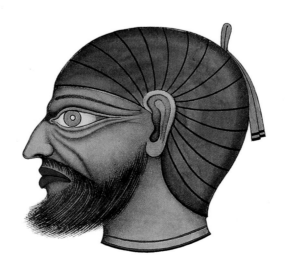

Salvatore Cherubini, *Abu Simbel, Great Speos*. Lithograph from *Monuments de l'Égypte et de la Nubie...*, 1835-45.

OPPOSITE:
Ippolito Rosellini, *Abu Simbel, Great Temple, south partition, heads of foreigners*. Lithographs from *Monuments de l'Égypte et de la Nubie...*, 1835-45.

Guiseppe Angelelli, *Franco-Tuscan literary expedition to Egypt*, 1828-9. Centre, seated, Champollion; on his right, standing, Ippolito Rosellini; foreground, seated, the painter Alexandre Duchesne. Oil on canvas. Florence, Museo archeologico.

was born: Egyptology. His posthumous works, published by his brother Champollion-Figeac, who had supported him throughout his researches, are landmarks: *Lettres écrites d'Égypte et de Nubie* (1833), *Grammaire égyptienne ...* (1836-41), *Dictionnaire égyptien ...* (1841) and *Monuments de l'Égypte et de la Nubie ...* (1835-45).

He was also the first to have thought of protecting the monuments in Egypt. While he was there he noted the monuments' deterioration—in some cases total destruction—which was due not just to the dealers in antiquities and their clandestine excavations but also to the modernization of the country, since ancient buildings were being demolished and their stones used to build modern ones. At the end of his stay in Alexandria he sent Mohammed Ali a report on the need to preserve the ruins:

It is of the highest importance for Egypt that Your Highness's government address the overall preservation of the ancient buildings and monuments the destruction of which is so deeply deplored by the whole of scholarly Europe.... It is well known that the barbarous demolition of these monuments has been carried out despite the liberal opinions and known intentions of Your Majesty by those incapable of appreciating the damage they are thus innocently causing the country, but that does not make the loss of these monuments any the less irreparable ... the worst sort of devastation is daily carried out ... by the fellahin, either on their own behalf or for the dealers in antiquities who have them in their pay.... In the interests of science it is essential that, rather than interrupt the excavations from which it continually gains new knowledge and unexpected discoveries, the diggers be subject to a regulation which will ensure that the preservation of tombs discovered today or in the future will be fully assured and that they will be given proper protection against ignorance or blind greed.[59]

This report was to bear fruit a few years later when Mohammed Ali instituted administrative measures concerning the antiquities. An order of 15 August 1835 forbade the export of remains out of Egypt and ensured their protection:

In consideration, therefore, of the importance which Europeans attach to the ancient monuments and the advantages they draw from the study of antiquity, and also in consideration of the abundant riches of that kind which Egypt, that marvel of all time, possesses, the government council of Egypt considers it to be just that:

1 The export of ancient artefacts of all kinds be severely prohibited in future.

2 That all artefacts of a similar nature already in the possession of the government, as well as all those that it might acquire through future researches and excavations, should be placed in a specially designed location in Cairo, in which they can be preserved and properly classified, so that the people may visit them, and travellers and foreigners especially be daily attracted to these lands to see them.

3 That not only should the destruction of the ancient monuments of Upper Egypt be expressly forbidden in future, but that the government should also take the necessary measures to ensure their overall preservation.[60]

Ippolito Rosellini, *Abu Simbel, Great Temple, east partition, head of a foreigner*. Lithograph taken from *Monuments de l'Égypte et de la Nubie...*, 1835-45.

Ippolito Rosellini, *Musicians* (detail). Lithograph
from *I Monumenti dell' Egitto
e della Nubia...*, 1832-44.

Ippolito Rosellini, *Scene of an offering before Amore.*
Lithograph from *I Monumenti dell' Egitto e della Nubia...*, 1832-44.

Ippolito Rosellini, *Biban al Maluk, tomb of Rameses Meriamon.*
Lithograph from *I Monumenti dell' Egitto e della Nubia...*, 1832-44.

CHAMPOLLION'S SUCCESSORS

The progress of Egyptology advanced rapidly in the wake of Champollion's pioneering work on the hieroglyphs. Scientific expeditions proliferated. A multitude of increasingly accurate notes, copies and surveys were brought back to swell the number of major publications. Floods of travellers were attracted to the cradle of civilization, where they visited the best-known sites and monuments, sketching and publishing accounts of their expeditions on their return. The French architect Hector Horeau (1801-72), for example, published a *Panorama d'égypte et de Nubie* after his visit in 1837, and the mineralogist Frédéric Cailliaud (1787-1869), for forty years curator of the Muséum d'Histoire Naturelle in Nantes, made several trips to Egypt and collaborated with Jomard in the publication of *Voyage à l'oasis de Thèbes ...* (1821), *Voyage à Méroé ...* (1826-7) and *Recherche sur les arts, les usages de la vie civile et domestique des anciens peuples d'Égypte, de la Nubie et de l'Éthiopie ...* (1831).

The German Karl Richard Lepsius (1810-84), an Egyptologist of Champollion's stature, dedicated himself to the study of Egyptian writing and language and in 1837 published his *Lettre à M. le Professeur Rosellini sur l'alphabet hiéroglyphique*. He spent four years visiting the principal Egyptian collections in England, Holland and Italy to broaden his knowledge of ancient Egypt, and in 1842-5 he led an important Prussian expedition in Egypt and Nubia

BELOW AND OPPOSITE:
Hector Horeau, *The principal monuments of Egypt*. Lithographs from *Panorama d'Égypte et de Nubie*, 1841.

where his excavations included the Hawarah labyrinth in the Fayyum. He formed a large collection of antiquities for the Berlin museum and brought back detailed drawings of inscriptions and monuments. In 1846 he became a professor at Berlin University and director of the Egyptian department of the city's museum. On his second expedition to Egypt, in 1866, he discovered the Canopus Decree at Tanis. His considerable writings were published in his twelve-volume *Denkmäler aus Aegypten und Aethiopien* (1849-59), illustrated with 894 plates.

Another pioneer was the Englishman John Gardner Wilkinson (1797-1875), who first went to Egypt in 1822, travelling through the ancient sites and excavating around Thebes. His copies of texts and other drawings are extremely precise. His notes, now in the Bodleian Library in Oxford, are a mass of information on various aspects of ancient Egypt. In 1837 he published a major book in three volumes on daily life under the pharaohs, *The Manners and Customs of the Ancient Egyptians* . . . , which is still used as a reference today.

Another who left his mark on Egyptology was the French archaeologist Émile Prisse d'Avennes (1807-79). Mohammed Ali hired him as an engineer from 1826 to 1836. He became professor of topography at the Egyptian Military Staff Academy, then professor of fortifications at the Infantry School in Damietta. After that he abandoned teaching for archaeology and, outdoing Lepsius, he removed the reliefs from the Ancestors' Hall in the temple at Karnak, now in the Louvre. His name is linked to the celebrated Prisse papyrus bought in Qurnah, now in the Bibliothèque Nationale. His many drawings, notes and surveys were published in

OPPOSITE: Karl Richard Lepsius, *View of the interior of the Great Temple at Abu Simbel.* Lithograph from *Denkmäler aus Aegypten und Aethiopien,* 1849-59.

François Christian Gau, *Abu Simbel, monument carved in the rock.* Engraving from *Antiquités de la Nubie ou Monuments des bords du Nil,* 1822.

Karl Richard Lepsius, *Thebes, view of the interior of the hypostyle hall at Karnak.* Lithograph from
Denkmäler aus Aegypten und Aethiopien, 1849-59.

the two-volume *Histoire de l'art égyptien d'après les monuments depuis les temps les plus reculés jusqu'à la domination romaine* (1879).

Amongst those who continued Champollion's work was Auguste Mariette (1821-81). From 1850 to 1880 he fought for the conservation of the archaeological treasures of Egypt, founding the Egyptian Antiquities Service and the Cairo Museum (the first national museum to be established in the Near East). He directed many excavations throughout the country and discovered, among other things, the Memphis Serapeum in the Saqqarah necropolis. He donated some of his finds to the Louvre, including the famous Seated Scribe and the beautiful statue of the bull Apis, and housed others in a little museum in Bulaq on the outskirts of Cairo, the ancestor of the present museum. In 1858 the Viceroy Said Pasha appointed him '*maamour*' or director of works for antiquities. It was then that he formed what was to become the Egyptian Antiquities Service, entrusted with the protection, preservation and even the beginnings of the restoration of the monuments, thus putting an end to the systematic pillaging of their remains. We owe to him the discovery of many masterpieces such as the statues of Chephren from Giza and the monuments of the Hyksos of Tanis. After his death the great French Egyptologist Gaston Maspero (1846-1916) succeeded him as director of the Antiquities Service.

With the invention of photography in 1839 scholars were quick to realize the immense possibilities of such a process for archaeology:

> It would take legions of draughtsmen many years to reproduce the millions and millions of hieroglyphs that cover even the outsides of the great monuments of Thebes, Memphis and Karnak. With the daguerreotype a single man could complete the task. Were the Egyptian Institute to be provided with two or three of M. Daguerre's devices, many of the large plates in the celebrated work which is the fruit of our immortal expedition could be filled with great spreads of real hieroglyphs in place of invented or purely conventional ones. Throughout, drawings would surpass the works of the finest painters in their faithfulness and local colour, and the photographic plates, after the application of a few simple geometric rules, would enable us to arrive at the exact dimensions of the highest parts of the most inaccessible buildings.[61]

The first 'archaeological photographers' began to descend on Egypt, among them Maxime du Camp, who arrived in November 1849 on an official mission for the Ministry of Public Education:

> Although the principal monuments on the banks of the Nile have been surveyed with care and drawn with accuracy, it would be useful to have general views and close-ups of architectural details taken with the daguerreotype. The special nature of photography, its indisputable accuracy and its minute exactitude in reproducing the faintest details renders everything it produces invaluable.[62]

His friend Gustave Flaubert was with him for the eight months he spent in Egypt, during which they travelled up the Nile, visiting Nubia and stopping at almost all the sites. Maxime du Camp explored every ruin and temple, taking rubbings and casts, measuring, making notes and photographing everything he could whilst his friend Flaubert let himself be seduced by the 'oriental balm'. 'I don't know how Maxime hasn't killed himself with his photographic fever, at which, by the way, he is very successful.'[63] Du Camp brought back a mass of negatives, the sheer number of which make him one of the first major photographers of Egypt. They appeared in an album published in 1852, *Égypte, Nubie, Palestine et Syrie. Dessins photographiques*...

Du Camp published an account of his work in 1855 in *Le Nil (Égypte et Nubie)*, in the form of letters to Théophile Gautier:

Maxime du Camp, *Abu Simbel, general view of the speos of Reo.* 'Photographic drawing' from
Egypt, Nubia, Palestine and Syria, 1852.

OPPOSITE: John Gardner Wilkinson, *Thebes, head of a Graeco-Egyptian mummy, c* 1822.
Watercolour. Paris, Bibliothèque Nationale.

Believe me, when the dullness of our cold nation enfeebles your heart, when you desire
to enter into direct contact with nature and drink deeply from the source of things, then
cross the Mediterranean, disembark on the ancient soil of Egypt, travel up and down the
peaceful Nile, admire its ruins, grow drunk on its landscapes, listen to the wonderful song
it murmurs into the ears of those who can understand it and wander bravely in the lonely
deserts, and you will feel younger, stronger, more productive, more ardent and closer to
God![64]

258

GLOSSARY OF TITLES AND TERMS

BEY Turkish title meaning 'prince' or 'lord'; governor of a province or district in the Turkish dominions.

DIVAN Council of government or state.

DJERM Nile sailing ship, similar to FELUCCA.

EFFENDI Turkish title meaning 'lord' or 'master', chiefly applied to officials and professional men.

EMIR Arabic title given to a military commander, ruler of a province or prince.

EMIR AL HADJ Leader of the annual pilgrimage to Mecca from Cairo.

FELLAH (pl. FELLAHIN) Arab peasant or labourer.

FELUCCA Mediterranean sailing vessel with two masts, lateen sails, oars and often a rudder at each end.

GRAND VIZIER Chief minister and head of the armed forces of the sultan of Turkey.

HYPOGEUM Underground vault or tomb.

HYPOSTYLE HALL Columned chamber, usually the largest in a temple.

KACHEF Subgovernor responsible to a bey for administering a province and collecting taxes.

MAMELUKE One of the ruling warrior-princes of Egypt, nominally subject to the Ottoman sultan; driven out by the viceroy Mohammed Ali in 1811.

NAOS Sanctuary or shrine where statues of gods were kept.

PASHA Turkish title given to high military officials and governors of provinces.

PORTE (also SUBLIME PORTE) The Ottoman court in Constantinople, seat of the imperial government (so called from the gate of the sultan's palace where justice was administered).

SHERIF Arab title given to certain princes and governors of Mecca and other cities.

SPEOS Cave or grotto.

STELE Slab of wood or stone, carved or inscribed.

ULEMA Body of professional theologians, authorities on Mohammedan law.

URAEUS Sacred golden cobra worn by a king on his forehead.

NOTES

1 *Description de l'Égypte, Antiquités descriptions*, Paris, 2nd edn, 1821-6, vol. 1, foreword, pp. cxxxii, cxxxiii, cxxxv.

2 Dominique Vivant Denon, *Voyage dans la Basse et la Haute Égypte pendant les campagnes du général Bonaparte*, 4th edn, Paris, 1803, pt II, p. 296.

3 Gaspard Antoine Chalbrand, *Les Français en Égypte ou Souvenirs des campagnes d'Égypte et de Syrie par un officier de l'expédition*, Just Jean Étienne Roy, ed., Tours, 1855, p. 16.

4 Jacques Bénigne Bossuet, *Discours sur l'histoire universelle à Monseigneur le Dauphin*, Lyons, 1697, pt II, pp. 249-50.

5 *Notices sur M. de Villiers du Terrage... par M. M. Mary, Alfred Maury et Jomard*, Paris, undated.

6 *Correspondance de Napoléon 1er publiée par ordre de l'empereur Napoléon III*, Paris, 1870, pt XXIX, p. 381.

7 François Bernoyer, *Avec Bonaparte en Égypte et en Syrie, 1798-1800, 19 lettres inédites présentées par Christian Tortel*, Poët-Laval, 1981, p. 84.

8 See Fernand Beaucour, *La Campagne d'Égypte (1798-1801) d'après les dessins inédits de Noël Dejuine...*, Levallois, 1983, vol. 1.

9 *Correspondance de Napoléon 1er...*, pt XXIX, p. 517.

10 Dominique Vivant Denon, *op. cit.*, pt I, pp. viii-ix.

11 *ibid.*, pt II, pp. 1-2.

12 *ibid.*, pt II, pp. 270-71.

13 *ibid.*, pt I, p. 11.

14 *ibid.*, pt II, pp. 11-12.

15 *ibid.*, pt II, p. 78.

16 Jean Baptiste Prosper Jollois, *Journal d'un ingénieur attaché à l'expédition d'Égypte 1798-1802*, Paris, 1904, pt VI, p. 85.

17 *ibid.*, p. 65.

18 Édouard de Villiers du Terrage, *Journal et souvenirs sur l'expédition d'Égypte (1798-1801)*, Paris, 1899, pp. 166-7.

19 *ibid.*, p. 167.

20 Prosper Jollois, *op. cit.*, p. 117.

21 *ibid.*, p. 95.

22 Édouard de Villiers du Terrage, *op. cit.*, pp. 134-5, 138.

23 *Les Français en Égypte...*, pp. 204-5.

24 Antoine Galland, *Tableau de l'Égypte pendant le séjour de l'armée française suivi de l'état militaire et civil de l'armée d'Orient*, Paris, 1804, pp. 211-12.

25 *Les Français en Égypte...*, pp. 211-12.

26 S. Martin, *Histoire de l'expédition française en Égypte*, Paris, 1815, pp. 287-8.

27 *ibid.*, pp. 289-90.

28 Joseph François Louis Grobert, *Description des pyramides de Ghizé, de la ville du Kaire et de ses environs*, Paris, 1801, pp. 109-11.

29 Dominique Vivant Denon, *op. cit.*, pt II, pp. 302-4.

30 *ibid.*, pt II, pp. 19-20.

31 *ibid.*, pt II, p. 161.

32 *ibid.*, pt I, p. 182.

33 See Jean Édouard Goby, *Les quarante éditions, traductions et adaptations du 'Voyage dans la Basse et la Haute Égypte' de Vivant Denon, Cahiers d'histoire égyptienne*, 4th series, pts 5-6, Cairo, 1952, pp. 290-97.

34 Édouard de Villiers du Terrage, *op. cit.*, pp. 232-3.

35 *Description de l'Égypte, Antiquités descriptions*, vol. 1, foreword.

36 *Description de l'Égypte, Antiquités*, pl. 1.

37 *Description de l'Égypte, Antiquités Descriptions*, vol. 1, foreword, pp. x-xi, cxxxvi-cxxxvii.

38 Edme François Jomard, 'Des nouvelles découvertes faites en Égypte et de l'influence qu'elles peuvent avoir sur l'étude des antiquités historiques', *Revue encyclopédique ou Analyse raisonnée des productions les plus remarquables dans la littérature, les sciences et les arts, année 1819*, Paris, 1829, pt II, pp. 334, 336-8.

39 Jean Humbert, 'Égyptologie et égyptomanie: imprégnation dans l'art occidental de quatre siècles d'une cohabitation harmonieuse', *Les Collections égyptiennes dans les musées de Saône-et-Loire*, exhibition, Autun, 27 May-3 October 1988, p. 51.

40 Charles Percier and Pierre François Léonard Fontaine, *Recueil des décorations intérieures...*, Paris, 1812, pl. VIII, p. 22.

41 *ibid.*, p. 11.

42 Théophile Gautier, *Portraits contemporains*, Paris, 1886, pp. 353-4.

43 François René de Chateaubriand, *Itinéraire de Paris à Jérusalem*, Paris, 1811, p. 71.

44 *Les Lettres d'Égypte de Gustave Flaubert*, Antoine Youssef Naaman, ed., Paris, 1965, p. 133.

45 Giovanni Battista Belzoni, *Voyages en Égypte et en Nubie*, Paris, 1979, p. 67.

46 *ibid.*, p. 175.

47 See Sydney Aufrère, *Collections égyptiennes des musées départementaux de Seine-Maritime*, Rouen, 1987.

48 Camille Lagier, *Autour de la pierre de Rosette*, Brussels, 1927, p. 21.

49 *ibid.*, pp. 24-5.

50 *ibid.*, p. 37.

51 *ibid.*, p. 34.

52 Raymond Verninac de Saint-Maur, *Voyage du Luxor en Égypte...*, Paris, 1835.

53 *Correspondance de Napoléon 1er...* pt XXIX, p. 379.

54 Ernest Doblhofer, *Le Déchiffrement des écritures*, Paris, 1959, p. 58.

55 *ibid.*, p. 60.

56 Jean François Champollion, *Précis du système hiéroglyphique des anciens Égyptiens...*, Paris, 1828, p. 79.

57 *idem, Lettres à M. le duc de Blacas d'Aulps relatives au Musée royal égyptien de Turin*, Paris, 1824-6, 1st letter, p. 5.

58 *idem, Lettres et journaux écrits pendant le voyage d'Égypte*, collected and annotated by Hermine Hartleben, Paris, 1909, pt xxxi, p. 181.

59 *idem, Note remise au vice-roi pour la conservation des monuments d'Égypte*, Alexandria, November 1829.

60 'Antiquités égyptiennes...', *Bulletin de la Société de géographie*, vol. 5, January 1836, pp. 67-8.

61 François Arago, quoted in *En Égypte au temps de Flaubert: les premiers photographes, 1839-1860*, exhibition catalogue, undated, p. 1.

62 'Rapport de la Commission nommée par l'Académie des inscriptions pour rédiger les instructions du voyage de M. Maxime du Camp (extrait du procès-verbal de la séance de vendredi 7 septembre 1849)', in Michel Dewachter and Daniel Oster, *Un voyageur en Égypte vers 1850: le Nil de Maxime du Camp*, Paris, 1987, p. 14.

63 *Les Lettres d'Égypte de Gustave Flaubert*, p. 133.

64 Maxime du Camp, *Le Nil (Égypte et Nubie)*, Paris, 1852, p. 348.

CHRONOLOGY

1795

25 OCTOBER After the dissolution of the academies of the Ancien Régime, the Convention creates the National Institute. It is divided into three classes: Physical Sciences and Mathematics; Literature and Fine Arts; Political Science and Ethics.

1797

17 OCTOBER Bonaparte signs the Treaty of Campo Formio with Austria, thus ensuring peace in Europe.

26 OCTOBER The Directoire plans to use the armies made available by the new peace to invade England. Bonaparte is appointed commander-in-chief.

25 DECEMBER Bonaparte is elected to the First Class of the National Institute.

1798

12 JANUARY The Directoire orders the formation of the Army of England.

14 FEBRUARY Foreign Minister Talleyrand submits a report to the Directoire advocating a military intervention in the East to bar the English route to India.

23 FEBRUARY On Bonaparte's advice the invasion of England is abandoned.

5 MARCH The Directoire decides upon the Egyptian expedition.

16 MARCH The Directoire issues an instruction creating the Commission for Arts and Sciences.

12 APRIL Formation of the Army of the Orient. Bonaparte is appointed commander-in-chief.

MAY Nelson is detached from the Cadiz blockade and sent to determine the movements of the French fleet, for the English still have no concrete information about the planned expedition.

19 MAY The fleet, comprising nearly 300 ships under the command of Admiral Brueys and carrying 54,000 civilians and servicemen, sails for Malta where it will join up with the convoys raised in Italy under the command of Major-General Desaix.

11 JUNE Bonaparte takes the island of Malta.

17 JUNE Nelson, who had followed the Italian coast in search of the French, learns that they are at Malta and sets off in pursuit.

19 JUNE Leaving an occupation force in Malta, Bonaparte and the French fleet sail for Egypt.

20 JUNE Reaching Messina, Nelson learns of the fall of Malta and discovers the destination of the expedition.

28 JUNE Nelson passes the French fleet in the night and arrives at Alexandria two days ahead of them. Failing to obtain any information as to their whereabouts, he sails for Syracuse to refit.

1 JULY The French arrive before Alexandria. The forces disembark in a violent storm during which the *Patriote* runs aground.

2 JULY Bonaparte storms the gates of Alexandria which falls at nightfall.

4 JULY The leading sheiks in Alexandria agree to lend their support to the French. The scholars disembark.

5 JULY The fleet anchors off Aboukir.

7 JULY Bonaparte leaves Alexandria and takes the desert route to Cairo.

10 JULY Bonaparte disperses the mamelukes at al Rahmaniya.

13 JULY Bonaparte disperses the mamelukes at Shubra Khayt. They regroup round Cairo.

20 JULY Nelson reaches Syracuse, still looking for the French.

21 JULY Battle of the Pyramids. Bonaparte routes the mameluke forces led by Murad Bey and Ibrahim Bey. Cairo falls. Ibrahim Bey regroups at Bilbays while Murad Bey retreats to Upper Egypt.

1 AUGUST Battle of the Nile. Nelson destroys the French fleet at Aboukir. From now on communications with France will be hampered by the British blockade.

7 AUGUST Bonaparte leaves Cairo for Bilbays in pursuit of Ibrahim Bey.

11 AUGUST After a skirmish at Salihiyya, near Bilbays, Ibrahim Bey flees to Syria.

14 AUGUST Bonaparte returns to Cairo where he learns of the destruction of the French fleet.

22 AUGUST Foundation of the Egyptian Institute.

25 AUGUST General Desaix is sent into Upper Egypt after Murad Bey, who had rejected Bonaparte's peace overtures in the wake of the Battle of the Nile.

29 AUGUST Publication of the first issue of the *Courier de l'Égypte*.

31 AUGUST Desaix reaches Bani Suwayf and begins a fruitless search for Murad Bey.

SEPTEMBER Bonaparte deploys his occupation forces throughout Lower Egypt.

9 SEPTEMBER Turkey declares war on France.

19 SEPTEMBER Bonaparte visits the pyramids at Giza.

1 OCTOBER Publication of the first issue of *La Décade égyptienne*. Brigadier Andréossy conducts the exploration of Lake Manzalah.

7 OCTOBER Desaix defeats Murad Bey at Sediman, temporarily putting him out of action, and takes control of the province of the Fayyum.

19 OCTOBER Two Turkish frigates appear before Alexandria.

21 OCTOBER The inhabitants of Cairo stage a revolt fomented by emissaries from the Ottoman Empire.

24 OCTOBER The Turkish frigates are reinforced by a further sixteen Russian and English men-of-war. An unsuccessful attack is made on the fort at Aboukir.

1 NOVEMBER The Directoire opens peace negotiations with England and the Ottoman Empire.

Vivant Denon leaves Cairo to join Belliard's 21st Regiment in Upper Egypt.

7 DECEMBER General Bon occupies the port of Suez.

23 DECEMBER The Ottoman Empire signs a treaty of alliance with Russia.

26 DECEMBER Bonaparte occupies Suez, where he plans a defensive naval force for the Red Sea.

29 DECEMBER Russia, England and the Kingdom of Naples and Sicily sign a treaty of alliance against France.

1799

5 JANUARY The Ottoman Empire signs a treaty of alliance with England.

6 JANUARY Bonaparte decides to take the offensive against Syria in order to prevent the Ottoman Empire from joining forces with its allies on the Egyptian coast, thus forcing them into a negotiation. By the same token, British ships would be prevented from revictualling in Syria.

22 JANUARY Desaix disperses the mamelukes south of Girga and pursues them as far as the cataracts. Brigadier Andréossy conducts a first exploration of the Natron Lakes.

1 FEBRUARY Desaix takes Syene, thus establishing the conquest of Upper Egypt.

10 FEBRUARY Bonaparte leaves Cairo to open the Syrian campaign.

20 FEBRUARY Fall of al Arish.

25 FEBRUARY Bonaparte enters Gaza.

3 MARCH Commodore Sidney Smith is appointed commander of the English squadron before Alexandria. Corfu, the last of the Ionian Islands in French hands, capitulates to the Russo-Turkish forces after a long siege.

7 MARCH Fall of Jaffa, where the army will contract the plague.

14 MARCH Leaving Jaffa, Bonaparte marches on Acre, taking Haifa on the way. The English squadron arrives before Acre, bringing Turkish reinforcements to Djezzar Pasha.

19 MARCH The siege of Acre begins.

11 APRIL Reaching Nazareth, Kléber attacks the enemy at Canaan and flings it back towards the Jordan.

16 APRIL Battle of Mount Tabor. Bonaparte's intervention in aid of Kléber carries the day.

24 APRIL Unrest is growing in Lower Egypt. A fanatic called al Mahdi incites the local population to massacre the 1,500-strong garrison at Damanhur.

9 MAY Al Mahdi's troops are dispersed at Damanhur and the town is looted, burned and sacked as an example.

20 MAY Bonaparte abandons the siege of Acre. The retreat begins.

14 JUNE Bonaparte makes a triumphant entry to Cairo on his return from the Syrian campaign.

11 JULY The English squadron, carrying the Turkish forces, reappears before Alexandria.

17 JULY The Turks capture Aboukir.

25 JULY Bonaparte routs the Turkish forces at Aboukir, although the fort will hold out for several weeks longer.

29 JULY Momentous sitting of the Egyptian Institute at which the discovery of the Rosetta stone shortly before is announced.

11 AUGUST Learning of the precarious situation in Europe and that the Directoire wish him to return to France, Bonaparte decides to leave Egypt.

14-16 AUGUST The English attack Qusayr from the Red Sea but are repulsed by Donzelot.

17 AUGUST Bonaparte renews peace overtures to the Ottoman Empire, but the negotiations are prevented by the British.

23 AUGUST Bonaparte leaves for France.

24 AUGUST Kléber becomes general-in-chief of the Army of the Orient.

16 OCTOBER Bonaparte reaches Paris.

NOVEMBER The Turkish offensive reopens at Damietta. They are repulsed by Brigadier Verdier.

Deciding to evacuate Egypt, Kléber opens negotiations with the Grand Vizier.

9 NOVEMBER *Coup d'état* of 18 Brumaire. Bonaparte becomes First Consul of France.

1800

24 JANUARY Convention of al Arish, whereby the French are to leave with arms and baggage and General Kléber is to return all conquered territories to the Turks.

FEBRUARY The British cabinet demands that the capitulation of the French be unconditional. By this time Kléber has given all the positions on the right bank of the Nile and in Upper Egypt back to the Turks. Countermanding his orders to the army, he recalls it to defend Cairo against the Grand Vizier.

20 MARCH Battle of Heliopolis. Kléber puts the Grand Vizier's army to flight.

21 MARCH Kléber marches on Bilbays and captures the remaining Turkish forces.

24 MARCH Kléber leaves Salihiyya for Cairo after retaking Damietta and all the positions in the delta lost through the al Arish agreement.

25 MARCH A second uprising in Cairo is bloodily suppressed.

27 MARCH Kléber reaches Cairo and pardons the insurgents.

19 APRIL The English are routed at Suez. Alliance with Murad Bey.

14 JUNE Kléber is murdered in Cairo by Suleiman al Halebi, a young fanatic sent by the defeated Grand Vizier. General Menou takes his place as supreme commander of the French forces in Egypt.

5 SEPTEMBER Malta falls to the British.

1801

8 MARCH The English land at Aboukir. Menou stays in Cairo and sends Lanusse to stop the English taking Alexandria.

18 MARCH The British take Aboukir.

21 MARCH Menou is defeated at Canopus. The British blockade Alexandria. Plague breaks out amongst Belliard's troops in Cairo.

22 APRIL Death of Murad Bey.

10 MAY The British take al Rahmaniya. Lagrange retreats to Cairo.

18 JUNE The British land at Qusayr and march on Qena under command of General Baird.

27 JUNE Belliard negotiates the evacuation of Cairo with arms and baggage.

8 JULY The English reach Qena, where the inhabitants are already demolishing the forts.

21 AUGUST The English take the fort at Marabut and master the channels in the old port of Alexandria.

2 SEPTEMBER Menou capitulates and agrees to hand the scholars' works and all their collections to the English. A group of scholars visits General Hutchinson and persuades him to at least let them take their work and personal collections with them. Major works of art, including the Rosetta stone, will nevertheless be confiscated by the English. By the end of the month most of the French will have left for France.

18 OCTOBER Menou embarks for France.

1802

Denon publishes his *Voyage dans la Basse et la Haute Égypte*.

18 FEBRUARY The scholars are convened to a meeting ordered by the Consuls in order to select a publishing commission for the *Description de l'Égypte*.

25 MARCH The peace treaty between England and France is signed in Amiens.

1803

1 JANUARY Marcel becomes head of the State Press which will print the *Description de l'Égypte*.

1808

1 JANUARY A delegation from the commission presents the Emperor Napoleon with the first volume of the *Description de l'Égypte*.

1814
The Empire collapses. Louis XVIII gives his patronage to the *Description de l'Égypte*.

1815
1 JANUARY Economies are ordered and Marcel is removed from the Presses of the Republic. Jomard begins to search for funding. From now on the book advances very slowly.

1816
17 NOVEMBER In Thebes Belzoni manages to load the bust of Rameses II on to the boat that will transport it to Cairo.

1817
1 AUGUST Belzoni enters the interior of the temple of Abu Simbel.
OCTOBER Belzoni discovers the tombs of Rameses I and Seti I.

1818
Belzoni opens up the second pyramid at Giza. Henry Salt sells his first collection of Egyptian antiquities to the British Museum.

1820
Charles Louis Panckoucke is authorized by Louis XVIII to publish a second edition of the *Description de l'Égypte*.

1822
Louis XVIII purchases the Dendera zodiac.
27 SEPTEMBER Champollion reads his *Lettre à M. Dacier...* to the Académie. He has discovered the key to the hieroglyphs.

1824
Drovetti sells his first collection of Egyptian antiquities to the king of Sardinia, Charles Felix. Henry Salt sells his second collection to the king of France.

1826
6 JANUARY Jomard presents Charles X with the final plates of the *Description de l'Égypte*.

1827
Inauguration of the two Egyptian rooms in the Musée Charles X at the Louvre. Charles X purchases Drovetti's second collection for the Louvre.

1836
Drovetti sells his third collection to the king of Prussia.
25 OCTOBER The Luxor obelisk is erected in the Place de la Concorde.

1842-5
Lepsius's expedition to Egypt and Nubia.

1858
Auguste Mariette is appointed director of works on Egyptian antiquities by the viceroy of Egypt, Said Pasha.

1862
The Institut d'Égypte is re-formed in Cairo under the name Institut égyptien.

BIBLIOGRAPHY

GENERAL

Bonaparte en Égypte, exhibition, Musée de l'Orangerie, Paris, 1938.

CARRÉ, Jean Marie, *Voyageurs et écrivains français en Égypte*, 2 vols, Institut français d'archéologie orientale, Paris, 1956.

CLAYTON, Peter A., *The Rediscovery of Ancient Egypt: artists and travellers in the nineteenth century*, Thames and Hudson, London, 1982.

DAWSON, Warren R. and UPHILL, Eric P., *Who was Who in Egyptology*, 2nd edn, The Egypt Exploration Society, London, 1972.

Dictionnaire Napoléon, Jean Tulard, ed., Fayard, Paris, 1987.

Égypte-France, exhibition, Musée des arts décoratifs, Pavillon de Marsan, Paris, 1949, Les Presses artistiques, Paris, 1949.

FAGAN, Brian M., *L'Aventure archéologique en Égypte: voleurs de tombes, touristes et archéologues en Égypte*, Pygmalion/Gérard Watelet, Paris, 1981.

MONTET, Pierre, *Isis, ou À la recherche de l'Égypte ensevelie*, Hachette, Paris, 1956.

THIERS, Adolphe, *Histoire de la Révolution française*, Furne, Jouvet, Paris, 1870-72.

Histoire du Consulat et de l'Empire, Paulin, Paris, 1845-69.

VERCOUTIER, Jean, *À la recherche de l'Égypte oubliée*, Découvertes Gallimard no. 1, Gallimard, Paris, 1986.

RELATIONS BETWEEN EGYPT AND EUROPE PRIOR TO BONAPARTE'S EXPEDITION

BEAUCOUR, Fernand, *Lettres, décisions et actes de Napoléon à Pont-de-Briques et au camp de Boulogne*, pt I, Société de Sauvegarde du château impérial de Pont-de-Briques, Levallois, 1979.

BOSSUET, Jacques Bénigne, *Discours sur l'histoire universelle à Monseigneur le Dauphin*, 2 parts in 1 volume, Jacques Guerrier, Lyons, 1697.

SAVARY, Claude Étienne, *Lettres sur l'Égypte*, 3 vols, Bleuet Jeune, Paris, 1785-6.

SOLÉ, Jacques, 'L'Égyptomanie du XVIe au XVIIe siècle', *Annales économies sociétés civilisations*, no. 2, March-April 1972, pp. 473-82.

VOLNEY, Constantin François de Chassebœuf, Comte, *Voyages en Syrie et en Égypte, pendant les années 1783, 1784 et 1785*, 2 vols, Volland, Desenne, Paris, 1789.

BONAPARTE'S EXPEDITION TO EGYPT

AL JABARTI, Abd al Rahman, *Journal d'un notable du Caire durant l'expédition française 1798-1801*, Albin Michel, Paris, 1979.

Annuaire de la République française, calculé pour le méridien du Caire, l'an IX de l'ère française, Imprimerie nationale, Cairo, 1800-1801.

ARMANT CALLIAT, Louis, *Vivant Denon 1747-1825 article nécrologique*, Musée de Chalon-sur-Saône, Chalon-sur-Saône, 1964.

BALLIÈRE, Henri, *En Égypte—Alexandrie—Port Saïd—Suez—Le Caire—Journal d'un touriste*, J. B. Baillière, Paris, 1867.

BEAUCOUR, Fernand, *La Campagne d'Égypte (1798-1801) d'après les dessins inédits de Noël Dejuine, du 20e régiment de Dragons*, Société de Sauvegarde du château impérial du Pont-de-Briques, Levallois, 1983.

'Noël Dejuine d'après "Sous dix Rois" de Boucher de Perthes', *Études napoléoniennes*, 1986.

0 'L'Institut d'Égypte et ses travaux', *Souvenir napoléonien*, July 1970.

BERNOYER, François, *Avec Bonaparte en Égypte et en Syrie 1798-1800, 19 lettres inédites présentées par Christian Tortel*, Poët-Laval, 1981.

BERTHIER, Louis Alexandre, *Mémoires. Campagne d'Égypte*, Baudouin Frères, Paris, 1827.

CAILLEUX, Pierre Louis, 'Campagne d'Égypte et de Syrie', *Carnet de la Sabretache*, January—February 1932.

CHALBRAND, Gaspard Antoine, *Les Français en Égypte ou Souvenirs des campagnes d'Égypte et de Syrie par un officier de l'expédition*, Just Jean Étienne Roy, ed., A. Mame, Tours, 1875.

La Chalcographie du Louvre, Histoire et description des collections, annexe I, La Description de l'Égypte (nos. 4529-5435), Paris, 1930.

CHARLES-ROUX, François, *Bonaparte gouverneur d'Égypte*, Plon, Paris, 1936.

Les Origines de l'expédition d'Égypte, Plon, Paris, 1910.

CHATELAIN, Jean, *Dominique Vivant Denon et le Louvre de Napoléon*, Librairie académique Perrin, Paris, 1973.

Courier de l'Égypte, Cairo, 1798-1801.

La Décade égyptienne, Journal littéraire et d'économie politique, Cairo, 1798-1801.

DEHÉRAIN, Henri, 'La dernière phase de la Commission des sciences et des arts de l'expédition d'Égypte', *Comité des Travaux historiques et scientifiques, Bulletin de la section de géographie*, pt XLIX, 1934, pp. 133-45.

L'Égypte turque. Pachas et mamalouks du XVIe au XVIIe siècle. L'expédition du général Bonaparte, Plon, Paris, 1931.

'L'exploration de la Haute-Égypte par la Commission des sciences et des arts de l'armée d'Orient en 1799', *Revue historique*, March-April 1931, pp. 256-65.

'L'Institut d'Égypte', *Revue Bleue*, January—December 1932, pp. 644-650.

DENON, Dominique Vivant, *Point de lendemain, par Monsieur Dominique Vivant Denon suivie d'une notice historique d'Anatole France*, Jean Jacques Pauvert, 1959.

Voyage dans la Basse et la Haute Égypte pendant les campagnes du général Bonaparte, Didot, Paris, 1802.

DESAIX, Louis Charles Antoine, 'Notes de voyage', *Carnet de Sabretache*, 1898, 1899.

Description de l'Égypte, Paris, 1809-26; 2nd edn, Panckoucke, Paris, 1821-6.

DESVERNOIS, Nicolas Philibert, *Mémoires*, Plon, Paris, 1898.

DESVOYES, M., 'Les Débuts de l'imprimerie en Égypte', *Institut Napoléon. Recueil de travaux et documents*, 1942.

DOGUEREAU, Jean Pierre, *Journal de l'expédition d'Égypte*, Perrin, Paris, 1904.

L'Égypte et l'expédition française de 1798 à 1801, exhibition, Donjon Lacataye, Mont-de-Marsan, 1978-9.

ESTRE, Henry d', *Bonaparte le mirage oriental, Égypte, 1798-9*, Plon, Paris, 1946.

FAIVRE D'ARCIER, Amaury, *Les Agents français en Égypte sous le Consulat et l'Empire*, École pratique des hautes études, thesis, Paris, 1988.

GALLAND, Antoine, *Tableau de l'Égypte pendant le séjour de l'armée française suivi de l'état militaire et civil de l'armée d'Orient*, 2 vols, Galland, Paris, 1804.

GAUTHIER, Henri, 'Vivant Denon en Égypte (juillet 1798—août 1799)', *Bulletin de l'Institut d'Égypte*, pt V, no. 2, 1922-3, pp. 163-93.

GILLISPIE, Charles Coulston and DEWACHTER, Michel, *Monuments de l'Égypte: édition impériale de 1809*, 2 vols, Hazan, Paris, 1988.

GOBY, Jean Édouard, 'Les quarante éditions, traductions et adaptations du "Voyage dans la basse et la Haute Égypte" de Vivant Denon', *Cahiers d'histoire égyptienne*, IV, nos. 5-6, Cairo, December 1952, pp. 290-316.

'Les travaux d'un siècle en Égypte sur l'expédition française de 1798-1801', *Revue de l'Institut Napoléon*, no. 54, January 1955, pp. 4-16.

'Nouvelle contribution à la bibliographie de l'expédition de l'Égypte', *Revue de l'Institut Napoléon*, no. 132, 1976, pp. 207-213.

GODET, Maurice, 'Mémoires', *Carnet de la Sabretache*, 1927.

GODLEWSKA, Anna, *The Napoleonic Survey of Egypt. A Masterpiece of Cartographic and Early Nineteenth-Century Fieldwork*, University of Toronto Press, 1988.

GROBERT, Joseph François Louis, *Description des pyramides de Ghizé, de la ville du Kaire et de ses environs*, Logeret-Petiet, Paris, 1801.

GUEMARD, Gabriel, 'Essai d'histoire de l'Institut d'Égypte', *Bulletin de l'Institut d'Égypte*, pt VI, 1923-4, pp. 42-84.

HERMANT, Abel, 'L'Égypte en 1798 d'après le journal

de H. J. Redouté', *Revue bleue*, pt III, 32nd year, 1st semester 1895, pp. 48-52, 173-8, 235-41, 304-10.

HEROLD, Jean Christopher, *Bonaparte in Egypt*, Hamish Hamilton, London, 1962.

HOUDARD, L., 'Bonaparte à el-Arich', *Institut Napoléon. Recueil de travaux et documents*, 1942.

HOUTH, 'Jomard l'Égyptien', *Bulletin de l'Institut d'Égypte*, pt XV, 1932-3, pp. 259-66.

HUBERT, Emmanuelle, 'À propos d'un bicentenaire: Napoléon Bonaparte et l'égyptologie', *Archeologia*, no. 28, May—June 1969, pp. 82-5.

JOLLOIS, Jean Baptiste Prosper, *Journal d'un ingénieur attaché à l'expédition d'Égypte 1798-1802 publié par P. Lefèvre-Pontalis. Notes de voyage et d'archéologie rédigées par Prosper Jollois avec des fragments tirés des journaux de Fourier, Jomard, Delille, [sic], Saint-Genis, Descotils, Balzac et Coraboeuf, Bibliothèque égyptologique*, pt VI, Ernest Leroux, Paris, 1904.

LA JONQUIÈRE, C. de, *L'Expédition d'Égypte, 1798-1801*, 5 vols, Charles-Lavauzelle, Paris, 1899-1907.

Journal d'un Dragon d'Égypte (14e Dragons). Notes recueillies par le commandant Merruau, Paris, 1899.

KÖSEOGLU, Hamdi, *Histoire des forces armées turques. Période ottomane, 1789-1802: la guerre franco-ottomane (l'expédition de Napoléon en Égypte)* (in Turkish), Genelkurmay Baskanligi, Ankara, 1987.

LAURENS, Henry, *Les Origines intellectuelles de l'expédition d'Égypte. L'Orientalisme islamisant en France (1698-1798)*, Isis, Paris, 1987.

Kléber en Égypte, 1798-1800. Kléber et Bonaparte, 1798-1799, 2 pts, IFAO, Cairo, 1988.

LEGRAIN, Georges, 'Inscriptions françaises de Haute Égypte (Thèbes, Esneh, Edfou, Assouan, Philae)', *Séances et travaux de l'Académie des sciences morales et politiques*, Paris 1911.

MARTIN, S., *Histoire de l'expédition française en Égypte*, 2 vols, Eberhart, Paris, 1815.

MARY, M.M., MAURY, Alfred and JOMARD, Edme François, *Notices sur M. de Villiers du Terrage, Inspecteur général des ponts et chaussées*, Dunod, Paris, undated.

Mémoires sur l'Égypte publiés pendant les campagnes du général Bonaparte dans les années VI et VII, 4 vols, P. Didot *l'aîné*, Paris, 1799-1800.

METZ, Jean de, and LEGRAIN, Georges, *Aux pays de Napoléon. L'Égypte*, J. Rey, Grenoble, 1913.

MICHALON, R. and VERNET, J., 'Adaptation d'une armée française de la fin du XVIIIe siècle à un théâtre d'opérations proche-oriental (Égypte, 1798-1801)', *La Revue internationale d'histoire militaire*, no. 49, 1980.

MIOT, Jacques François, *Mémoires pour servir à l'histoire des expéditions en Égypte et en Syrie*, revised 2nd edn, le Normant, Paris, 1814.

MOIRET, Joseph Marie, *Mémoires sur l'expédition d'Égypte*, P. Belfond, Paris, 1984.

MUNIER, Henri, *Tables de la 'Description de l'Égypte' suivis d'une bibliographie sur l'expédition française de Bonaparte*, Institut français d'archéologie orientale, Cairo, 1943. (Publications de la Société royale de géographie d'Égypte.)

NAPOLEON I, *Correspondance de Napoléon Ier publiée par ordre de l'empereur Napoléon III*, Plon-Nourrit, Paris, pt IV, 5 March—21 September 1798; pt XXIX: Napoleon's works at St Helena, 1870.

Mémoires pour servir à l'histoire de France sous Napoléon, écrits à Sainte-Hélène... publiées sur les manuscrits entièrement corrigés de la main de Napoléon... écrits par le général Gourgaud, 2 vols, Didot père et fils, Paris, 1823.

NOË, de, *Mémoires relatifs à l'expédition anglaise*, Paris, 1826.

NORRY, C., *Relations de l'expédition d'Égypte*, Charles Pougens, Paris, 1798-9.

PIETRO, D. di, *Voyage historique en Égypte pendant*

les campagnes des généraux Bonaparte, Kléber et Menou, l'Huillier, Paris, 1818.

REYBAUD, L., *Histoire scientifique et militaire de l'expédition française en Égypte et atlas*, 10 vols texts, 2 vols plates, A. J. Denin, Paris, 1800-36.

REYNIER, Jean Louis, *Mémoires. Campagne d'Égypte*, Baudouin Frères, Paris, 1827.

SCHNEPP, Dr B., 'Discours prononcé sur la tombe de Jomard', *Mémoires de l'Institut égyptien*, pt I, 1862, pp. 11-15.

SCHWOB, 'Notices sur Jomard', *Bulletin de l'Institut égyptien*, no. 8, 1862-3, pp. 48-51.

THIRY, Baron Jean, *Napoléon Bonaparte. Bonaparte en Égypte, décembre 1797—24 août 1799*, Berger Levrault, Paris, 1973.

THOUMAS, General, *L'Agenda de Malus. Souvenirs de l'expédition d'Égypte (1798-1801)*, H. Champion, Paris, 1892.

GENERAL V..., 'Les tenues spéciales à l'armée d'Égypte (1798-1799)', *Carnet de la Sabretache*.

VERTRAY, Captain, *Journal d'un officier de l'armée d'Égypte (le capitaine Vertray). L'armée française en Égypte 1798-1801.* Manuscript edited and published by Henri Gallichet, known as H. Galli, G. Charpentier, Paris, 1883.

VIGO-ROUSSILLON, François, *Journal de campagne*, France-Empire, Paris, 1981.

VILLIERS DU TERRAGE, Édouard de, *Journal et souvenirs sur l'expédition d'Égypte (1798-1801)*, Plon-Nourrit, Paris, 1899.

WASSER, Amin Sami, *L'Information et la presse officielle en Égypte jusqu'à la fin de l'occupation française*, Institut français d'archéologie orientale, Cairo, 1975.

THE EGYPTIAN REVIVAL

BALTRUSAITIS, Jurgis, *Essai sur la légende d'un mythe, la quête d'Isis, introduction à l'égyptomanie*, Jeu Savant collection, O. Perrin, Paris, 1967.

BELLONCLE, Michel, *La Ville et son eau, Paris et ses fontaines*, Serg, Paris, 1978.

BRUNET, Marcelle and PRÉAUD, Tamara, *Sèvres: des origines à nos jours*, Office du Livre, Fribourg, 1978.

CARROTT, Richard G., *The Egyptian Revival, its Sources, Monuments and Meaning 1808-1858*, University of California Press, Berkeley, Los Angeles/London, 1978.

CONNER, Patrick, *The Inspiration of Egypt, its Influence on British Artists, Travellers and Designers 1700—1900*, exhibition, Brighton Museum, 7 May—17 July 1983; Manchester City Art Gallery, 4 August—17 September 1983.

De David à Delacroix: la peinture française de 1774 à 1830, exhibition, Grand Palais, Paris, 16 November 1974—3 February 1975, Musées nationaux, Paris, 1974.

GAUTIER, Théophile, *Portraits contemporains*, Charpentiers, Paris, 1886.

Les Lettres d'Égypte de Gustave Flaubert d'après les manuscrits autographes: édition critique, Antoine Youssef Naaman, ed., A. G. Nizet, Paris, 1965.

GRANDJEAN, Serge, 'Les Fournitures de la manufacture de Sèvres à l'empereur Napoléon Ier', *Bulletin des musées de France*, September—October 1947, pp. 32-4.

'L'Influence égyptienne à Sèvres', *Publicaties Van het Genootschap voor Napoleontische studien*, September 1955, pp. 99-105.

HAUTECŒUR, Louis, 'L'Expédition d'Égypte et l'art français', *Revue des études napoléoniennes*, pt XXIX, January—June 1925, pp. 81-7.

HUMBERT, Jean, 'Aïda entre l'égyptologie et l'égyptomanie', *L'Avant-scène*, July—August 1976, pp. 9-14.

'À propos de l'égyptomanie dans l'œuvre de Verdi: attribution à Auguste Mariette d'un scénario anonyme de l'opéra Aïda', *Revue de musicologie*, pt LXII, no. 2, pp. 229-55.

'L'Égyptomanie dans l'art occidental', *Silex*, no. 13, 1979, pp. 105-14.

'Égyptologie et égyptomanie: imprégnation dans l'art occidental de quatre siècles d'une cohabitation harmonieuse', *Les Collections égyptiennes dans les musées de Saône-et-Loire*, exhibition, Bibliothèque municipale, Musée Rollin, Muséum national d'histoire naturelle, Autun, 27 May—3 October 1988; Musée des Ursulines, Mâcon, 21 October 1988—15 January 1989.

'Les monuments égyptiens et égyptisants de Paris', *Bulletin de la Société française d'égyptologie*, October 1971, pp. 25-62.

Quand l'Égypte fleurit à Paris, Touring Club de France, Paris, 1976.

JUIN, Hubert and NIEPCE, Janine, *Fontaines et bassins*, ACE, Paris, 1981.

LACROIX-SPACENSKA, Bernadette, *Aqueducs et fontaines: Bordeaux XIXe siècle*, Office de Tourisme, Bordeaux, 1987.

LECLANT, Jean, 'En quête de l'égyptomanie', *Revue de l'art*, no. 5, 1969, pp. 82-8.

Le Néoclassicisme français: dessins des musées de Province, exhibition, Grand Palais, Paris, 6 December 1974—10 February 1975, Musées nationaux, Paris, 1974.

PERCIER, Charles and FONTAINE, Pierre François Léonard, *Recueil des décorations intérieures comprenant tout ce qui a rapport à l'ameublement...*, Paris, 1812.

THORNTON, Lynne, *Les Orientalistes peintres voyageurs 1828-1908*, ACR, Paris, 1983.

THE CONSULS IN EGYPT AND THE EUROPEAN COLLECTIONS

AUFRÈRE, Sydney, *Collections égyptiennes des musées départementaux de Seine-Maritime*, Musées départementaux de la Seine-Maritime, Rouen, 1987.

BELZONI, Giovanni Battista, *Voyages en Égypte et en Nubie*, Pygmalion/Gérard Watelet, Paris, 1979.

Narrative of the Operations and Recent Discoveries within the Pyramids, Temples, Tombs and Excavations, in Egypt and Nubia; and a journey to the coast of the Red Sea, in search of the ancient Berenice; and another to the oasis of Jupiter Ammon, John Murray, London, 1820.

CHAMPOLLION, Jean François, *Notice descriptive des monuments égyptiens du musée Charles X*, Crapelet, Paris, 1827.

CLOT, Dr Antoine-Barthélmi, known as CLOT BEY, *Aperçu général sur l'Égypte*, 2 vols, Méline, Cans, Brussels, 1840.

CURTO, Silvio, *Storia del Museo di Torino*, Turin, 1976.

De la place Louis-XV à la place de la Concorde, exhibition, Musée Carnavalet, Paris, 17 May—14 August 1982.

HALLS, J. J., *The Life and Correspondence of Henry Salt... Consul-General in Egypt*, 2 vols, Richard Bentley, London, 1834.

HUMBERT, Jean, 'Les Obélisques de Paris, projets et réalisations', *Revue de l'Art*, no. 23, 1974, pp. 9-29.

JOANNIS, Léon de, *Campagne pittoresque du Luxor*, Mme Huzard, Paris, 1835.

KANAWATY, Monique, 'Les Acquisitions du musée Charles X', *Bulletin de la Société française d'égyptologie*, no. 104, October 1985, p. 31.

'Identification de pièces de la collection Drovetti au musée du Louvre', *Revue d'égyptologie*, pt XXXVII, 1986.

LEBAS, Jean Baptiste Apollinaire, *L'Obélisque de Luxor. Historique de sa translation à Paris, description des travaux auxquels il a donné lieu...*, Carilian-Gœury et V. Dalmont, Paris, 1839.

L'HÔTE, Nestor, *Notice bibliographique sur les obélisques égyptiens et en particulier sur l'obélisque de Louqsor*, Leleux, Paris, 1836.

NELSON, Monique and PIERINI, Gisèle, *Catalogue des Antiquités égyptiennes*, Musée Borely, Marseilles, 1978.

RIFAUD, Jean Jacques, *Tableau de l'Égypte, de la Nubie et des lieux circonvoisins*, Treuttel et Wurtz, Paris, 1830.

Voyage en Égypte en Nubie et lieux circonvoisins depuis 1805 jusqu'en 1827, Paris, undated.

ROUGÉ, Emmanuel, *'Rapport adressé à M. le Directeur général des musées nationaux sur l'expédition scientifique des principales collections égyptiennes renfermées dans les divers musées publics de l'Europe'*, *Moniteur universel*, 7 and 8 March 1851.

VERCOUTTER, Jean, *'L'Obélisque de la place de la Concorde'*, *Archeologia*, no. 234, April 1988, pp. 36-9.

VERNINAC DE SAINT-MAUR, Raymond, *Voyage du Luxor en Égypte entrepris par ordre du roi pour transporter de Thèbes à Paris l'un des obélisques de Sésotris*, Arthur Bertrand, Paris, 1835.

DECIPHERING THE HIEROGLYPHS

'Antiquités égyptiennes: mesures administratives récemment prises a ce sujet sur le vice-roi d'Égypte', *Bulletin de la société de géographie*, pt V, January 1836, pp. 65-70.

BARGUET, Paul, *'L'Œuvre de Champollion'*, *Archeologia*, no. 52, November 1972, pp. 30-36.

CHAMPOLLION, Jean François, *Aperçu des résultats historiques de la découverte de l'alphabet hiéroglyphique égyptien*, Fain, Paris, 1827.

Dictionnaire égyptien en écriture hiéroglyphique, publié d'après les manuscrits autographes et sous les auspices de M. Villemain par M. Champollion-Figeac, Firmin Didot Frères, Paris, 1841.

Grammaire égyptienne, ou Principes généraux de l'écriture sacrée égyptienne appliquée à la représentation de la langue parlée, Firmin Didot Frères, Paris, 1836-41.

Lettres à M. le duc de Blacas d'Aulps relatives au Musée royal égyptien de Turin, Firmin Didot, Paris, 1824-26.

Lettres et journaux écrits pendant le voyage d'Égypte, collected and annotated by Hermine Hartleben, *Bibliothèque égyptologique*, pt XXXI, Ernest Leroux, Paris, 1909.

Monuments de l'Égypte et de la Nubie d'après les dessins exécutés sur les lieux sous la direction de Champollion le jeune et les descriptions autographes qu'il a laissées, 4 vols, Firmin Didot Frères, Paris, 1835-45.

Précis du système hiéroglyphique des anciens Égyptiens ou Recherches sur les éléments premiers de cette écriture sacrée, 2e éd. revue par l'auteur et augmentée de la Lettre à M. Dacier... relative à l'alphabet des hiéroglyphes phonétiques..., Imprimerie royale, Paris, 1828.

CHAMPOLLION-FIGEAC, Aimé, *Les Deux Champollion, leur vie et leur œuvre, leur correspondance archéologique relative au Dauphiné et à l'Égypte, étude complète de la biographie et de la bibliographie 1778—1867 d'après des documents inédits*, X. Drevet, Grenoble, 1887.

CURTO, SILVIO, *'Champollion en Italie et en Égypte'*, *Archeologia*, no. 52, November 1972, pp. 21-5.

DAUMAS, François, *'Champollion le jeune déchiffre les hiéroglyphes'*, *Archeologia*, no. 52, November 1972, pp. 10-20.

DOBLHOFER, Ernest, *Le Déchiffrement des écritures*, Signe des Temps, Arthaud, Paris, 1959.

DUJARDIN, Dr., *'Les Hiéroglyphes de la langue égyptienne à propos de la grammaire de M. Champol-*

lion', *Revue des deux mondes*, pt VII, 1836, pp. 199-213.

DUPONT-SOMMER, André, *Champollion et l'Académie des inscriptions et belles-lettres; Discours pour la cérémonie du 20 octobre 1972 en l'honneur de Champollion*, Institut de France, Paris, 1972.

Champollion et ses amis: Lecture faite dans la séance publique annuelle du 24 novembre 1972, Institut de France, Paris, 1972.

HARTLEBEN, Hermine, *Champollion: sa vie et son œuvre 1790-1832*, Pygmalion/Gérard Watelet, Paris, 1983.

LACOUTURE, Jean, *Champollion une vie de lumières*, Bernard Grasset, Paris, 1988.

LAGIER, Camille, *Autour de la pierre de Rosette*, Fondation égyptologique, Brussels, 1927.

LECLANT, Jean, *'Champollion et le collège de France'*, *Bulletin de la Société française d'égyptologie*, no. 95, October 1982, pp. 32-46.

'Sur Huyot et l'Hôte', *Bulletin de la Société française d'égyptologie*, no. 32, December 1961, pp. 35-42.

Naissance de l'écriture cunéiforme et hiéroglyphes, exhibition, Galerie nationale du Grand Palais, Paris, 7 May-9 August 1932, Réunion des musées nationaux, Paris, 1982.

QUONIAM, Pierre, *'Champollion et le musée du Louvre'*, *Bulletin de la Société française d'égyptologie*, no. 95, October 1982, pp. 47-61.

ROSELLINI, Ippolito, *I Monumenti dell'Egitto e della Nubia disegnati dalla spedizione scientifico-letteraria toscana in Egitto, distribuiti in ordine di materie interpretati ed illustrati dal dott. Ippolito Rosellini*, N. Capurro, Pisa, 1832-44.

SACY, Antoine Isaac Silvestre de, *Lettre au citoyen Chaptal au sujet de l'inscription égyptienne du monument trouvé à Rosette*, Imprimerie de la République, Paris, 1801-2.

SAULCY, F. de, *'Les Hiéroglyphes de la langue égyptienne, à propos d'une critique de la grammaire de Champollion par feu le docteur Dujardin'*, *Revue archéologique*, pt 1, 15 April-15 September 1844, pp. 341-62.

VANDIER D'ABBADIE, J., *Nestor l'Hôte (1804-1842): choix de documents conservés à la Bibliothèque nationale et aux archives du musée du Louvre*, E. J. Brill, Leyden, 1963.

VERCOUTTER, Jean, *'Dans les pas de Champollion'*, *Bulletin de la Société française d'égyptologie*, no. 95, October 1982, pp. 5-8.

YOUNG, Thomas, *An Account of Some Recent Discoveries in Hieroglyphical Literature and Egyptian Antiquities including the author's original alphabet as extended by Mr Champollion with a translation of five unpublished Greek and Egyptian manuscripts*, John Murray, London, 1823.

YOYOTTE, Jean, *'Le Panthéon égyptien de Jean-François Champollion'*, *Bulletin de la Société française d'égyptologie*, no. 95, October 1982, pp. 76-108.

'Champollion', *Archeologia*, no. 52, November 1972, pp. 8-9.

TRAVELLERS AND EGYPTOLOGISTS

BURCKHARDT, John Lewis, *Travels in Nubia*, John Murray, London, 1822.

CAILLIAUD, Frédéric, *Recherche sur les arts, les usages de la vie civile et domestique des anciens peuples de l'Égypte, de la Nubie et de l'Éthiopie, suivie de détails sur les mœurs et coutumes des peuples modernes des mêmes contrées...*, Debure Frères, Paris, 1831.

Voyage à l'oasis de Thèbes et dans les déserts situés à l'orient et à l'occident de la Thébaïde, fait pendant les années 1815, 1816, 1817 et 1818 par M. Frédéric

Cailliaud... rédigé et publié par Jomard... contenant 1° le voyage à l'oasis de Dakel, par M. le Chevalier Drovetti... 2° le journal du premier voyage de M. Cailliaud en Nubie... 3° des recherches sur les oasis..., Imprimerie royale, Paris, 1821.

Voyage à Méroé, au fleuve Blanc au delà de Fâzoql, dans le midi du royaume de Sennâr, à Syouah et dans cinq autres oasis, fait dans les années 1819, 1820, 1821 et 1822, Imprimerie royale, Paris, 1826-27.

CURTO, Silvio, *'Jean-François Champollion et l'Italie'*, *Bulletin de la Société française d'égyptologie*, no. 65, October 1972, pp. 13-24.

DU CAMP, Maxime, *Égypte, Nubie, Palestine et Syrie. Dessins photographiques recueillis pendant les années 1849, 1850 et 1851, accompagnés d'un texte explicatif et précédés d'une introduction*, Paris, 1852.

Le Nil (Égypte et Nubie), Librairie Nouvelle, Paris, 1855.

En Égypte au temps de Flaubert: les premier photographes 1839-1860, exhibition by the public relations department of Kodak-Pathé designed by Marie-Thérèse and André Jammes, undated.

Hector Horeau: 1801-1872, Exhibition, Musée des arts décoratifs, Paris, 27 April—1 July 1979.

HOREAU, Hector, *Panorama d'Égypte et de Nubie*, Paris, 1841.

LEPSIUS, Karl Richard, *Denkmäler aus Aegypten und Aethiopien*, 12 vols, Nicolai, Berlin, 1841-1859.

MAYER, Luigi, *Views in Egypt from the original drawings in the possession of Sir R. Ainslie... with historical observations*, R. Bowyer, London, 1801.

PRISSE D'AVENNES, Émile, *'Archéologie égyptienne. Lettre à M. Champollion-Figeac, du Thouthmoséium de Karnak le 27 Mai 1843'*, *Revue archéologique*, pt II, 15 October 1844-15 March 1845, pp. 723-34.

Histoire de l'art égyptien d'après les monuments depuis les temps les plus reculés jusqu'à la domination romaine, Arthur Bertrand, Paris, 1879.

Monuments égyptiens, bas-relief, peintures, inscriptions, etc... d'après les dessins exécutés sur les lieux pour faire suite aux 'Monuments de l'Egypte et de la Nubie' de Champollion le jeune, Firmin Didot, Paris, 1847.

ROBERTS, David, *Egypt and Nubia, with Historical Descriptions by Wild [William] Brockledon*, London, 1846-50.

Un voyageur en Égypte vers 1850: le Nil de Maxime Du Camp, Michel Dewachter and Daniel Oster with a preface by Jean Leclant, Sand/Conti, Paris, 1987.

WILKINSON, John Gardner, *The Manners and Customs of the Ancient Egyptians including their private 'life, government, laws, arts, manufactures, religion, and early history; derived from a comparison of the paintings, sculptures, and monuments still existing, with the accounts of ancient authors*, 3 vols, John Murray, London, 1837.

MANUSCRIPT AND ICONOGRAPHIC SOURCES

The following are the major sources used in the writing of the present work:

CHAMPOLLION, Jean François, *Monuments de l'Égypte et de la Nubie*, original drawings, Paris, Bibliothèque nationale, MS N.A.F. 20358-60.

Papiers de J. Fr. Champollion le Jeune (1790-1832), Paris, Bibliothèque nationale, MS N.A.F. 20303-09.

Commission d'Égypte, 'Antiquités', drawings, Paris, Bibliothèque nationale, Prints, Ub. 181.

HUYOT, Jean Nicolas, *Albums des voyages de J. N. Huyot à Smyrne et en Asie Mineure à Constantinople, en Égypte et en Grèce 1817-1821*, Paris, Bibliothèque nationale, MS N.A.F. 5080-81.

LIST OF ILLUSTRATIONS

The numbers refer to the pages on which the illustrations appear. For reasons of convenience the watercolours painted during the Egyptian campaign, or worked up from sketches done *in situ* by the scholars, have been uniformly dated 1798-1801. This does not exclude the fact that some of them may have been altered or completed after the scholars' return to France.

Etat moderne, vol. II, pl. F. Paris, Bibliothèque Nationale, Department of Prints. Photo BN.

77 André Dutertre, *An Egyptian*, 1798-1801. Watercolour heightened with pastel. Engraved for the *Description de l'Égypte*, 1809-26, *État moderne*, vol. II, pl. E. Paris, Bibliothèque Nationale, Department of Prints. Photo BN.

78-9 Henri Joseph Redouté, *Outskirts of Rosetta*, 1798-1801. Pen and wash. Paris, Bibliothèque Nationale, Department of Prints.

80 Nicolas Jacques Conté, *Cairo, view of Sultan Hasan's mosque*, 1798-1801. Watercolour. Engraved for the *Description de l'Égypte*, 1809-26, *État moderne*, vol. I, pl. 32. Paris, Bibliothèque Nationale, Department of Prints. Photo BN.

82 Jean Constantin Protain, *View of the interior of one of the great halls in Hasan Kachef's house, used for meetings of the Institute*, 1798-9. Pen and wash heightened with gouache. Engraved for the *Description de l'Égypte*, 1809-26, *État moderne*, vol. I, pl. 55. Paris, Bibliothèque Nationale, Department of Prints. Photo BN.

82-3 André Dutertre, *A meeting of the scholars from the Commission for Arts and Sciences in the gardens of the Institute*, 1798-9. Pen and watercolour. Paris, Bibliothèque Nationale, Department of Prints. Photo BN.

84 André Dutertre, *Outskirts of Cairo, water being drawn from the Cairo canal and the festivities held at the opening of the dyke*, 1799. Watercolour. Engraved for the *Description de l'Égypte*, 1809-26, *État moderne*, vol. I, pl. 19. Paris, Bibliothèque Nationale, Department of Prints. Photo BN.

85 Nicolas Jacques Conté, *View of the interior of a weaver's workshop*, 1798-1801. Watercolour. Engraved for the *Description de l'Égypte*, 1809-26, *État moderne*, vol. I, pl. XIII. Private collection.

86 André Dutertre, *Oriental dancing girl's red silk dress*, 1798-1801. Watercolour. Engraved for the *Description de l'Égypte*, 1809-26, *État moderne*, vol. II, pl. LL. Paris, Bibliothèque Nationale, Department of Prints. Photo BN.

87 André Dutertre, *Woman wearing traditional Egyptian costume*, 1798-1801. Watercolour. Engraved for the *Description de l'Égypte*, 1809-26, *État moderne*, vol. II, pl. LL. Paris, Bibliothèque Nationale, Department of Prints. Photo BN.

88 Nicolas Jacques Conté, *View of the interior of an oil press*, 1798-1801. Watercolour and wash. Engraved for the *Description de l'Égypte*, 1809-26, *État moderne*, vol. I, pl. XII. Private collection.

89 Nicolas Jacques Conté, *The glass bottle maker*, 1798-1801. Watercolour and wash. Engraved for the *Description de l'Égypte*, 1809-26, *État moderne*, vol. II, pl. XXIII. Private collection.

90-91 Nicolas Jacques Conté, *View of the sundial in one of the courtyards of Hasan Kachef's house*, 1798-1801. Watercolour. Engraved for the *Description de l'Égypte*, 1809-26, *État moderne*, vol. I, pl. 60. Private collection.

92 A. Burckhardt, engraved portrait of Nicolas Jacques Conté.

93 Nicolas Jacques Conté, *The maker of wooden locks and the carpenter's tools*, 1798-1801. Watercolour and wash. Engraved for the *Description de l'Égypte*, 1809-26, *État moderne*, vol. II, pl. XV. Private collection.

94-5 Charles Louis Balzac, *Cairo, the Citadel, view of the exterior of Joseph's Divan*, 1798-1801. Pen and watercolour. Engraved for the *Description de l'Égypte*, 1809-26, *État moderne*, vol. I, pl. 71. Paris, Bibliothèque Nationale, Department of Prints. Photo BN.

95 André Dutertre, *An Alexandrian child*, 1798-1801. Watercolour heightened with pastel. Engraved for the *Description de l'Égypte*, 1809-26, *État moderne*, vol. II, pl. F. Paris, Bibliothèque Nationale, Department of Prints. Photo BN.

96 *La Décade égyptienne, journal littéraire et d'économie politique*. The first issue, published on 1 October 1798. Photo Flammarion.

96 The *Courier de l'Égypte*. The first issue, published on 29 August 1798. Photo Flammarion.

98 André Dutertre, engraved portrait of Édouard de Villiers du Terrage.

99 Alire Delile, *Arabian desert, view of the Gabal Gharib*, 1798-1801. Watercolour and wash. Engraved for the *Description de l'Égypte*, 1809-26, *État moderne*, vol. II, pl. 100. Paris, Bibliothèque Nationale, Department of Prints. Photo BN.

100 *General map of Bulaq, Cairo, the island of Rawdah, Old Cairo and Giza*. Drawn up by Jacotin, Simonel, Lathuille, Jomard, Bertre and Lecesne. Engraving from the *Description de l'Égypte*, 1809-26, *État moderne*, vol. I, pl. 15. Photo BN.

101 Antoine Poiteau, *Artemisia monosperma*, 1798-1801. Wash. Engraved for the *Description de l'Égypte*, 1809-26, *Histoire naturelle*, vol. II, '*Botanique*', pl. 43. Private collection. Photo Flammarion.

101 Henri Joseph Redouté, *Crucifera thebaica*, 1798-1801. Watercolour. Engraved for the *Description de l'Égypte*, 1809-26, *Histoire naturelle*, vol. II, '*Botanique*', pl. 1. Paris, Bibliothèque du Muséum National d'Histoire Naturelle. Photo Flammarion.

102 Henri Joseph Redouté, *Tetrodon fahaca*, 1798-1801. Watercolour. Engraved for the *Description de l'Égypte*, 1809-26, *Histoire naturelle*, vol. I, '*Poissons*', pl. 1. Paris, Bibliothèque du Muséum National d'Histoire Naturelle. Photo Flammarion.

103 Jacques Barraband, *Adult haje viper*, 1798-1801. Watercolour. Engraved for the *Description de l'Égypte*, 1809-26, *Histoire naturelle*, vol. I, '*Reptiles*', pl. 7. Paris, Bibliothèque du Muséum National d'Histoire Naturelle. Photo Flammarion.

104 Dominique Vivant Denon, *Self-portrait*, *c* 1780. Pastel. Chalon-sur-Saône, Musée Vivant Denon. Photo Giraudon.

104 Dominique Vivant Denon, *View of Miqyas*, 1798-9. Pen and wash. Engraved for *Voyage dans la Basse et la Haute Égypte*, 1802, pl. 22. London, British Museum, Department of Prints and Drawings. Photo BM.

105 Dominique Vivant Denon, *Vivant Denon at the ruins of Hierconpolis*, 1798-9. Pen and wash. Engraved for *Voyage dans la Basse et la Haute Égypte*, 1802, pl. 54 *bis*. London, British Museum, Department of Prints and Drawings. Photo BM.

106 Dominique Vivant Denon, *The Egyptian barber*, 1798-9. Pen and wash. Engraved for *Voyage dans la Basse et la Haute Égypte*, 1802, pl. 92. London, British Museum, Department of Prints and Drawings. Photo BM.

107 Dominique Vivant Denon, *The Egyptian bath*, 1798-9. Pen and wash. Engraved for *Voyage dans la Basse et la Haute Égypte*, 1802, pl. 35. London, British Museum, Department of Prints and Drawings. Photo BM.

108 Dominique Vivant Denon, *Arabian desert grasshopper*, 1798-9. Pen and wash. Engraved for *Voyage dans la Basse et la Haute Égypte*, 1802, pl. 111. London, British Museum, Department of Prints and Drawings. Photo BM.

109 Dominique Vivant Denon, *Head study*, 1798-9. Pen and wash. Engraved for *Voyage dans la Basse et la Haute Égypte*, 1802, pl. 104. London, British Museum, Department of Prints and Drawings. Photo BM.

110 Cloquet, *Fossil of a shell from the shores of the Red Sea*, 1798-1801. Watercolour. Engraved for the *Description de l'Égypte*, 1809-26, *Histoire naturelle*, vol. II, '*Minéralogie*', pl. 11. Paris, Bibliothèque Nationale, Department of Prints. Photo BN.

110 Henri Joseph Redouté, *The Polypterus bichir*, 1798-1801. Watercolour. Engraved for the *Description de l'Égypte*, 1809-26, *Histoire naturelle*, vol. I, '*Poissons*', pl. 3. Paris, Bibliothèque du Muséum National d'Histoire Naturelle. Photo Flammarion.

111 Ringuet, *Memnonian puddingstone from the Gabal al Silsilah*, 1798-1801. Watercolour. Engraved for the *Description de l'Égypte*, 1809-26, *Histoire naturelle*, vol. II, '*Minéralogie*', pl. 4. Paris, Bibliothèque Nationale, Department of Prints. Photo BN.

111 Henri Joseph Redouté, *Three-clawed emys or Nile tortoise*, 1798-1801. Watercolour. Engraved for the *Description de l'Égypte*, 1809-26, *Histoire naturelle*, vol. I, '*Reptiles*', pl. 1. Paris, Bibliothèque du Muséum National d'Histoire Naturelle. Photo Flammarion.

112 Dominique Vivant Denon, *Study of a dromedary's head*, 1798-9. Pen and pencil. Engraved for *Voyage dans la Basse et la Haute Égypte*, 1802, pl. 109. London, British Museum, Department of Prints and Drawings. Photo BM.

113 Dominique Vivant Denon, *General headquarters in the tombs near Naqada*, 1798-9. Pen and wash. Engraved for *Voyage dans la Basse et la Haute Égypte*, 1802, pl. 79. London, British Museum, Department of Prints and Drawings. Photo BM.

114-5 Cécile and Balzac, *Thebes, view of the ruins of Karnak*, 1798-1801. Watercolour. Engraved for the *Description de l'Égypte*, 1809-26, *Antiquités*, vol. III, pl. 18. Paris, Bibliothèque Nationale, Department of Prints. Photo BN.

116 André Dutertre, engraved portrait of Louis Costaz.

117 Caristie, *The Fayyum, view of the Begig obelisk*, 1798-1801. Pen and wash. Engraved for the *Description de l'Égypte*, 1809-26, *Antiquités*, vol. IV, pl. 71. Paris, Bibliothèque Nationale, Department of Prints. Photo BN.

118-19 Cécile, *Thebes, Karnak, general view of the propylaea and the ruins of the palace seen from the north-east*, 1798-1801. Watercolour. Engraved for the *Description de l'Égypte*, 1809-26, *Antiquités*, vol. III, pl. 43. Paris, Musée du Louvre. Photo Flammarion.

120 Jean Constantin Protain, *Cairo, perspective view of part of the City of the Tombs*, 1798-1801. Pen and wash. Engraved for the *Description de l'Égypte*, 1809-26, *État moderne*, vol. I, pl. 66. Paris, Bibliothèque Nationale, Department of Prints. Photo BN.

121 Jean Constantin Protain, *Elevation of Hasan Kachef's house (the Institute) facing the courtyard and garden*, 1798-1801. Pen and wash. Engraved for the *Description de l'Égypte*, 1809-26, *État moderne*, vol. I, pl. 54. Paris, Bibliothèque Nationale, Department of Prints. Photo BN.

122 André Dutertre and Edme François Jomard, *Thebes, ibis mummies found in the hypogaea*. Coloured engraving from the *Description de l'Égypte*, 1809-26, *Antiquités*, vol. II, pl. 52. Photo Flammarion.

123 Nicolas Jacques Conté, *View of the pyramids at Giza*, 1798-1801. Watercolour. Private collection.

124, 125 *Portable bed for the wounded invented by the surgeon Dominique Larrey*, 1798-1801. Graphite. Engraved for the *Description de l'Égypte*, 1809-26, *État moderne*, vol. II, pl. 31. Paris, Bibliothèque Nationale, Department of Prints. Photo BN.

126-7 Edme François Jomard, *Night view of the Qasr Qarun temple situated at the western edge of the lake known as Birkat al Qarun*, 1798-1801. Watercolour. Engraved for the *Description de l'Égypte*, 1809-26, *Antiquités*, vol. IV, pl. 69. Paris, Bibliothèque Nationale, Department of Prints. Photo BN.

129 Nicolas Maréchal, *Mongoose*, 1802. Watercolour on vellum. Engraved for the *Description de l'Égypte*, 1809-26, *Histoire naturelle*, vol. I, '*Mammifères*', pl. 6. Paris, Bibliothèque du Muséum National d'Histoire Naturelle. Photo Flammarion.

130 Henri Joseph Redouté, *Nefaschia citharus*, 1798-1801. Watercolour. Engraved for the *Description de l'Égypte*, 1809-26, *Histoire naturelle*, vol. I, '*Poissons*', pl. 5. Paris, Bibliothèque du Muséum National d'Histoire Naturelle. Photo Flammarion.

130 Henri Joseph Redouté, *Malapterus electricus*, 1798-1801. Watercolour. Engraved for the *Description de l'Égypte*, 1809-26, *Histoire naturelle*, vol. I, '*Poissons*', pl. 12. Paris, Bibliothèque du Muséum National d'Histoire Naturelle. Photo Flammarion.

131 Edme François Jomard, *Middle Egypt, view of Turah* (detail), 1798-1801. Watercolour. Engraved for the *Description de l'Égypte*, 1809-26,

Etat moderne, vol. I, pl. 8. Paris, Bibliothèque Nationale, Department of Prints. Photo BN.

132 Nicolas Huet, *Desert monitor*, 1804. Watercolour. Engraved for the *Description de l'Égypte*, 1809-26, *Histoire naturelle*, vol. I, 'Reptiles', pl. 3. Paris, Bibliothèque du Muséum National d'Histoire Naturelle. Photo Flammarion.

132 Nicolas Huet, *Egyptian hare*, 1806. Watercolour on vellum. Engraved for the *Description de l'Égypte*, 1809-26, *Histoire naturelle*, vol. I, 'Mammifères', pl. 6. Paris, Bibliothèque du Muséum National d'Histoire Naturelle. Photo Flammarion.

133 Léon de Wailly, *Ram with a thick tail*, 1805. Watercolour on vellum. Engraved for the *Description de l'Égypte*, 1809-26, *Histoire naturelle*, vol. I, 'Mammifères', pl. 7. Paris, Bibliothèque du Muséum National d'Histoire Naturelle. Photo Flammarion.

134 Cécile, *Mameluke dagger*, 1798-1801. Gouached watercolour. Engraved for the *Description de l'Égypte*, 1809-26, *État moderne*, vol. II, pl. NN (detail). Paris, Bibliothèque Nationale, Department of Prints. Photo BN.

135 Edme François Jomard, *Abyssinian tray made out of dum leaves*, 1798-1801. Gouached watercolour. Engraved for the *Description de l'Égypte*, 1809-26, *État moderne*, vol. II, pl. DD (detail). Paris, Bibliothèque Nationale, Department of Prints. Photo BN.

THE ARCHAEOLOGICAL CONQUEST

136 Jean Baptiste Lepère, *Thebes, Memnonium, perspective view of the painted interior of the western temple*. Coloured engraving from the *Description de l'Égypte*, 1809-26, *Antiquités*, vol. II, pl. 37. Photo Flammarion.

138-9 Claude Sicard, *Map of the deserts of Lower Thebais*, 1717. Pen and watercolour. Paris, Bibliothèque Nationale, Department of Maps and Charts. Photo BN.

140 John Greaves, *The first pyramid*. Engraving from *Pyramidographia, or a description of the pyramids in Aegypt*, London, 1646. Paris, Bibliothèque Nationale, Department of Prints. Photo Flammarion.

141 Athanasius Kircher, *The temple of Isis Campensis in Rome*. Engraving from *Obelisci aegyptiaci*, Rome, 1666. Photo Flammarion.

142 André Dutertre, *Karnak, view of a colossus at the entrance of the hypostyle hall of the palace*, 1798-1801. Pen and wash. Engraved for the *Description de l'Égypte*, 1809-26, *Antiquités*, vol. III, pl. 20. Paris, Bibliothèque Nationale, Department of Prints. Photo BN.

142-3 Cécile, *Thebes, Madinat Habu, view of the propylaea of the temple and of the pavilion taken from the south side*, 1798-1801. Watercolour. Engraved for the *Description de l'Égypte*, 1809-26, *Antiquités*, vol. II, pl. 3. Paris, Musée du Louvre. Photo Flammarion.

144 Friderik Norden, *View of the main gate of the antiquities at Luxor*. Engraving from his *Travels*, 1751. Paris, Bibliothèque Nationale, Department of Prints. Photo BN.

145 Charles Louis Balzac, *Thebes, Madinat Habu, view of the interior of the palace peristyle*, 1798-1801. Pen and wash. Engraved for the *Description de l'Égypte*, 1809-26, *Antiquités*, vol. II, pl. 14. Paris, Bibliothèque Nationale, Department of Prints. Photo BN.

146 Henri Joseph Redouté, *Thebes, Karnak, bas-relief carved in the corridor round the granite apartments of the palace*, 1798-1801. Wash. Engraved for the *Description de l'Égypte*, 1809-26, *Antiquités*, vol. III, pl. 35. Paris, Bibliothèque Nationale, Department of Prints. Photo BN.

147 Edme François Jomard, *Elephantine, view of a granite rock with traces of quarrying* (detail), 1798-1801. Watercolour. Engraved for the *Description de l'Égypte*, 1809-26, *Antiquités*, vol. I, pl. 32. Paris, Bibliothèque Nationale, Department of Prints. Photo BN.

148 Dominique Vivant Denon, *Elevation of the portico at Dendera*, 1798-9. Pen and wash. Engraved for *Voyage dans la Basse et la Haute Égypte*, 1802, pl. 39. London, British Museum, Department of Prints and Drawings. Photo BM.

149 Edme François Jomard and Michel Ange Lancret, *Island of Philae, bas-relief carved under the gallery of the western temple*, 1798-1801. Pen and wash. Engraved for the *Description de l'Égypte*, 1809-26, *Antiquités*, vol. I, pl. 22-3. Paris, Bibliothèque Nationale, Department of Prints. Photo BN.

150 Benjamin Zix, *Allegorical portrait of Vivant Denon*, 1811. Pen and brown ink. Paris, Musée du Louvre, Department of Drawings. Photo Musées Nationaux.

151 Dominique Vivant Denon, *Alexandria, Vivant Denon measuring Pompey's pillar*, July 1798. Watercolour. London, Victoria and Albert Museum, Searight Collection. Photo V & A.

152 Dominique Vivant Denon, *Temple of Dendera*, 1798-9. Pen and wash. Engraved for *Voyage dans la Basse et la Haute Égypte*, 1802, pl. 38. London, British Museum, Department of Prints and Drawings. Photo BM.

153 Cécile, *Dendera, view of the façade of the Great Temple*, 1798-1801. Watercolour. Engraved for the *Description de l'Égypte*, 1809-26, *Antiquités*, vol. IV, pl. 7. Paris, Musée du Louvre. Photo Flammarion.

154 André Dutertre, *Thebes, Memnonium, view of the two colossi*, 1798-1801. Pen and wash. Engraved for the *Description de l'Égypte*, 1809-26, *Antiquités*, vol. III, pl. 3. Paris, Bibliothèque Nationale, Department of Prints. Photo BN.

155 Dominique Vivant Denon, *Elephantine, ruins of a temple*, 1798-9. Pen and wash. Engraved for *Voyage dans la Basse et la Haute Égypte*, 1802, pl. 65. London, British Museum, Department of Prints and Drawings. Photo BM.

156-7 Cécile, *Thebes, Luxor, view of the palace gates*, 1798-1801. Watercolour. Engraved for the *Description de l'Égypte*, 1809-26, *Antiquités*, vol. III, pl. 3. Paris, Musée du Louvre. Photo Flammarion.

158 André Dutertre, *Memphis, view of the second pyramid taken from the east side*, 1798-1801. Pen and wash. Engraved for the *Description de l'Égypte*, 1809-26, *Antiquités*, vol. V, pl. 10. Paris, Bibliothèque Nationale, Department of Prints. Photo BN.

159 Cécile, *Memphis, views of the high gallery in the Great Pyramid taken from the upper and lower landings*. Engraving from the *Description de l'Égypte*, 1809-26, *Antiquités*, vol. V, pl. 13. Photo BN.

160 Nicolas Jacques Conté, *Memphis, view of the sphinx and the Great Pyramid taken from the south-east*, 1798-1801. Watercolour. Engraved for the *Description de l'Égypte*, 1809-26, *Antiquités*, vol. V, pl. 11. Private collection.

161 Henri Joseph Redouté, *Thebes, Madinat Habu, painted bas-relief carved in the southern gallery of the palace peristyle*, 1798-1801. Watercolour and wash. Engraved for the *Description de l'Égypte*, 1809-26, *Antiquités*, vol. II, pl. 12. Paris, Bibliothèque Nationale, Department of Prints. Photo BN.

162 André Dutertre, *View of the island of Philae and of the surrounding granite mountains*, 1789-1801. Pen and wash. Engraved for the *Description de l'Égypte*, 1809-26, *Antiquités*, vol. I, pl. 4. Paris, Bibliothèque Nationale, Department of Prints. Photo BN.

163 Edme François Jomard, *View of a brick pyramid east of the Fayyum*, 1798-1801. Watercolour. Engraved for the *Description de l'Égypte*, 1809-26, *Antiquités*, vol. IV, pl. 72. Paris, Bibliothèque Nationale, Department of Prints. Photo BN.

164 Prosper Jollois and Édouard de Villiers du Terrage, *Thebes, Memnonium, detail of the colossal statue of Memnon*, 1798-1801. Watercolour and pen. Engraved for the *Description de l'Égypte*, 1809-26, *Antiquités*, vol. II, pl. 22. Paris, Bibliothèque Nationale, Department of Prints. Photo BN.

164 Henri Joseph Redouté, *Esna, Latopolis, interior decorations on a wall between the pillars of the portico*, 1798-1801. Wash. Engraved for the *Description de l'Égypte*, 1809-26, *Antiquités*, vol. I, pl. 81. Paris, Bibliothèque Nationale, Department of Prints. Photo BN.

165 Prosper Jollois and Édouard de Villiers du Terrage, *Thebes, Biban al Maluk, lid of a vase found in the hypogaea*, 1798-1801. Gouached watercolour. Engraved for the *Description de l'Égypte*, 1809-26, *Antiquités*, vol. II, pl. 81 (detail). Paris, Bibliothèque Nationale, Department of Prints. Photo BN.

166 Prosper Jollois and Édouard de Villiers du Terrage, *Thebes, Memnonium, bas-relief carved in the hypostyle hall*, 1798-1801. Pen and wash. Engraved for the *Description de l'Égypte*, 1809-26, *Antiquités*, vol. II, pl. 31. Paris, Bibliothèque Nationale, Department of Prints. Photo BN.

167 Dominique Vivant Denon, *Zodiac in the small apartment in the temple at Dendera*. Engraving from *Voyage dans la Basse et la Haute Égypte*, 1802. Photo BN.

168-9 Cécile, *Thebes, Luxor, characteristic view of the palace taken from the south*, 1798-1801. Watercolour. Engraved for the *Description de l'Égypte*, 1809-26, *Antiquités*, vol. III, pl. 4. Paris, Musée du Louvre. Photo Flammarion.

170 André Dutertre, *Thebes, bronze statuette found in the hypogaea*, 1798-1801. Watercolour. Engraved for the *Description de l'Égypte*, 1809-26, *Antiquités*, vol. II, pl. 56 (detail). Paris, Bibliothèque Nationale, Department of Prints. Photo BN.

170-71 Cécile, *Thebes, Karnak, view of the gate and the southern temples*, 1788-1801. Pen, wash and pencil. Engraved for the *Description de l'Égypte*, 1809-26, *Antiquités*, vol. III, pl. 49. Paris, Bibliothèque Nationale, Department of Prints. Photo BN.

172 Cécile, *Al Kab, view of an ancient quarry*. Engraving from the *Description de l'Égypte*, 1809-26, *Antiquités*, vol. II, pl. 67. Photo Flammarion.

172-3 Charles Louis Balzac, *Gabal al Silsilah, view of the grottoes cut at the entrances to the ancient quarries*, 1798-1801. Watercolour. Engraved for the *Description de l'Égypte*, 1809-26, *Antiquités*, vol. I, pl. 47. Paris, Bibliothèque Nationale, Department of Prints. Photo BN.

174 The Rosetta stone (detail). London, British Museum, Department of Egyptian Antiquities. Photo BM.

175 Henri Joseph Redouté, *Rosetta and its outskirts, view of the hill known as Tell Abu Mina*, 1798-1801. Watercolour. Engraved for the *Description de l'Égypte*, 1809-26, *Antiquités*, vol. I, pl. 80. Paris, Bibliothèque Nationale, Department of Prints. Photo BN.

176 Henri Joseph Redouté, *Thebes, Biban al Maluk, paintings in the fifth tomb of the kings to the east and bas-reliefs at the entrance of the same tomb*, 1798-1801. Watercolour. Engraved for the *Description de l'Égypte*, 1809-26, *Antiquités*, vol. II, pl. 87. Paris, Bibliothèque Nationale, Department of Prints. Photo BN.

177 Henri Joseph Redouté, *Island of Philae, collection of stained, carved and painted vases in the Great Temple*, 1798-1801. Watercolour. Engraved for the *Description de l'Égypte*, 1809-26, *Antiquités*, vol. I, pl. 15. Paris, Bibliothèque nationale, Department of Prints. Photo BN.

178 André Dutertre, *Thebes, Karnak, bas-reliefs carved on the stelae and walls of the granite apartments of the palace* (detail), 1798-1801. Watercolour. Engraved for the *Description de l'Égypte*, 1809-26, *Antiquités*, vol. III, pl. 36. Paris, Bibliothèque Nationale, Department of Prints. Photo BN.

180 Hand of the statue of Rameses II found at Memphis. Granite. London, British Museum, Department of Egyptian Antiquities. Photo BM.

180 Charles Louis Balzac, *Fist (and its measurements) of a colossus at Memphis*, 1798-1801. Pencil and wash. Engraved for the *Description de l'Égypte*, 1809-26, *Antiquités*, vol. V, pl. 4. Paris, Bibliothèque Nationale, Department of Prints. Photo BN.

181 André Dutertre, *Memphis, view of the ruins taken from the south-east*, 1798-1801. Watercolour

and pastel. Engraved for the *Description de l'Égypte*, 1809-26, *Antiquités*, vol. V, pl. 3. Paris, Bibliothèque Nationale, Department of Prints. Photo BN.

182 Dominique Vivant Denon, *Egyptian heads* (detail). Engraving from *Voyage dans la Basse et la Haute Égypte*, 1802, pl. 104. Photo BN.

182-3 Michel Rigo, *Egyptian costume*. Engraving from Vivant Denon, *Voyage dans la Basse et la Haute Égypte*, 1802, pl. 101. Photo BN.

184 Michel Rigo, *The sphinx near the pyramids*. Engraving from Vivant Denon, *Voyage dans la Basse et la Haute Égypte*, 1802, pl. 20 *bis*. Photo BN.

185 Dominique Vivant Denon, *Egyptian baker's oven near Naqada*, 1798-9. Pen and wash. Engraved for *Voyage dans la Basse et la Haute Égypte*, 1802, pl. 79. London, British Museum, Department of Prints and Drawings. Photo BM.

186 Charles Louis Balzac, *Island of Elephantine, view of the south temple*, 1798-1801. Pen and wash. Engraved for the *Description de l'Égypte*, 1809-26, *Antiquités*, vol. I, pl. 34. Paris, Bibliothèque Nationale, Department of Prints. Photo BN.

186 Prosper Jollois and Édouard de Villiers du Terrage, *Thebes, Biban al Maluk, cover of a vase found in the hypogaea*, 1798-1801. Gouached watercolour. Engraved for the *Description de l'Égypte*, 1809-26, *Antiquités*, vol. II, pl. 81 (detail). Paris, Bibliothèque Nationale, Department of Prints. Photo BN.

187 André Dutertre, *Qaw al Kabir, view of the temple taken from the west side*, 1798-1801. Pen and wash. Engraved for the *Description de l'Égypte*, 1809-26, *Antiquités*, vol. IV, pl. 39. Paris, Bibliothèque Nationale, Department of Prints. Photo BN.

188 Cécile, frontispiece of the *Description de l'Égypte*, 1809-26, *Antiquités*, vol. I. Engraving. Photo BN.

188 Title-page of the *Description de l'Égypte*, 1809-26, *Antiquités*, vol. I. Photo Flammarion.

189 André Dutertre, *Thebes, Biban al Maluk, painting in the Hall of Harps in the fifth tomb of the kings to the east*, 1798-1801. Watercolour. Engraved for the *Description de l'Égypte*, 1809-26, *Antiquités*, vol. II, pl. 91. Paris, Bibliothèque Nationale, Department of Prints. Photo BN.

190 Jean Baptiste Lepère, *Thebes, Madinat Habu, plan and longitudinal section of the temple, its propylaea, the palace and the pavilion*. Engraving from the *Description de l'Égypte*, 1809-26, *Antiquités*, vol. II, pl. 4. Photo Flammarion.

191 *Thebes, hypogaea, manuscript on papyrus*. Engraving from the *Description de l'Égypte*, 1809-26, *Antiquités*, vol. II, pl. 60. Photo Flammarion.

192-3 Jean Baptiste Lepère, *Island of Philae, perspective view of the painted interior of the Great Temple taken from the portico*. Engraving from the *Description de l'Égypte*, 1809-26, *Antiquités*, vol. I, pl. 18. Photo BN.

194 André Dutertre, *Edfu, view of the Great Temple*. Engraving from the *Description de l'Égypte*, 1809-26, *Antiquités*, vol. I, pl. 49. Photo Flammarion.

195 Prosper Jollois and Édouard de Villiers du Terrage, *Dendera, perspective view of the interior of the portico of the Great Temple*, 1798-1801. Engraving from the *Description de l'Égypte*, 1809-26, *Antiquités*, vol. I, pl. 30. Photo BN.

196 André Dutertre, *Thebes, hypogaea, paintings of mummy cases* (detail), 1798-1801. Watercolour. Engraved for the *Description de l'Égypte*, 1809-26, *Antiquités*, vol. II, pl. 56. Paris, Bibliothèque Nationale, Department of Prints. Photo BN.

197 André Dutertre, *Details of a tunic found in the tombs of Saqqarah*, 1798-1801. Watercolour. Engraved for the *Description de l'Égypte*, 1809-26, *Antiquités*, vol. V, pl. 5. Paris, Bibliothèque Nationale, Department of Prints. Photo BN.

198 The Rosetta stone. London, British Museum. Photo BM.

199 Edme François Jomard, *Copy of the Rosetta stone, detail of the hieroglyphic section*, 1799-1801. Pen and wash. Engraved for the *Description de l'Égypte*, 1809-26, *Antiquités*, vol. V, pl. 52. Paris,

Bibliothèque Nationale, Department of Prints. Photo BN.

200 André Dutertre, *Thebes, Biban al Maluk, various chairs and armchairs painted in the fifth tomb of the kings to the east*, 1798-1801. Watercolour. Engraved for the *Description de l'Égypte*, 1809-26, *Antiquités*, vol. II, pl. 89 (detail). Paris, Bibliothèque Nationale, Department of Prints. Photo BN.

201 Edme François Jomard and Gilbert Joseph Chabrol de Volvic, *Dendera, perspective view of the north gate*. Reconstruction. Engraving from the *Description de l'Égypte*, 1809-26, *Antiquités*, vol. IV, pl. 6. Photo Flammarion.

THE BIRTH OF EGYPTOLOGY

202 David Roberts, *The ruins of Karnak*. Coloured lithograph from *Egypt and Nubia*, 1846-50, vol. I. Photo Jean Louis Nou.

204 Giovanni Battista Piranesi, chimneypiece. Engraving from *Différentes Manières d'orner les cheminées*, 1769. Photo BN.

204 Charles Monnet, *The Fontaine de la régénération erected on the debris of the Bastille on 10 August 1793*. Photo Bulloz.

205 Auguste Hibon, *Place du Châtelet*, Paris. Watercolour. Paris, Musée Carnavalet. Photo Bulloz.

206-7 Jean Julien Deltil, *The Battle of Heliopolis*. Wallpaper. Rixheim, Musée du Papier Peint, Carlhian Collection. Photo Sotheby's.

208 T. H. Stepherd, *The Egyptian Hall, Piccadilly*, 1812. Engraving. London, British Museum, Department of Prints and Drawings. Photo BM.

208 Bralle and Beauvallet, *The Fountain of the Fellah*, 1806-9. Paris, 42 rue de Sèvres. Photo Flammarion.

209 Thomas Hope, armchair designed for the Egyptian room in his house, 1804. London, H. Blairman & Sons Collection. Photo H. Blairman & Sons.

209 Jacob Desmalter, armchair, 1803-5. Mahogany and gilded bronze. Paris, Musée des Arts Décoratifs. Photo Musée des Arts Décoratifs.

210 Charles Morel, cabinet designed to hold the volumes of the *Description de l'Égypte*, 1813-36. Carved walnut. Paris, Bibliothèque du Sénat. Photo Flammarion.

211 Jacob Desmalter and Guillaume Biennais, Dominique Vivant Denon's medal cabinet, 1806. Mahogany and silver. New York, Metropolitan Museum of Art, Collis P. Huntington Donation. Photo MMA.

212 Sugar bowl from the second Sèvres Egyptian service, 1812. Porcelain. London, Victoria and Albert Museum, Duke of Wellington Collection. Photo V & A.

213 Ice-bucket from the second Sèvres Egyptian service, 1812. Porcelain. London, Victoria and Albert Museum, Duke of Wellington Collection. Photo V & A.

214 Adrien Dauzats, *The mosque of al Azhar*, 1831. Oil on canvas. Paris, Assemblée Nationale. Photo Jean Loup Charmet.

215 Prosper Marilhat, *The Nile valley with the ruins of the temple of Seti I*, 1844. Watercolour heightened with gouache. Paris, Musée du Louvre. Department of Drawings. Photo Musées Nationaux.

216 Jean Michel Moreau le Jeune, *Egyptian initiation scene*, 1792. Pen and wash. Quimper, Musée des Beaux-Arts. Photo Le Grand.

217 David Roberts, *Great Entrance of the temple at Luxor* (detail). Coloured lithograph from *Egypt and Nubia*, 1846-50, vol. II. Photo Jean Louis Nou.

218-9 David Roberts, *Temple of Philae, known as the Pharaoh's Bed*. Coloured lithograph from *Egypt and Nubia*, 1846-50, vol. II. Photo Jean Louis Nou.

220 Maxime du Camp, *Flaubert in Cairo, 9 January 1850*. Photograph. Paris, Bibliothèque de l'Institut. Photo Jean Loup Charmet.

221 David Robert, *Edfu* (detail). Coloured lithograph from *Egypt and Nubia*, 1846-50. Photo Jean Louis Nou.

222 Frederick Schinkel, backdrop for Mozart's *The Magic Flute*, act II, scene vii, Berlin, 1815. Aquatint. Paris, Bibliothèque de l'Opéra. Photo BN.

223 Goblet given to General Thoutii by Tuthmosis III, 18th Dynasty. Gold repoussé. Paris, Musée du Louvre, Drovetti Collection. Photo Musées Nationaux.

224 Amenophis I. Turin, Museo Egizio, Drovetti Collection. Photographed by the museum.

224 Funeral urn of Rameses III, 20th Dynasty. Pink granite. Paris, Musée du Louvre, Salt Collection. Photo Musées Nationaux.

224 M. Nicolosino, *A hall in the Egyptian museum in Turin*. Pen and sepia. Turin, private collection.

225 *The large Egyptian gallery in the British Museum*, 1854. Paris, Bibliothèque des Arts Décoratifs. Photo Jean Loup Charmet.

225 A. Reagis, *Egyptian room in the Musée Charles X*. Engraving from *Paris illustré, nouveau guide de l'étranger et du Parisien*, 1863. Photo BN.

226 Henry Salt, *The pyramids seen from Cairo*. Lithograph from *Twenty-four Views Taken in St. Helena, the Cape, India, Ceylon, Abyssinia and Egypt*, 1809, pl. 24. Paris, Bibliothèque Nationale, Department of Prints. Photo BN.

227 Jean Pierre Granger, *Bernardino Drovetti and his entourage measuring a fragment of a colossus in Upper Egypt*. Black chalk on buff paper. Paris, Musée du Louvre, Department of Prints. Photo Musées Nationaux.

228 Amenophis III, 18th Dynasty. Black granite. London, British Museum, Department of Egyptian Antiquities, Salt Collection. Photo BM.

229 Giovanni Battista Belzoni, *Transporting the bust of Memnon*. Engraving from *Narrative of the Operations and Recent Discoveries... in Egypt and Nubia...*, 1820, pl. 2. Paris, Bibliothèque Nationale, Department of Printed Books. Photo BN.

230-31 Giovanni Battista Belzoni, *View of the interior of the temple of Abu Simbel*. Engraving from *Narrative of the Operations and Recent Discoveries... in Egypt and Nubia...*, 1820, pl. 43. Paris, Bibliothèque Nationale, Department of Printed Books. Photo BN.

232 Prosper Jollois and Édouard de Villiers du Terrage, *Dendera, zodiac carved on the ceiling of one of the upper halls in the Great Temple*. Engraving from the *Description de l'Égypte*, 1809-26, *Antiquités*, vol. IV, pl. 21. Photo Flammarion.

233 The zodiac from Dendera, Paris, Musée du Louvre. Photo Musées Nationaux.

234 Nicolas Huyot, *Erecting an obelisk*. Watercolour. Drawn for the history of architecture classes, Bibliothèque de l'École Nationale Supérieure des Beaux-Arts, Paris. Photo ENSBA.

234 Prosper Jollois and Édouard de Villiers du Terrage, *Thebes, Luxor, elevation of the palace façade*, 1798-1801. Graphite, pen and wash. Engraved for the *Description de l'Égypte*, 1809-26, *Antiquités*, vol. III, pl. 6. Paris, Bibliothèque Nationale, Department of Prints. Photo BN.

235 Léon de Joannis, *Luxor, view of the eastern section of the route to the ship taken by the obelisk*. Engraving from *Campagne pittoresque du Luxor*, 1835, pl. 4. Paris, Bibliothèque Nationale, Department of Prints. Photo BN.

235 François Dubois, *Erection of the Luxor obelisk, 25 October 1836*. Oil on canvas. Paris, Musée Carnavalet. Photo Musées de la ville de Paris, © Spadem.

236 David Roberts, *Great Entrance of the temple at Luxor*. Coloured lithograph from *Egypt and Nubia*, 1846-50, vol. II. Photo Jean Louis Nou.

237 Jean François Champollion, *Luxor, inscription engraved on the southern wall of one of the palace halls*. Engraving from *Monuments de l'Égypte et de la Nubie...*, 1835-45, vol. IV, pl. 349. Paris, Bibliothèque Nationale, Department of Prints. Photo BN.

237 Jean François Champollion, *Lettre à*

INDEX

271